Also by Norman Eisen

The Last Palace

Democracy's Defenders (ed.)

A Case *for the* American People

A Case *for the* American People

The United States v. Donald J. Trump

Norman Eisen

Published in the United States by Crown, an imprint of Random House,
a division of Penguin Random House LLC, New York.

Crown and the Crown colophon are registered trademarks of
Penguin Random House LLC.

Hardback ISBN 978-0-593-23843-1
Ebook ISBN 978-0-593-23844-8

Printed in the United States of America on acid-free paper

crownpublishing.com

2 4 6 8 9 7 5 3 1

First Edition

Book design by Susan Turner

To my father, Irvin Eisen, who taught me everything I know about not *compromising*

This is the lesson: never give in, never give in, never, never, never, never, never—in nothing, great or small, large or petty—never give in except to convictions of honour and good sense.

—Winston Churchill

Contents

A Case *for the* American People

Opening Statement

I have a case for the American people. It is to deliver the ultimate verdict on the high crimes and misdemeanors of Donald J. Trump. You are the witnesses, the victims, and—most important—the judges and jury. Only you can stop him—or allow his high-crime spree to continue. All other remedies available under our constitutional system have been tried. Some have worked, some have failed, and now the final judgment is up to you.

I ought to know. For over three years now I have been pursuing President Trump for his offenses against the law. First as one of Trump's frequent litigation adversaries, involved in almost three hundred legal matters opened against him, his administration, or his allies. Then as special counsel to the House Judiciary Committee for an entire year of intense activity that culminated in my sitting on the floor of the House and then of the Senate as those two awesome chambers—the most powerful legislature in the world—debated and adjudicated the articles of impeachment.

Indeed, I helped lead the writing of those articles. I was the first staff member to begin drafting them, the last to approve final edits, and involved at every stage in between. They revealed, and the trial proved, that the president's shocking behavior toward Ukraine and his political opponents was part of a long-running, ongoing pattern of Trump's abusing his power and then covering that up. The articles showed that the president has violated the public interest to further his selfish personal and political gain for years, without regard for how it would hurt each of you and our country. Most urgently, the articles made it clear that when the next crisis came—as we warned it would—he would repeat the pattern of abuse and cover-up, to all of our peril.

Despite alerting American institutions to the misconduct of the president, and despite some other successes along the way, our collective efforts have thus far fallen short of removing Trump. Federal and state prosecutors have not ultimately stopped him. Nor have the courts. And Congress has not halted him. As a result, the crises rage on. This is why I'm appealing directly to the highest adjudicating body in our democracy. You, the people.

From a number of angles, I have helped rain down legal, political, and public pressure on the president, exposing his misdeeds. These blows would have driven a lesser offender to apologize, recant, and perhaps even resign. Instead, President Trump repeatedly did what he has always done, since the beginning of his career: dodge, deny, and degrade the rule of law. As a result, over the course of my year as special counsel, I contemplated a vast array of impeachment articles. All of them displayed, and were intended to disrupt, Trump's cycle of abusive, obstructive, and criminal misconduct. Within the Judiciary Committee, we maintained a secret running indictment: ten articles of impeachment in all. Ten articles, not two, ladies and gentlemen of the jury. Every one of them will be revealed and explained, for the first time, in the trial that awaits you in these pages. They would have been sufficient to end Trump's presidency in a normal world. The two articles that made it to judgment in the Senate certainly should have been. But ours is no normal world, and Trump is no ordinary criminal.

Our president's offenses unquestionably include "high Crimes and Misdemeanors" under our Constitution. Abuse of power in pressuring foreign governments to investigate his U.S. political opponents. Obstruction of justice and of Congress, making true his pledge to "fight all the subpoenas." Both the abuse and the obstruction are of a kind we have never seen before in American history. They are paired with other corruption, from offering hush money to mistresses to aid his campaign to the acceptance of forbidden foreign and domestic emoluments after he won. Abuse, obstruction, corruption: Trump has violated the law at a rate and scale unimagined by our founders, such as Franklin, Madison, and Jefferson, all of whom must be spinning with outrage in their tombs.

Ladies and gentlemen of the jury, I will guide you through the unvarnished story of the president's crimes and their prosecution. Along the way, we will go backstage for a full year of impeachment efforts, starting in February 2019 and ending twelve months later with the conclusion of the Senate impeachment trial. If you have been following this tale, you may be wondering what essential evidence and which elements have evaded the American collective consciousness, including because they were blurred in the chaos. The portrait reflected in conventional wisdom and the media is lacking in crucial features—ones that yield new insights into the repeated strategy, defenses, and tactics used by our president and his often-felonious cohorts.

As we go through this impeachment year together, you will be able to see his pattern of misconduct from a fresh angle, and be better able to trace the through line of Trump's life, candidacy, and presidency: his radical selfishness and assault on our national interest. He asserts his will and then manages the outcome—immorally, illegally, repeatedly.

These revelations foreshadow the dangerous, even deadly moves he has made since the impeachment and trial, is making as you read this, and will continue to make in the months leading up to the election. The president's response to COVID-19 follows a pattern of abuse and obstruction similar to the one that got him impeached. He is yet again putting his own personal and political interests first in his response to the pandemic—not America First, but Trump First. The same propensity for quid pro quos that led to his 2016 statement to Russia that "you will probably be rewarded mightily," or his 2019 one to Ukraine to "do us a favor though," has characterized his treatment of governors seeking aid in the current crisis: "If we do that, we will have to get something for it." The president's obstruction continues, too. The nonstop flow of lies, the attacks on inspectors general and whistleblowers, the refusal to cooperate with congressional investigators—it is all of a piece, only now it has turned deadly. We warned of exactly this during the president's impeachment and trial. It will not only continue; it will get worse, unless you stop him.

Some of you may be skeptical. You may think I am being too extreme. I understand your position. I too once urged that people keep an open mind regarding the Trump presidency. I even went as far as assisting his presidential transition, starting before he was elected. I was prepared to play a role in easing him into his presidency. I have dined with the president. I am acquainted with his daughter and son-in-law and many of those around him. I once hoped, sincerely, that Trump could be an ethical president. I learned better. I later held on to the desperate, optimistic belief that Trump's behavior would change, or that his systematic, reckless wrongdoing could be curbed. I now know that, too, to be false.

I will explain why I believe this so you can make your own decision. If, after you weigh the case, you agree that he is guilty, you have the power to bring this illicit cycle to a halt. He will not change. His crime spree will continue unless we, as a nation, get in his way. All of you, and you alone, can stop him. So now my optimism lies with the American people.

For those of you who might not have followed the barrage of headlines, who long ago threw up your hands, or who perhaps sense that the president is a bad guy but do not believe there is anything new to learn or anything to be done, welcome. I ask you to keep an open mind as we revisit proof of wrongdoing that has eluded sustained public attention in the dizzying stream of events. The danger we are facing is unprecedented and more terrifying than has been acknowledged. It affects every one of us. As you are reading this, the cancer of Trump's presidency is metastasizing throughout America and indeed our world. I beseech you not to underestimate its power, for unless something is done, its consequences will be felt for generations.

What follows is the evidence required for you, the ultimate judges and jury, to render a decisive verdict come November. This fight is not over. Change remains within our grasp, and we have the ability, and the duty, to hold the president accountable. Even with the last chapter unwritten, what follows is the story of our time, shaped by villains and heroes of all varieties who have ushered this nation through waves of crushing disappointment and surges of genuine triumph and vindication.

Each one of you is a participant in that story. The last chapter is yours to write; the verdict remains in the balance. Your decision will be made in November 2020, in the ultimate impeachment trial of Donald J. Trump.

CHAPTER ONE

The Illegal President

ELECTION DAY, NOVEMBER 8, 2016, 11:45 P.M. I KEPT ONE EYE ON our television, the returns growing ever larger for Donald Trump as I attempted to comfort my disconsolate college professor wife and our weeping fifteen-year-old climate-change-obsessed daughter. Periodically, I refreshed the screen of my phone. Earlier the *New York Times* election prediction needle had swung wildly between Clinton and Trump, like a broken compass. Now it remained firmly and deeply in the Republican red.

One part of me felt sick. As the former Obama ethics czar, how could I not? From 2009 to 2011, I had served as White House special counsel for ethics and government reform. I had earned the moniker Mr. No, helping to make integrity a hallmark of the Obama years and to deliver what experts called the most scandal-free administration in modern history. Trump threatened the opposite. Financial, sexual, and political scandals, including welcoming Russian attacks on our election, marred his career and campaign. Now it looked as if he were going to be elected.

But it was not only dismay I felt as I tucked my daughter into bed, kissing her forehead, and then said good night to my wife, telling her that everything would work out. I had a secret as I exited the bedroom, walked through our darkened home, returned to the living room, and flipped open my laptop, the television silently flickering in front of me. I doubled-clicked to open a document: Draft Presidential Ethics Order.

I was doing my part to help Donald Trump prepare to take the reins of our government, and side by side with my sadness I felt some measure of hope that he might do a good job.

It might seem hypocritical that, despite my misgivings about Trump, I was secretly helping his presidential transition and potential administration with government ethics and compliance. If I had noted and even sounded an alarm bell on his risk factors, why would I help? Because he would be the president of all of us, including my family. I am also—as my wife says—a desperate optimist.

I had worked on two tracks after the Republican Party nominated Trump that summer of 2016. On one, I spoke out vociferously about the ethical quagmire a Trump presidency could present. To do so, I partnered with my Republican ethics counterpart, Richard Painter. The gray-haired law professor was an East Coast WASP with Harvard and Yale degrees who had served as President George W. Bush's ethics counsel from 2005 to 2007. He was as tightly laced as I was expressive. He had a deadpan sense of humor, was careful not to smile unless absolutely necessary, and never under any circumstances to grin. But whatever our stylistic and political differences, we were equally alarmed by Trump's ethics—above all, that he had failed to commit to fully divesting from his multiple businesses, were he elected. He proposed handing over his companies to his children, but that was not enough. On TV, on radio, and in print, Painter and I explained why not. As long as Trump's profits landed in his pockets, his potential for conflicts was astronomical. If elected, he would have to sell his interests and put the proceeds in a blind trust—one where he wouldn't know how the trustee managed them. That was just one of many things Trump would be required to do to govern ethically (along with releasing his tax returns, making transparent with whom he was doing business).

The press was surprisingly resistant to investigating these concerns. The story of the age of Trump is the story of how our institutions have fared, and none has been more important than the media. But that does not mean their record is unblemished. Reporter after reporter called me that fall, but usually to talk about Clinton's emails, family foundation, or other potential ethics issues. My wife, Lindsay, often heard me say, "But what about Trump?" Only to be told variations of "Trump? Oh, we'll call you back about that if he wins."

They seemed to discount that possibility. I was not as sanguine. So while I was publicly voicing my apprehension about Trump's business affairs, I was privately doing what I could to ameliorate them. Starting in midsummer, I was part of a series of meetings with representatives of both Clinton's and Trump's presidential transitions. We gathered in an office building in downtown D.C., sitting around a large square table with government experts from both Democratic and Republican administrations. Governor Chris Christie of New Jersey was running the Trump transition in the event of his victory in November and had put together a competent team of professionals, including the former chairman of his campaign, the New Jersey lawyer Bill Palatucci. Bill was a burly, none-too-gentle survivor of New Jersey's brutal political scene. But he and his colleagues had federal and state experience and seemed to listen attentively and to ask questions as incisive as those asked by the Clinton transition representatives.

Painter and I decided that we would work quietly with a small group of other ethics experts to devise improvements to the Obama ethics program, then offer them to a President Trump (if elected) to sign into law, just as Obama had done. We made our efforts known to my new friends on the Trump transition team. The upshot: I was invited to meet privately with Palatucci in October to discuss our new and improved ethics plan. I hope you will not think less of me for believing that ethical progress was possible in a Trump presidency. But I did. Trump had said his children would take over the management of his companies while he was serving as president. As vague as that commitment was, I thought that with a bipartisan nudge from Painter and me he really might cut himself off from the Trump Organization and its profits and otherwise put some distance between himself and his scandalous past should he secure the presidency.

It was a strange experience to visit the Trump transition headquarters on October 20, 2016. The office was on the upper floor of a nondescript building a block away from the White House. Remembering the frenzied, excited activity of the Obama transition, I was taken aback when the elevator doors dinged open and we stepped into a hushed atmosphere, with very few people on the premises and mostly empty offices and cubicles. Were we on the right floor? I was accompanied by two other ethicists, one of whom whispered to me, "I guess they don't think they are really going to have a transition." Like the reporters I had spoken to, the transition team itself was doubtful about a Trump presidency.

Palatucci welcomed us into his spacious quarters, where he razzed me Jersey-style about some controversial ethics exceptions I made under Obama and I gave it right back to him about Governor Christie, but the back-and-forth was good-natured. We quickly got down to a serious, detailed conversation about why our revision to the federal ethics regime was an improvement. The meeting was cordial and comprehensive, giving me every reason to believe that the transition team took our proposal seriously. The seemingly shared desire for improvement would give me that chaser of hope to follow my shot of horror on election night.

After Trump won the election, I doubled down on my optimism. I reached out to Steve Bannon's ethics guru (yes, he had one), Peter Schweizer. The resident Breitbart muckraker was the author of *Clinton Cash,* a purported exposé of the Clinton family. That November and December, I negotiated a package of ethics proposals that Peter and I jointly endorsed and published in *The Washington Post*. They included the improved version of the Obama ethics plan that I had pitched to the transition team, and Schweizer also joined the call for Trump to divest his businesses into a blind trust, as Painter and I had insisted upon for months. With Schweizer and (I hoped) Bannon having endorsed the plan, I greeted the New Year thinking we might have a real influence on Trump's governance. Lindsay was a bit glum as we raised a glass of champagne to toast January 1, 2017, but I allowed myself some effervescence of hope as the bubbles tickled my tongue.

My abrupt collision with reality occurred a week and a half later, on January 11, as I watched Trump's first press conference as president-elect. All morning, Painter and I fielded calls from reporters, who kept telling us that Trump was going to announce his intention to keep his businesses. Still, I found myself floored as I tuned in and heard Trump announce his intent. He pointed to the heaps of files on the tables in front of him, said they contained documentation for transferring his businesses to his family, and explained that the form of transferring control would be in a "trust," before brashly declaring,

> I have a no-conflict situation because I'm president.
>
> My two sons . . . They are going to be running it in a very professional manner. They're not going to discuss it with me.

Wait—he *what*? This was all wrong. No president had ever done anything like this. The others had sold their businesses and put their interests in a blind trust (or the equivalent) so they would not know about their investments or sources of income. Trump's plan of handing day-to-day control to his sons meant that he would keep his interest in his businesses, keep the profits, and invite in a world of conflicts. Technically, it was a trust, but it bore no resemblance whatsoever to the blind trusts that presidents before him had used. It was the opposite: a seeing-eye trust.

Even worse, what Trump was proposing was unconstitutional. The emoluments clauses of the Constitution state that a president cannot accept anything of value from foreign or even local U.S. governments (other than his salary and routine benefits available to all, like Social Security). Our founders included those protections because they were worried about the conflicts that foreign and domestic government payments could create for a president. They were obsessed with historical examples like the British king Charles II, who was funded by the French king Louis XIV, with corresponding damaging effects on British policy. Through his businesses, Trump would have such payments pouring into his pocket every day. What was he talking about: the president cannot have a conflict of interest? On the contrary, Trump was about to have the mother of them all.

Reporters started calling Richard and me for comment before the press conference even ended. I was certain they would see it as we did: an abomination. To my dismay, however, some of our nation's most sophisticated journalists were already falling for Trump's inaccuracies. One extremely skeptical, razor-sharp reporter with whom I had worked for years argued with me: "What's the problem here, Norm? He said that he's handing over control and he's setting up a trust . . . Why is that not good enough?" It's an insufficient safeguard! I explained. He would personally benefit from his companies' business, have conflicts up the wazoo, and unconstitutional ones to boot. That was why no other American president had done this. It was the realization of our founders' worst fear: Trump's plan would enable governments, both foreign and domestic, to use the president's wallet to influence him.

This reporter and others that day shocked me by replying, "Well, isn't that what the American people voted for?"

"No," I said. "No! He told the American people he was going to separate from his businesses." This was a flimflam show. When reason failed, I attempted humor: "It's Three Card emolu-Monte!" I exclaimed. None of them, however, seemed to understand.

I paused for a moment to take stock. Like a basic code illuminating within a matrix, the simple, terrifying pattern of Trump's illegality crystallized in my mind. There I was, fending off reporters and begging them not to fall for it, without fully appreciating that for far too long *I* had fallen for it. Part of my vehemence with the reporters sprang from the reality that I was talking to myself.

What a fool I had been to believe that I could somehow usher this president inside *any* ethical boundaries. To help me navigate the era of Trump, I sometimes reminded myself that in World War II, FDR and Churchill had gone so far as to partner with Stalin. (Unfortunately, I had thought too little about how Stalin had come to abuse their trust.) My penchant for finding compromise—the trait that had enabled me to thrive in a bipartisan way in Washington for almost three decades—had led me astray. That press conference was the moment when my hope for the Trump presidency was lost. There would be no partnering with Donald Trump.

But I had little time to dwell on that. Painter and I could tell we were losing the battle with the press. Their opinions, and Trump's narrative, were already gaining widespread acceptance. Conventional wisdom sets quickly. If the media sounded the theme that what Trump was doing was okay, we would have to live with it for the next four years.

I swung into action, calling the one person I could think of who could explode the narrative before it hardened into concrete. He was the man who was about to become Trump's most senior career ethics official, the head of the Office of Government Ethics (OGE), Walter Shaub. If he spoke out, it could make a difference, but it also might destroy him.

WALT HAD DEDICATED HIS LIFE'S work to making sure our government functioned smoothly and effectively for the benefit of all Americans. He had gone to the Office of Government Ethics as a mid-level staffer, worked his way up through the ranks, earned a series of important appointments, and became the head of the office in 2013. OGE has always been rigorously nonpartisan, and Shaub had worked brilliantly with both Painter when he was Bush's ethics adviser and me when I filled the ethics czar role for Obama. (Our jobs differed from Walt's, in that we were political appointees serving in the White House, whereas he was a career expert, working from an outside agency.)

Walt picked up immediately when I called. To his credit, he was equally stunned by what he had just seen. Because he was already privy to all kinds of information in his government job, he was careful with his words—confining himself only to commenting on what was public. But he felt compelled to express horror about Trump's admission and showed a moral clarity that was a breeze of fresh air compared with Trump's blast of swamp gas. He too had just come to the realization that Trump was not going off the rails; instead, Trump believed that there were no rails.

"Norm, this is unethical. What we just saw in that press conference is just plain wrong. I'm not going to stand for it." That was it. If the government's chief independent career ethicist, who was about to be working for Trump, condemned his future boss, the narrative would be transformed. He needed to be heard publicly as soon as possible. I seized the moment.

"Let's do a press conference. It will be a bipartisan one. We'll have Painter and me flanking you and we'll allow you to speak out." I had no idea if we could pull it together, but I kept talking: "Just give us a couple hours, Walt, we will find a venue, and we'll have a press conference later today." We needed to counter Trump before the next day's papers.

Without skipping a beat, he responded, "Just tell me when to be there."

I called Richard, who agreed that we needed to make a statement—not just a statement, but a knockout punch. The two of us launched a furious onslaught, reaching out to everyone we knew.

The president's gaslighting had become a five-alarm fire. We scrambled to book a room, recruiting as many reporters as possible, and managed to pull together a full press conference.

At 4:00 P.M. that day—in time for reporters to make their filing deadlines—this courageous official, the most senior sitting authority on ethics in the U.S. government, explained to the American public (while flanked by the Bush and Obama ethics gurus) that what had just happened was flat-out wrong.

After a brief introduction from Painter and me, he began, "I wish circumstances were different and I didn't feel the need to make public remarks today. You don't hear about ethics when things are going well. We've been hearing a lot about ethics lately. I need to talk about ethics today because the plan the president has announced doesn't meet the standards that his nominees are meeting, and that every president in the last four decades has met." What Shaub said was as straightforward as the president's plan was crooked. He expressed a genuine desire to help Trump reach an understanding of and abide by an ethically sound plan. He went on to emphasize that the notion of handing his businesses off to his sons was simply "meaningless from a conflict-of-interest perspective."

He succeeded in transforming the news of the day. Instead of the narrative being a president-elect saying that his conduct was perfectly legal, the headline was that Trump's own government had rejected his conflicts and emoluments as unethical. In story after story, the narrative flipped. The same reporters who were preparing accounts of a reasonably adequate press conference instead wrote about the controversy and Shaub's immediate blowback. Every major paper included Shaub's denunciation of his incoming boss. *The New York Times* headlined with "It 'Falls Short in Every Respect': Ethics Experts Pan Trump's Conflicts Plan," while *The Wall Street Journal* and *The Washington Post* led with "Government Ethics Chief Says Trump's Conflict-of-Interest Plan Isn't Good Enough" and "Federal Ethics Chief Blasts Trump's Plan to Break from Businesses, Calling It 'Meaningless,'" respectively.

Today I know that there was never any chance that Trump was going to give up his emoluments. I did not realize how debased he was. We still cannot be certain what the depths are with Trump, as his former personal lawyer and fixer, among many others, would later warn me. That is why I am appealing to you, the American people, to check him. Everybody has the opportunity to be a patriot. I am arguing this case to you because I believe the brake to be in your hands, and in your hands alone.

ON THE NIGHT OF JANUARY 11, once I had a moment to catch my breath following Shaub's press conference, I realized what I had overlooked about Trump. It was his pattern, one that was brought into sharp relief by that day's events. As I scanned the details of Trump's life from a fresh perspective, the blinders about what lay ahead were torn from my eyes. He had abused the law, then covered it up through confusion and spectacle for decades. In 1973, just shy of half a century ago, the Department of Justice (DOJ) alleged that Trump's family business was denying apartments to black tenants, and charged the company with racial discrimination. Despite the profuse evidence, the twenty-seven-year-old president of the company, Donald Trump, responded that the charges "are absolutely ridiculous. We never have discriminated, and we never would. There have been a number of local actions against us, and we've won them all." They retained the notorious alley-fighter Roy Cohn to assist in the case, and ultimately reached a settlement. Trump Management later noted that there had been no admission of guilt in the agreement. And Trump said he was satisfied that the law would not require his company to accept the applications of persons on welfare, unless they were as qualified as other tenants. This pattern of misconduct, cover-up, and denial spanned Trump's entire career. He consorted with mobsters, refused to pay debts, and created phony organizations to place ads that blocked the construction of casinos that might compete with his operations in Atlantic City (though his went bankrupt). He faced a series of litigated fraud suits, like the Trump University case that he settled on the eve of his inauguration, in addition to myriad allegations of personal harassment. Every time, in the face of overwhelming wrongdoing, he found somebody else to blame and obfuscated his own misconduct, settling when he had to and moving on to the next rip-off. What had I been thinking in believing that he would change?

I realized now that he would repeat this pattern as president. He had started with the emoluments; it was anyone's guess what law he might violate next. I knew that as soon as he removed his hand from the Bible and finished taking his oath of office, he would be committing a grave constitutional violation. His flimsy cover-up methods had already been put on full display with the piles of folders he had by his side for his first presidential performance routine, purportedly as "some of the many documents I've signed turning over complete and total control to my sons." He did not, however, display the documents, and commentators speculated that the folders were full of blank sheets of paper. He was a sham, and we had just witnessed the launch of his next cycle of misconduct.

The frequency and consistency of his questionable acts are another part of the strategy. One forgets about what happened yesterday, what happened last month, or what happened three years ago, because every day delivers a fresh batch of horrific or offensive behavior with which we must contend. He keeps the rotation going; it is a key feature of his modus operandi: to perpetually obscure our vision with successive bursts of scandal and incessant public commentary, or worse. Every headline announcing his latest misstep further blinds us. He engineers a system overload.

That night, after our daughter had gone to bed, Lindsay and I stayed up late talking. She asked me if I had lost hope. I admitted I had—but only in Trump. Not in our institutions. Keeping him in check was going to be harder than I thought. But if Trump would not voluntarily give up his emoluments, I had an idea on how to make him.

• • •

It is as true in politics as in any other human endeavor: if you want to get something done, you need alliances, from both within your own party and across the aisle. In that spirit of bipartisanship, Richard Painter agreed to join the board of Citizens for Responsibility and Ethics in Washington (CREW), the government watchdog group that I had founded years before and recently rejoined. Together with our executive director, Noah Bookbinder, we limbered up to hold the president accountable. A Stanford Law grad and former corruption prosecutor, Noah was slight, with an amiable affect that concealed a relentless hunger for justice. On the wall of his office was a poster of his favorite band, their name offering an apt title for our plans: the Clash.

The moment after Trump was sworn in on Friday, January 20, we filed a complaint with the General Services Administration targeting ground zero of Trump's illegal emoluments: his D.C. hotel, a magnet for foreign and domestic government spending. The lease provided that no party could hold a government position. Trump was now in violation of the lease, and we demanded it be canceled under federal law. Three days later, on Monday, Trump's first actual workday in office, we followed that up with a second sally. This time we sued Trump in federal court in Manhattan over his acceptance of emoluments. Noah and I put together a dream team to work on the litigation, including America's leading constitutional scholar, Larry Tribe.

We didn't stop there. Those were merely the first two of a deluge of almost three hundred legal matters that CREW opened during my return as board chair. We lodged criminal complaints against the president and those around him. We filed ethics charges, Freedom of Information Act requests, regulatory complaints—every arrow in the litigation quiver. Our docket alone could have been a law school curriculum. If Trump was going to deploy a system overload strategy, then we would match him blow for blow. That included a second emoluments case, this one working with the State of Maryland and the District of Columbia, whose attorneys general, Brian Frosh and Karl Racine, stepped up to oppose the president's unconstitutional acts.

We also linked arms with other groups who were determined to use the rule of law to rein in this lawless president. This de facto legal department of the Resistance started conferring soon after the inauguration, with calls at noon every Friday and more often when needed. As Trump's offenses escalated by the day and often by the hour, the opposition ballooned to more than a hundred groups, with thousands of lawyers, other professionals, and volunteers preparing countless legal actions. Our legal Resistance group included those who fought Russian interference, the Muslim ban, possible Hatch Act violations, Jared Kushner's security clearance; we even fought Trump on using the presidential seal at his golf course.

My strategies for fighting Trump had an unlikely inspiration. For guidance in how to wage legal war, I pulled down off my shelf my well-worn six-volume set of Churchill's history of World War II. Dust jackets missing or crumbling, spines faded, it remains the single most instructive book I know for detailing how to strategically fight a sustained battle against long odds. Like many titans of history, Churchill has a complicated record, to say the least. But his book has many virtues, including as a reminder of how frequently things went south for Sir Winston, and all the moments when success seemed impossible. He overcame that by, among other things, building alliances and seeing them through all their stresses and strains.

In the months that followed, it became clear that there were two distinct camps among the legal Resistance: those who favored maximum escalation against the president, and those who wanted to proceed more cautiously, building bipartisan public support. The former was led by John Bonifaz, my friend of more than thirty years. Named a MacArthur genius for his pro-democracy organizing, he was whippet thin, with intense eyes burning behind round spectacles. John and I attended both college and law school together. We had joined forces on an array of issues ranging from fighting electronic voting machines (too hackable) to litigating election recounts to working for campaign finance reform.

John had called me even before the inauguration to start work on the ultimate constitutional weapon against a president: impeachment. The Constitution provides grave remedies if the president commits "high Crimes and Misdemeanors," that is, offenses against the political order itself, like accepting emoluments or otherwise violating the Constitution. You need not have ordinary statutory crimes, although they certainly did not hurt. But if the president commits high crimes, the House is empowered to impeach him or her on a majority vote. Impeachment then moves to the Senate, where the president can be removed from office if sixty-seven senators vote to convict.

"John," I replied when he called. "How can you impeach the man? He hasn't even taken office yet!" The Republicans controlled both houses of Congress. They were not going to vote for impeachment now—maybe not ever. John, with his entrepreneurial vision and out-of-the-box organizational thinking, countered that the president would be accepting emoluments and violating the Constitution. He felt it was a moral and a political duty, and that if we led the way we would eventually bring Congress around. He continued to push me and others in our weekly discussions to publicly call for impeachment. A minority of the more left-leaning of our lawyers and groups concurred.

To John's affable disappointment, I helped lead the majority camp opposing immediate impeachment. I did so with other leading voices, including my watchdog mentor, Fred Wertheimer, the pugnacious dean of government reformers. He was the oldest dog in the kennel, with wisps of white hair floating around his head, but his bark was ferocious and his bite even worse. We conceded that Trump had gone beyond any other president in recent history in terms of the breadth and depth of his constitutional offenses, but we also knew that we needed to bring you, the American people, along first. In other words, we had to be patient. Like any campaign, it needed time to garner public support, ideally from both sides.

That campaign would soon get a boost from the unlikeliest of helpers: Donald Trump.

RICHARD AND I HAD WARNED that if Trump set a tone of illegality with his emoluments and other conflicts, worse depths would soon be plumbed.

A critical turning point arrived less than a month into the presidency. On February 13, National Security Adviser Michael Flynn resigned, amid allegations that he had misled the FBI about secret conversations that he had with the Russian ambassador during the transition. The Justice Department was digging into that along with other connections to Russia and its attack on our democracy by Trump's campaign and his associates. There they were: allegations of abuse and cover-up, the pattern that had characterized Trump's entire career. Now they were swirling around his White House.

As the Russia scandal metastasized in mid-February, it became clear under the ethics rules that Attorney General Jeff Sessions should not be overseeing it. This was not a close call. If you worked on a campaign, as Sessions had, you cannot oversee an investigation of that campaign. Following one of the legal Resistance's Friday calls, I helped lead the public effort to call upon the attorney general to recuse himself. Unlike Trump, Sessions proved to have some shame. The diminutive Alabamian with jug ears did not pull the Trumpian abuse-and-obstruct maneuver. He did the right thing: on March 2, he stepped away from the Trump-Russia investigation.

Trump was enraged. He lashed out uncontrollably, especially on Twitter, his temper reaching a keystroke fever pitch. Sessions's recusal meant Trump was unable to bring his own executive branch to heel, thereby highlighting the limits of his power. The functioning of our institutions is central to the story of the Trump presidency, and here is an example. Even his own executive branch's internal checks and balances were working—a balm for my congenital optimism.

The president's reaction provided a crucial insight. Hell hath no fury like a Trump defied. I began to see that his rage was his tell. If he had simply admitted Russian interference, accepted Flynn's prosecution and Sessions's recusal, and left well enough alone, I would have a far weaker case to make to you. He might very well be cruising into a comfortable 2020 electoral position. But as the world witnessed Trump's mania, I began to understand the chink in his armor through which everyone could see his true nature. Trump's temper tantrums are a fissure in his power.

With Trump hemorrhaging credibility, Painter and I helped lead the charge for a special counsel to investigate the Russian electoral attack. When there is a scandal that potentially involves the president or those around him, there has been a long tradition in the United States of appointing independent lawyers to look into the matter. Think Archibald Cox during Watergate, or—more controversially—Ken Starr with Clinton. Now we needed one for DOJ's Russia investigation. True to emerging form, it was Trump himself who ensured that our wish would come true.

LIKE A NUCLEAR CHAIN REACTION, Trump's disdain for ethics would only set off escalating crises, culminating in scandals rivaling or exceeding Watergate. The most dramatic acceleration we had yet seen occurred on May 9, with the firing of the FBI director, James Comey. The facts that emerged in the immediate aftermath were shocking, even by Trump's subterranean standards. After learning of Flynn's troubles, Trump had demanded Comey's loyalty. Then, the day after Flynn had been asked to resign, Trump had told Comey, "I hope you can see your way clear to letting this go, to letting Flynn go." When Comey refused and intensified the investigation, Trump fired him, admitting he did so with the "Russia thing" in mind. It would prove to be an inflection point. Trump was illustrating that he was his own worst enemy—or, put differently, the best friend the legal Resistance had.

I told my colleagues on our weekly calls that with this latest firestorm we were sure to get a special counsel. I had confidence in the man making the decision, the newly minted deputy attorney general, Rod Rosenstein. I first met Rosenstein after he got a DOJ job that I was angling for in 1993. I didn't like missing out on the gig, but couldn't kvetch about the tall, earnest, bespectacled young lawyer who had been chosen. I admired his career over the next quarter century. I viewed him as a smart, moderate Republican, the kind I could work with.

On May 17, 2017, Rosenstein came through. When the former FBI director Robert Mueller was appointed as special counsel, virtually everyone on the political spectrum agreed there could not have been a better choice. Everybody, that is, with the exception of President Trump, who would soon kick off a smear campaign, lashing out at Mueller and launching his refrain: "You are witnessing the single greatest WITCH HUNT in American political history—led by some very bad and conflicted people!" The president's absurd claims that Mueller had a conflict of interest, followed by his attacks on the other main players—Comey, Rosenstein, Sessions—served only to telegraph the response of a desperate, guilty man.

The president's conflicts of interest were obvious; the notion that he was claiming *Mueller* had them was idiotic—but predictable. Whataboutism was just another method of Trumpian chaos: turning an accusation around and accusing the accuser. I had known Bob for years and had worked with him when I was in the Obama administration. He was famous for his reticence, and I was certain he would not get into a tit for tat. Knowing that Mueller would remain silent, Painter and I rushed to help command the barricades around him. We also felt compelled to defend Rosenstein's reputation and integrity. We even stood up for Sessions, as odd as that felt. Ever mindful of the need to win the day's news cycle, we explained in op-eds, in television appearances, on radio, and on Twitter just how wrong Trump was, across the board. We were taking no chances on a repeat of Trump's "no conflicts" press conference.

In the events that followed, as you know, Trump's pattern of abuse regarding Russia continued to unfold. Thanks to a series of leaks and scoops, the media operated as a check on Trump, rocking him and the country with a series of revelations. We learned that Trump had been negotiating for a Trump Tower in Russia in 2016 despite his protestations of having no business with that country. Meanwhile, Russian emissaries had visited the New York Trump Tower before the election to offer dirt on his adversary. Predictably, the abuse came with a cover-up. As we would later learn, Trump had instructed his White House counsel, Don McGahn, to have Mueller fired. If true, that would constitute criminal (and impeachable) obstruction of justice.

Mueller and his colleagues racked up an impressive series of convictions and indictments during 2017 and 2018. My optimism soared as the special counsel seemed to be taking steps to hold those around him accountable. Flynn pleaded guilty to lying about his conversations with the Russian ambassador and began cooperating. The campaign adviser George Papadopoulos pleaded guilty to lying about conversations during the campaign with possible Russian agents about creating connections to Trump (although it was not clear if those connections ever materialized). The campaign chair Paul Manafort was indicted, and his campaign deputy and long-time business associate Rick Gates was also charged with personal financial crimes—but ones relating to pro-Russian clients in Ukraine. Three important institutions—law enforcement, the courts, and the press—were all functioning brilliantly. A fourth one, civil society, including CREW and other nonprofit watchdogs, wasn't doing so shabby either.

But my high hopes gradually settled back to earth as one figure evaded accountability: Trump himself.

THROUGHOUT 2017 AND INTO 2018, Trump repeatedly seemed on the verge of firing some combination of Mueller, Rosenstein, and Sessions—an action I was sure would bring him down. The legal Resistance did our best to stop it, furiously defending and praising Mueller. Perhaps we were too successful. Trump never quite went that far, displaying the instinct for survival that has allowed him to live on the bleeding edge of the law for all these decades.

My faith in the courts was gradually tempered by reality as well. The onslaught of private litigation was grinding painfully slowly through the legal system. Our emoluments litigation was representative, with preliminary successes and failures at the district court level, both of the cases on appeal, and no final order yet that Trump had to obey. The flock of cases brought by CREW and many others opposing presidential illegalities had a similarly mixed record. When the occasional case made it up to the Supreme Court for final review, like the Muslim ban, a compliant conservative five-justice majority protected the president more often than not. The Court also broke all records for helping a president through emergency stays of lower court orders against Trump or his administration.

Most sobering of all, as I surveyed Mueller's progress, I started to worry that he too would only go so far against Trump. His court filings had started to pile up, and they offered scant direct evidence against the president. According to press reports, Mueller seemed reluctant to get that evidence by subpoenaing the president, with the special counsel instead getting mired down in months-long negotiations to get answers to questions from Trump. Moreover, DOJ policy prohibited charging a sitting president. I disagreed as a matter of law, but Mueller was a DOJ employee, and one with a long reputation for going by the book. It seemed unlikely that he would defy his own employer by indicting Trump.

That left just one untapped force with the possible power to end Trump's pattern once and for all. For a variety of reasons, that contingency was far from assured. But as 2018 wore on I began to shift my gaze in that direction. It was toward the body that could initiate the impeachment proceedings that I had so far resisted but that increasingly seemed to constitute our best hope: the House Judiciary Committee.

At this point, my primary partner transitioned from Richard Painter to my friend Barry Berke. The six-foot-four-inch Berke was one of America's top trial lawyers, a larger-than-life presence in the courtroom, which would fill to standing room only for his legendary cross-examinations. We had briefly overlapped at Harvard Law School, we had since litigated together, and there was no one I trusted more to analyze the direction of the Mueller investigation. The president's ethics problems had foreshadowed the crisis, but it was now very much a criminal matter, and between us Barry and I had well over half a century of criminal law experience.

We were convinced that Mueller's most devastating blow against Trump was going to land in the area of obstruction of justice. It was not that we thought Trump was innocent in his engagement with Russia. Quite the opposite: his behavior with respect to that adversary and its attack on our democracy was shameful. But based upon what we were reading in the press, and our knowledge of the law, it didn't feel to us as if the evidence or Mueller's findings on collusion would be definite enough for Congress to take action—that is, to launch impeachment. It was just a guess, and we could have been wrong.

In contrast to the collusion, the evidence of barefaced obstruction—including press revelations that Trump had instructed his White House counsel, McGahn, to have Mueller fired and Trump's open tampering with the witnesses Manafort and Michael Cohen—made a powerful case, depending of course on what

Mueller finally said. But what was known seemed like a clear, overwhelming case finally to hold the president to account for his wrongdoing. We decided to go all in by writing and then updating a two-hundred-page report (joined by the executive director of CREW, Noah Bookbinder), laying out the obstruction-based case for impeachment and sharing it with members of Congress whenever they asked us about the situation. And they were starting to ask us about it a lot.

Traditionally, the president's party loses seats in the first midterm election (as happened with the cataclysmic loss of the House to the Tea Party in the Obama era). I felt optimistic that widespread popular revulsion for Trump was bound to trigger a wave of revolt and we'd get the seats back. If that happened, the House would enjoy a privileged place in the process of holding the president accountable—perhaps even being called upon to use the ultimate weapon of impeachment to stop him.

At various points over the course of 2017 and 2018, I was invited to speak to House Democrats singly, in small groups, and as an entire caucus. (I would have gladly accepted the same invitations from the Republican majority, but oddly they were not forthcoming.) I'd lay out the state of play on the Mueller investigation, emoluments, or other legal subjects.

Members of the House Judiciary Committee were regulars at these gatherings. They included the most senior committee Democrat, the former chair John Conyers, an elder statesman of the party who tended to listen more than he talked. Another habitué was his colleague Representative Jerry Nadler, a feisty New Yorker who always responded with pointed questions about emoluments, Trump's misconduct, Trump's ethics, and what it would indeed take to hold him responsible.

As our relationship developed, the committee's sage, longserving, minority staff director, Perry Apelbaum, began inviting me and my colleagues in to brief staff and the members, explain various issues, and field a broad range of questions. Eventually, I helped put together an informal group of experts to meet periodically with Judiciary and answer their queries, including lawyers with experience working as congressional staff. When I was first invited to come in and bring others with me in mid-2017, I told Perry that I thought it would be useful to have another litigator besides myself. I certainly had plenty of trial experience, but it had been ten years since I had tried a case. Perry initially suggested our common friend Abbe Lowell, who had represented the committee Democrats during the Clinton impeachment. A brilliant but prickly criminal litigator who sits behind me in synagogue, Abbe turned me down because of another representation he was about to take. It turned out to be Jared Kushner.

So I approached Barry Berke. It was a bonus that he was a New Yorker; he would bring a fresh perspective to the rest of the D.C.-heavy group I had organized. I told Barry about the situation, and we discussed the possibility—with history as the barometer—that Democrats would take the House back in the midterms. We agreed that, given the president's shenanigans, this could possibly lead to the most interesting legal assignment imaginable: impeachment. Barry is firmly of the defense lawyer school that he has a moral imperative to defend against an overreaching government. He saw Trump as the central talon of that overreach and agreed wholeheartedly about his disastrous pattern of abusing his office. He was on board. As part of welcoming him I shipped him a copy of my guidebook to doing battle with Trump: all six volumes of Churchill's World War II history.

Presidential impeachment was historical, and it was rare. I well remember being thirteen and watching the Watergate hearings on our little TV in my family's hamburger stand. I was transfixed, standing beside my dad, both of us gazing up at the grease-splattered screen as all the president's men testified under tough questioning by the members of Congress and their counsel. "They are fighting for

America," he said, indicating the questioners. It was what he and his generation had done, serving in World War II. I hoped my notion of going to work for Judiciary was compelled by that same sense of genuine, moral purposes—duty, justice, principle. I must admit that the thought of becoming a part of history, viewed by some parent and child out there, watching as *I* grilled witnesses in an impeachment proceeding, might have had something to do with it too.

So I was intrigued as our connection with the committee deepened throughout 2018. In the process, I developed a relationship with Jerry Nadler, a constitutional scholar and principled fighter for justice. I looked forward to his regaling me with stories about how he had refused to bend on matters of principle. If there's one thing that members of Congress respect, it's a spine of steel. His had set him on a course to becoming one of the most outspoken and powerful voices for the Constitution in the Democratic majority. When Representative Conyers, who was running the committee, stepped aside, Nadler ascended to ranking member status.

But there's another side to Jerry Nadler: he's a mensch, as we would say in Yiddish. He is a kind, decent, and warm person—qualities he exhibited when my brother passed and I was sitting shiva, in the fall of 2018. As I was surrounded by a jam-packed hodgepodge of Brookings colleagues, synagogue co-religionists, and former law firm partners, who should come through the door of my apartment but Jerry and his chief of staff, Amy Rutkin. Jerry impressed me, not just because he was able to follow the prayers in perfect Hebrew (as a former yeshiva boy—currently the only one in Congress—he was extremely knowledgeable), but also because of the calm and generous way he handled the swarm of people who quickly surrounded him, eager to bend his ear about a wide array of subjects. Conscious that he had practically been pinned down, I finally rose from the shiva chair and whispered to Lindsay, "Please rescue Jerry."

She approached the group to break it up, but Jerry graciously declined to be rescued. I commented to Amy, who has been working with him for over a decade, on what an impressive performance it was. She smiled and replied, "There is only one Jerry Nadler. The person you see at this shiva is the same person you see on the floor of the United States Congress."

For all his *haimish* (down-home) ways, from our earliest conversations it struck me that Jerry was exactly the man to take down Trump for his constitutional violations, if anyone could. In a long *Times* piece in the run-up to the election, I forecast that the American people would be disgusted by our high-criminal president and the two-headed monster he exhibited: abuse of power and obstruction of justice. Any impeachment of this beast would have to go through the House Judiciary Committee, hence my lack of subtlety when cultivating that relationship. When the Democrats indeed won in November, Jerry ascended to the chair and in December offered Barry and me positions as special counsels to the committee.

I discussed the offer over dinner that night with Lindsay. A college professor who is both a left-wing feminist and a devoutly religious Orthodox Jew, she pays little mind to the Washington scene and its artifice. This post would take a toll on our family, necessitating exceptionally long hours, inevitable media spotlight, and tunnel vision on my part.

I feigned the mandatory reluctance that has characterized all ambitious Americans since the time of George Washington. Lindsay immediately called my bluff, then got on with the reasons why I should take the job. "Well," she said. "Number one, it's imperative that we deal with the president—he's a criminal. Number two, you've spent the past two years obsessed with this, and your entire life preparing for this moment. Number three, it'll drive you crazy if somebody else takes the job, because you'll be jealous that you're not in the middle of it, and every time they make a mistake you're going to make me miserable criticizing the way it's going. And number four, dear, we both know that this is a pro forma conversation and you're going to do it, so just get it over with and say yes, would you?"

It's a good thing that was her answer, because I had already accepted the job. Barry informed me that he was in as well, and we were off to the races.

CHAPTER TWO

Bring It On

I'LL BE HONEST: THE HAMBURGER GREASE THAT SATURATED MY youth will forever remain embedded beneath my fingernails, even if I alone can feel it. Like me, Barry was a working-class kid and the first in his family to go to college; he even had the shared experience of flipping burgers, having worked in a McDonald's.

So yes, when the House Judiciary Committee announced on February 12, 2019, that Barry and I would be joining their staff, we enjoyed that our names were all over the media. But we had little time to savor the spotlight or to reflect on the trajectories we'd traveled. The new Congress was a month into its tenure, it had taken a while for us to get through the bureaucracy and be instated, and the press was rife with speculation that the Mueller Report could drop within a matter of weeks. If (as we expected) Mueller found Trump had obstructed justice over and over again, Congress would be squarely confronted with the question of whether to impeach. We had to be ready for that possibility. On our first morning, after weaving through cameras and reporters, Barry and I were led into the tightly packed warren of committee offices on the first floor of the Rayburn House Office Building. We would be sharing a rectangular, windowless office, barren apart from our two desks, a couch, and a bookcase containing random volumes of committee proceedings going back decades. It reminded me of getting my dorm room—complete with roommate—on the first day of college. (Except my dorm room had a window.) Placing my briefcase down, I surveyed the sparse setting until my eyes landed on Barry. Fresh from his high-rise corner office with floor-to-ceiling glass walls overlooking Manhattan, he shot me a "what have you gotten me into?" look—one I would become all too familiar with over the course of the year.

Our first order of business was not a meet and greet, nor was it a tour of the premises. We did not have the luxury of settling in. In no time at all, we were cycling through meetings with Chairman Nadler and his staff to figure out how first the committee, then the House, could do what the world had failed to do for the past four decades: hold Donald Trump accountable. Nadler's committee and staff were a reflection of Trump's worst nightmare. They included fiery liberals, outspoken feminists, people of color, those from the LGBTQ community, and accomplished children of immigrants. New Yorkers were well represented and Jews not exactly scarce. We began by huddling with the senior staff in the committee's private meeting room, which doubled as a conference room when the members were not using it. Our band included Amy Rutkin, Nadler's long-serving, tough, and savvy chief of staff (now also filling that role for the committee); Perry Apelbaum, the wise mastermind of congressional procedure who had been with the committee the longest—since before the Clinton impeachment days; Aaron Hiller, a brawny Texan who exuded calm but was ready to rumble at a moment's notice; and Arya Hariharan, the youngest and most intense of the crew, who shared several traits with the heroic assassin of the same name on *Game of Thrones,* short in stature and high in courage. Barry and I were the instant litigation department. The two of us had spent the better part of the past twenty-five years practicing criminal law, and the prior two years together studying one high criminal in particular: Trump.

The team looked to us expectantly. We launched the conversation by explaining two things we knew to be certain. One, our president was going to continue to act wrongly. And two, he was going to continue to cover it up. Those have been the resounding bass lines that have defined his entire professional life. They were easy to predict, because that pattern has been repeated for decades as he and his family have navigated civil suits, criminal investigations, and bankruptcies. Along the way, he has been blessed with unbelievable luck—somehow finding a way to dodge virtually every legal blow swung in his direction, including the punches I had tried and failed to land since the first days of his presidency. He'd successfully thrown any number of victims in front of him, unfazed by consequences reaped by others. There are words for this repetitive behavior. They would eventually define the articles of impeachment. And they are what I ask you, the American people, to keep in mind as you cast your vote in his ultimate trial: abuse and obstruction.

After that was established, I took a deep breath, then stated our intention. We were going to succeed in holding Donald Trump accountable for his misconduct and misdeeds. The team leaned forward as Barry picked up the baton, laying out our blueprint for the challenging part: *how*?

We proposed a two-pronged strategy for the staff's—and the chairman's and the committee's—consideration. First, we would anchor the committee's investigation in the Mueller Report and hearing from Bob Mueller himself. If he delivered the goods in writing and in person, we would capitalize on that by then considering whether those findings supported impeaching and removing the president. Based upon what was already public, the evidence for obstruction of justice looked powerful, but we would have to wait for the formal report and the man himself to, we hoped, call out the president's pattern.

But if Mueller didn't come through, despite our high hopes, we would be ready to do our own thing and see where that led. That brought us to the second prong: our own investigation of the president's abuse and obstruction, using a top-down approach. As quickly as possible, we needed to contact the most important individuals, companies, and agencies that had engaged in questionable dealings with Trump. We'd serve them all with document requests, starting with any records they had produced to all other investigators, enabling us to catch up quickly to the state of play.

We would pivot from documents to witnesses, bringing in as many as possible. We'd cast the net wide—not out of careless desperation, but because we had good reason to suspect that a great number of entities had known about, had witnessed, or had conspired in wrongdoing with the president. Trump's children and organizations. Michael Flynn. Jay Sekulow. The NRA. Corey Lewandowski. Paul Manafort. Steve Bannon. Cambridge Analytica. Don McGahn. Roger Stone. And many others. The letters, which we proposed sending out within days, would be straightforward, transparent, and public—thereby placing our actions in direct opposition to the president's habitually covert dealings.

When we finished, we invited our new congressional colleagues to have at the proposed plan, and they did, each taking a turn at honing our strategy. No time was wasted on pleasantries or decorum. They closely considered our approach, flyspecking it and criticizing any aspect that seemed misguided. The scene was an all-out, gloves-off, intellectual rough-and-tumble. Neither Barry nor I was deterred by a good brawl—quite the opposite. We enjoyed defending our approach, explaining the strategic considerations behind our recommendation, and working with our colleagues to figure out the best execution of the plan. We also knew, from decades of experience with letting teams grow, that cohesion was key, and we needed to present a unified front to the chairman and the committee.

Three particularly strong points of concern quickly emerged. We debated them at our initial meeting and in the days that followed. Indeed, the same three issues were bones of contention that we struggled with all year long.

The primary tension was how broad or narrow our claims should be. The president had a long, dirty laundry list of potential abuses of power—the Muslim ban, arrogating powers to himself, using billions of previously appropriated dollars by declaring a state of emergency at the southern border, consistent interference in investigations. His offenses had no end.

After days of internal debate (which, as much as we enjoyed it, felt more like a month of ceaseless back-and-forth), we agreed to an expansive list of claims. We included corruption—such as violations of the emoluments clauses, the president's involvement in hush money payments to mistresses, and the resulting potential conspiracies to violate federal campaign and financial reporting laws. We also agreed to broaden the aperture to keep an eye out for Trump's attacks on the press, judges, DOJ, and law enforcement, as well as misuse of the pardon power and other powers of Trump's office. But the core of our attention to abuse and obstruction remained Mueller's work.

The second issue that we wrestled with was our proposed top-down approach. Congress was used to slowly gathering documents with one or two requests at a time to lay a foundation, interviewing the small fry at the bottom of the food chain, digesting what had been learned, and, over months or even years, working its way up the line. Barry and I suggested starting at the top and getting the worst actors to appear in public hearings, posthaste. Given Trump's ongoing high-crime spree, we simply did not have the time to take the standard route, which would risk us getting lost in a tsunami of paperwork. On this point we won the day, persuading our new colleagues that—under these unique circumstances—we needed to go big or go home.

The final point of contention was how we would deal with Trump's anticipated stonewalling. Trump and those around him were not going to give us anything for free. We were going to have to fight. For *everything*. We advocated fast recourse to the courts to enforce our subpoenas. If we had to go to court to get materials as part of our investigation, so be it. That's what Barry and I did for a living. We would push the ball up the court fast, suing when called for, driving our cases forward.

Here, we encountered some hesitation, in particular about being too quick to sue before we knew the lay of the land. The compromise was to wait to see what was in the Mueller Report and *then* pick the best cases. We knew we would face frivolous but fierce "privilege" battles—that is, claims that documents and testimony we wanted were protected from disclosure under the law. Court clashes of this kind were highly unusual, so the law was undefined and susceptible to abuse. In fact, during the debate we were reminded that the House had only twice resorted to the courts to enforce a subpoena against the executive branch. We agreed that we would dig into the privilege issues and be thoroughly prepared to go to court should the need arise.

Once we had all agreed on the plan, we traipsed directly across the hall to run it by Nadler. Jerry had a long history of volatility with Trump; they had, in fact, been engaged in a decades-long running battle, originating in a heated conflict over a Trump real estate development that Jerry, then a member of the New York State Assembly, blocked. That was back in 1985, when Trump, an ambitious real estate developer known for cutting corners, purchased a run-down railroad yard in Nadler's assembly district and tried to turn it into an urban mega-development, including the world's tallest skyscraper. Nadler, an ambitious, liberal city politician, wanted to upgrade the rail system to assist with jobs in the transport community. According to *The Washington Post*, "When Nadler inquired about the purpose of the soaring skyscraper, Trump said he wasn't sure but knew he wanted to live in the penthouse, so high in the sky that he would have to call the concierge to find out what the weather was below." Nadler had found the whole project grotesque and worked for years to block the request for public funds, even into his time in Congress, fighting Trump to a draw. He knew precisely whom we were dealing with and was as well acquainted as anyone with the president's pattern of greed-driven misconduct, followed by excuses and cover-up tactics.

The chairman was enthroned behind his desk when Barry and I entered his office with our colleagues. Nadler's desk is an apt reflection of his character: neat stacks of paper reflecting the flow of committee business he manages; personal memorabilia scattered throughout; an oversized gavel near at hand symbolizing his ascension to the chair; a mahogany and silver *pushka,* or Jewish charity box; and one of the ever-present stacks of pocket Constitutions he carries with him at all times.

He leaned back in his chair, bespectacled and scholarly. Barry and I assumed the two black leather guest seats across from him and presented the revised two-pronged strategy. His preferred mode of engagement was like that of a justice of the Supreme Court: generally, he would listen impatiently for one or two minutes, then immediately move to peppering the presenter with questions. We didn't have to wait too long for him to engage us with a withering cross fire of questions, opening with "If the Mueller Report turns out to be a dud, will this entire strategy collapse?" But his highest concern—and a legitimate one—was the logistics of our enforcement plan. "Will the cases move quickly enough?"

Barry and I explained our belief, especially given the extraordinary stakes involved, that while the president would certainly engage in dilatory tactics, we would do everything in our power to push through these cases as briskly as possible once they were filed. The success of our strategy depended on it. Barry and I had both expedited high-profile cases, and we knew that we could not anticipate all the detours and delays that we might confront, but the longer we waited to proceed, the harder it would be to get timely decisions.

Next Nadler raised the question of impeachment and probed our views on whether and when to launch such proceedings. "Because—based on what we have right now—we are not there," he added. That skeptical reaction underscored why I felt so comfortable working for him. Even as I had been fighting since day one of Trump's presidency, I had remained on the more cautious wing of the legal Resistance. Nadler was never an obstacle to our presentation of the case of Trump's radical selfishness. He believed that Trump had committed impeachable offenses, including on emoluments. But he is a realist, and he knows his politics. He appreciates that the world does not look like his Brooklyn and Manhattan district. Even our committee—let alone our caucus and the Senate, where an impeachment would have to be tried—was not as open to impeachment as he was.

Switching gears from judge to professor, he explained his test for launching impeachment proceedings: One, has the president committed impeachable offenses? Two, do those offenses rise to such a level of gravity that it is worth putting the country through the trauma of such proceedings? And three, is the evidence so clear and are the offenses so grave that, once we've laid it all out, a good fraction of the voters will admit to themselves—however reluctantly—that we had to do it? He placed the most emphasis on this last point. Nadler believed in the importance of receiving the support of the American public—across party lines. In fact, nobody in that room was preset to impeach the president, unless we could deliver a sound argument to you, the people. There was ample public evidence that *should* concern all Americans. But Jerry knew that we needed hard evidence that *would* move the American people.

I too did not think the publicly available evidence was enough for overturning the will of the American people and for the congressional divisiveness and diversion of impeachment—yet. I wanted to see what Bob Mueller had to say. For the moment, we'd aim to secure documents and testimony on Trump's sundry instances of abuse, obstruction, and corruption.

After Nadler signed off, we presented our strategy to the House Judiciary Committee* on February 27. We wouldn't be able to move forward until they had endorsed our plan. We were a bit nervous as we gathered in the committee's auxiliary hearing room on the second

* Unless otherwise specified, references to the Judiciary Committee are to the Democratic majority, whom I represented and with whom I principally engaged.

floor of Rayburn, a smaller, more modern version of our primary chamber. House Judiciary draws some of Congress's most competitive, ideologically vibrant minds. In addition to the chairman, the committee included the likes of California's Zoe Lofgren, a constitutional authority who had worked on both the Nixon and the Clinton impeachments; Sheila Jackson Lee, a fiery Houston attorney serving her twenty-fifth year in Congress, who took no guff from anyone; Memphis's Steve Cohen, the funny, acerbic chair of the Subcommittee on the Constitution, Civil Rights, and Civil Liberties, who had already come out for impeachment; Hank Johnson of Georgia, whose elegant manner and charming southern drawl belie his steel-trap insight and cutting intellect; and almost twenty of their colleagues. All have litigious instincts and feel little compulsion to keep their opinions to themselves.

I laid out the overarching two-pronged plan: rely on Mueller but in the meantime do our own investigation. Then Barry dove into the details, predicting the roadblocks that we might hit and how we would have to surmount them in order to pierce Trump's defenses. We emphasized that we thought we would be able to collect a lot of information to develop proof of the president's abuse, obstruction, and corruption. And the recipients of the letters would not have the usual excuses of burden or privilege because they would have already gathered and produced the documents we were seeking. Once we finished, the members questioned us about our method. Some felt that there was already overwhelming evidence and that we should just be preparing to pivot to impeachment once we got the Mueller Report. Others questioned whether we would ever get sufficient evidence. Another concern was timing. Could we really enforce the subpoenas and drive those cases forward that quickly?

But our time with our colleagues and the chairman had armed us with answers, and we presented them energetically. Despite their questions, the committee as a whole appeared to be enthusiastic about the plan. Indeed, some were too enthusiastic, urging greater expedition than our already brisk pace. Nonetheless, it helped that the chairman had given us the green light, and as we left the grilling by the committee, we could exhale. We were cleared to move forward, with Godspeed.

WE BEGAN WITH SWEEPING DOCUMENT requests for materials that the key players had handed over to government investigators over the past two years. Even when one is seeking high-level witnesses as quickly as possible, a paper trail is essential. I undertook the task of leading the drafting of the document requests that would harvest the evidence of Trump's abuse of power and obstruction. Barry led on developing the list of people to target. As I began working with the team on drafting the letters, I was reminded of one of the biggest differences between government and my previous gigs: as a member of Jerry's lean, feisty crew, I had to do a lot of my own work. I had most recently been challenging Trump with the support of my colleagues at CREW, where I had almost thirty experienced litigators and other professionals working with me. Sometimes I had to fight to get to do real work on a case. Here, there were fewer staff members, and each of them had their hands full. I had to get started on my own.

Turns out, I was a little rusty. After I circulated my first effort at drafting, Barry called me on Saturday night, cleared his throat, and said, "Uh, bud, I hate to break it to you, but . . . this is . . . no good at all." I had basically written, "Give us the documents that were given to other investigators," then listed those investigations.

"You have to spell out, point by point, exactly what documents you want . . . for each of the recipients," Barry reminded me. "Nobody is going to just say, 'Oh, fine! I'll pull up the tractor trailer to your loading dock.'"

I looked back at my efforts, seeing that he was right and that I was going to be in for a world of pain that weekend. I needed to produce a detailed template that we could adapt for what was (at that point) nearing fifty individuals, with the list growing by the hour. I worked Saturday night, Sunday, and into the early hours of Monday morning. It would prove to be the first of many nights that afforded me little sleep. (That is perhaps why I now have an emerging skunk-like streak of white hair running down the middle of my head. I wouldn't be surprised if there was a similar, parallel scar on my brain, burned into it by the anxiety of my battles with Trump.)

From the time of Barry's call to Monday morning, I never made it out of my house—or my pajamas. But, somehow, I managed to get a reasonable set of requests together. From each recipient, we requested roughly three or four pages of specific records relating to Trump's abuses of power, corruption, and obstruction. In the meantime, Barry and the team were researching and further developing our list of recipients. I had been so absorbed in my task that I didn't pay much attention to how high the number had grown. I had estimated we'd be hitting somewhere just over fifty letters. To my astonishment, once the team had dug into all the people and entities who could offer insight into Trump's abuse of power and other misconduct—because they either were privy to details or were possible accomplices—the list cascaded down the page, totaling more than eighty.

"That's too many," was my first response. We wanted to go big, but maybe not quite *that* big. Our efforts might be seen as overbearing or lacking in focus. Trump world would respond with fury (and it did). But, as Arya said to me, "Look, his crimes are sprawling. If we want to capture them all, we need to send out a lot of letters." Barry concurred, and I eventually came around. We'd come in by storm and escalate our investigations by tackling all the primary contacts in one sweep.

I was starting to wonder what I had been thinking, taking this on (while also maintaining a substantial part-time role at Brookings). Feeling as if I were killing myself on a treadmill of work that was getting me nowhere, I'd send regular snarling texts to Barry, who was equally exhausted. Just as overloaded, he'd snarl right back at me, "Norm, what the hell have you gotten *me* into?"

It turned out that he had at least one greater reason to complain than I did.

On Monday, February 25, just as Barry and I were settling into our office, he got a call on his cell. After listening for a while, he began asking, with a rising decibel of incredulity, "*What?* What? What!" Naturally, my ears perked up, and I spun around in my chair, waiting for him to get off the phone. Finally, he hung up and turned to me, bewildered. "Norm. Donald Trump is saying that I have a conflict of interest because I'm *his* lawyer."

"*What?*"

Barry proceeded to explain the absurd logic. His firm in New York had previously done some work for companies related to the Trump Organization. The work was over, and Barry had been uninvolved with it. All the same, Trump's people were claiming Barry had a conflict of interest and that the House could not work with him. As with the president's earlier claims about Mueller's supposed conflicts, I knew this was nonsense. However, as an ethicist, I also knew that these kinds of allegations—even when frivolous—can prove consequential. If nothing else, they serve to harass, to create a distraction, and to make an excuse for delay: three of Trump's go-to tactics for dealing with challengers.

Sure enough, it wasn't long before the Republicans on the committee started complaining, firing vehement letters at Nadler. The ranking member, Doug Collins, whom we would develop a cordial relationship with over time, wrote an insinuating, accusatory missive to Nadler, throwing barbs at him for allowing "these two individuals to become the judge, jury and executioner regarding impeachment proceedings." (Now I was dragged into it as well.) Suddenly other committees were calling Judiciary, asking, "What is this? Your new consultant has a conflict?"

I told Barry not to worry; this was a standard part of doing battle in Washington. "It's just a reflection of their fear of you," I assured him. And, to the credit of our team, neither Nadler nor any of the other Judiciary majority or staff members so much as flinched at the allegations. These tough brawlers were also loyal, moral people who didn't recoil at flailing punches swung by lesser fighters. But Barry was wholly unaccustomed to having his ethics questioned, by the president of the United States no less. I continued insisting that this was business as usual in Washington. Barry—with the pained expression of a man who cared sincerely about having his reputation dragged through the mud—replied, in an anguished tone, "Then give me New York, any day." This became a recurring theme between us as he began referring to himself as a short-term visitor. On countless occasions I'd say, "It's just D.C., Barry," to which he'd hurl back, "Well, I'm only here on a tourist visa." Eventually, his usual cheer returned. We had work to do. In the end, the whole affair served only to further inform our understanding of Trump's response tactics: attack and keep attacking, with no regard for merits or the truth.

If the objective was to slow us down, it failed. On Monday, March 4, we launched our offensive and sent out the first salvo of eighty-one letters. They began, "The House Judiciary Committee is investigating a number of actions that threaten our nation's long-standing commitment to the rule of law, including allegations of obstruction of justice, public corruption, and other abuses of power." We had chosen those focus points very carefully. We did not doubt Trump's collusion with Russia, but the relevant events had largely occurred before he was president, and the evidence was murkier, making the legal violations less clear. By contrast, Trump's interference with Mueller's investigation had been committed when he was using his powers of office and in our view was a clear case of obstruction of justice. The same was true of his emoluments and myriad other acts of misconduct. We mostly left collusion to others, focusing instead on what we believed were the most egregious—and provable—sins within our committee's jurisdiction.

The letters had exactly the influence we hoped they would. By making them public, we let every curious American know what we believed the president had done wrong. They also created some internal blowback, including from our colleagues on the House Permanent Select Committee on Intelligence. We had informed them and other House committees in advance that we would be sending out some letters. But we had not determined the full scope of what we were doing ourselves, much less disclosed it to others. As a result, the Intelligence Committee felt, with some merit, that we were barging into their existing investigations dealing with many of the same issues.

On March 8, we received a visit from Dan Goldman and Maher Bitar, the chief investigative counsel and general counsel of the Intelligence Committee. I knew and liked both of them. Dan, whom I'd previously met through liberal lawyer circles, had spent a decade as a prosecutor in the elite Southern District of New York's U.S. Attorney's Office. Graduates of that office are known for their healthy sense of self, and he was no exception. Handsome and well-to-do, he is not shy about sharing his views. But neither am I. Maher is a lawyer and career foreign policy analyst whom I had first met when we were both working for the State Department. Soft-spoken, smart, intense, and hardworking, he usually sports a short beard that is little more than an overgrown five-o'clock shadow. Dan and Maher were one of those odd couples that made a balanced team: one forthright, one modest; one clean-shaven, one bearded; one an outsider to D.C., one a consummate insider.

Barry was out of the office, so Aaron, Arya, and I welcomed them. We hastened to explain that we did not intend to intrude on their jurisdiction; they were still free to lead on collusion issues. We were simply attempting to understand the full range of Trump's misconduct and wanted to work collaboratively with them. Goldman is a tough negotiator and clearly did not believe me. After he repeatedly rejected my explanation, I blew up, startling everyone. "Are you calling me a liar? Fuck you!" I said, and then, unfortunately, repeated it twice.

We went back and forth (giving Aaron and Arya a story they enjoyed sharing for quite some time thereafter). Eventually, we were able to convince our colleagues of our good faith and clear the air. But those nascent tensions over Judiciary's aggressive approach to investigating potential grounds for impeachment would prove a harbinger of the various frictions that would arise within Congress over the course of the year.

The letters would ultimately yield tens of thousands of documents revealing Trump's long-term pattern of abuse and obstruction and inform every step we took. And the letters were helpful not only for the records we received but also because they served as our calling card. Among other things, they flushed out the lawyers for the eighty-one recipients. Between us, Barry and I knew virtually every one of them. Countless conversations, revelations, and relationships sprang from that, each one contributing to the trajectory of our year.

Sometimes the lawyers connected us directly with their clients, which was how we got to know Michael Cohen. Cohen, the president's former personal lawyer and fixer, had offered a sequence of inconsistent testimonies to the authorities about Trump before eventually pleading guilty. His crimes included making false statements and violating campaign finance laws through his involvement in paying hush money to cover up Trump's affairs. Within six weeks he would be reporting to prison but nonetheless extended an invitation for us to come meet with him in New York City. I had to be in the city for other reasons, so we agreed to sit down on March 27. Barry and our newest colleague, Sarah Istel—a brilliant litigation associate who came to us from the law firm Paul, Weiss, Rifkind, Wharton & Garrison—would join by phone.

Cohen, with his familiar lachrymose expression above a well-tailored but rumpled blazer, struck me as having a sympathetic side. As we talked about how his life had converged with Trump's and then sharply split, I found—to my surprise—that Michael was genuinely remorseful. He discussed Trump's method of implicitly making demands in such a way that helped him evade getting caught while placing the blame on others. This is a man, he said, who is willing to do *anything*. No ethics, no shame, so I should be ready for that, he warned me.

Hearing Cohen explain Trump's behavior was like listening to a profiler at the FBI describe how a serial killer thinks. Michael had witnessed Trump commit crimes or cover-ups again and again. That day and at a follow-up meeting on May 3, Cohen walked us through the collusion allegations from the perspective of the man who had helped Trump secretly negotiate for a Trump Tower in Moscow during the campaign. Cohen told us about his involvement in a plan to offer Putin a $50 million penthouse in the development, revealing that he had discussed it with Trump, who liked the idea and thought it was funny. (Needless to say, it was not; on the contrary, it was a possible Foreign Corrupt Practices Act violation.) Cohen also illuminated the president's obstruction, explaining how it felt to be on the receiving end of Trump's blandishments to stop him from cooperating with the government—and after he did cooperate, the president's furious public assault on him and his family.

Then there were the illegalities around Trump's hush money payments, a scheme to which Cohen pled guilty. Cohen facilitated secret payments to two former mistresses of Trump—"Individual-1" in the prosecution's court filings. The payments were likely illegal campaign contributions because the silence they bought benefited the campaign. The last of them was made just days before ballots were cast, while the controversy was still swirling around Trump's *Access Hollywood* comments, and another sex scandal could have tilted the election. Cohen had used his own money to fund some of the payments, with the president repaying him while in office. That meant we were looking at not only a campaign finance crime but also a federal false statement violation by the president. It seemed he had intentionally omitted the debt he owed Cohen from his 2017 financial disclosures—filed under criminal penalties for such omissions.

Michael shared documents, played tape recordings, offered insights, and took us through Trump's sordid past—and present. At times, his candid observations became profoundly emotional. At one point he asked me in a quiet voice, laced with anguish, "Norm . . . how is it that I'm going to jail, while Donald Trump, who did *so many worse things,* is sitting in the White House, untouched?" Abuse, corruption, cover-up; abuse, corruption, cover-up. Trump had been doing it for decades; he began the cycle anew from the moment he was sworn in and returned to it time and again while sailing through his presidency, and there is no doubt that he will continue this pattern. Michael Cohen was a complicated figure. He had done terrible things himself. But I sensed a vein of decency as well, and felt sorry for the man when he was hauled off to Otisville prison in New York State (from where he would send me occasional messages, funny and bitter). He was a victim of his own worst tendencies, yes, but there could be no question they were encouraged by his proximity to Trump.

Barry, the team, and I debated about how we would present to Congress the pattern Cohen had dramatized for us. I submit it to you now. How long are we willing to accept this, from anybody? How has Trump gotten away with it for so long? The mystery of how Trump manages to live on the edge of criminality without ever being held accountable is one that with my faith in our institutions I still do not understand.

"No matter," I told Barry and my other colleagues upon my return from the Cohen interview. Trump was not going to get away with it anymore. Despite the roadblocks, the runarounds, and all the lies, my optimism was stronger than ever. After all, investigating the Trump abyss was the best possible man for the job: my former colleague the ex-FBI director Robert Mueller. Shortly before our March 27 Cohen meeting, we got word that Mueller's report was due to arrive any moment, bringing phase one of our investigation to the fore and surely complementing our own work to date on phase two.

With Mueller ready to report, Trump would finally face justice. Barry and I had been so confident of this outcome we had made a significant bet that it would impact our careers forever.

What could go wrong?

CHAPTER THREE

Spin Class

My confidence in Bob Mueller was so strong that I had quit both CREW and CNN to join the Judiciary Committee and gone part-time at Brookings (I would eventually transition to a full leave). Not everyone understood those choices. Impeachment seemed like a remote contingency to many, and as one of my TV colleagues said to me on my way out, "People go to work on the Hill to get a job at CNN, not vice versa." But I knew Bob, I knew the publicly available evidence, and I had seen a light in his eye when we had discussed bringing criminals to justice—the glint of a true lawman. To my mind, there was simply no way that he would let Trump off the hook.

Bob and I had first met decades before, when I was a defense lawyer and he was a widely respected federal prosecutor. I really got to know him when he paid a visit to Prague in his capacity as FBI director when I was serving as ambassador in April 2012. As he deplaned, I was welcoming an American hero. Mueller's tenure as director had begun a decade earlier, just one week before 9/11.

I picked him up at the airport in my heavily armored black Cadillac, pleased to see him again. His security detail traveled with us in the motorcade, along with a police escort. Anybody who has watched Bob Mueller, in action or otherwise, could gather that his personality leans toward the stern. In his own ex-marine, ex-prosecutor way, he is actually very friendly but disinclined toward small talk. As we sped downtown, he started grilling me about how I was liking the ambassadorship.

"What's not to like?" I asked cheerfully. Feeling as if I were on the verge of being subjected to one of his famous cross-examinations, I turned the tables and asked him for management advice. He responded by telling me about the first staff meeting he ran as director of the FBI. His office had a large conference table, which was occupied by top career officers. They all listened closely as he laid out his plans for the agency. After he finished, the silence was broken by his deputy, another career officer, who told the group, "Don't listen to him; he only *thinks* he runs this place." "So, you want my advice?" Bob concluded, with a hint of a smile. "My advice is to keep in mind . . . that you only *think* you run the place."

We remained in amicable touch after his visit, and I was even able to return the favor of his advice when he considered what to do post-FBI. I visited him in his vast office in the crumbling, brutalist bureau (where I also would later sit with his successor, Jim Comey), discussing life in the private sector. We had both worked at the same law firm (albeit at different times), a shared experience that helped me talk through his exit strategy and what to expect once he made the transition from the FBI.

Bob Mueller is one of the great Americans who has acted with grit and integrity throughout his life. He went from Princeton to the U.S. Marines after a beloved friend was killed in Vietnam; he and others enlisted, honoring their friend's memory. After earning a Purple Heart and a Bronze Star for valor, he began a lucrative law career in private practice. The call to serve led him back to working in the Department of Justice and as a U.S. Attorney. He then chose an unheard-of step down the career ladder to work again as an ordinary line prosecutor for the government doing something he loved: trying cases. From there, he ascended to the highest rank of public law enforcement. Then, of course, came his most relevant swan song of a role as special counsel, the one that will emblazon him in our nation's historical record.

Given this life of service and accomplishments, you will understand why betting on Mueller to deliver a hard-hitting report felt like a sound wager. Plus, the public facts of the obstruction of justice case were so clear. There was little question in my mind that the Mueller Report would be as just and unflinching on the president's obstruction crimes as the man himself—in other words, a bracing condemnation of a shameless, crooked president.

That said, as special counsel, Mueller ran an exceptionally leak-free ship. I knew as little about the conclusions of his investigation as anybody else. That included where he and his able gang of avengers would land on the other main issue: collusion by Trump and his circle with Russia. As profoundly rotten as that alleged conduct was, there is no federal offense of collusion, and I wasn't sure the evidence would quite rise to the level of conspiracy. For those and other reasons, Trump's pattern of obstruction of justice while in office seemed like the more obvious bet for an impeachable offense (or offenses).

I was painfully reminded on March 11 that not everyone agreed with me. Barry and I were sitting in Arya's office, discussing the rumors circulating that Mueller was wrapping up his investigation. She had CNN on, when the announcer said, "just in, House Speaker Nancy Pelosi just spoke to *The Washington Post* about President Trump and impeachment." Our heads simultaneously swiveled to the screen like in a cartoon. A slide with Pelosi's quotation filled the screen as the anchor read the words.

"I'm not for impeachment," Pelosi said. "Impeachment is so divisive to the country that unless there's something so compelling and overwhelming and bipartisan, I don't think we should go down that path, because it divides the country." She added an opinion she would repeat throughout the spring: "He's just not worth it."

There we were, plotting out our intensive strategy to open up the road to impeachment, just as the most powerful person in the House was announcing to America that she wouldn't consider going down it. The room felt heavier under the additional pressure: *unless there's something so compelling and overwhelming and bipartisan.* Barry flashed a wry, familiar grimace and said sarcastically, "Gee, thanks for telling me before I left my family and my law practice and moved to D.C. for impeachment." Arya straightened her posture, her defiant chin raised, and declared that we would just have to locate that compelling and overwhelming evidence. And we all knew where we might find it.

On Friday, March 22, the first official notice arrived that Mueller had concluded his investigation. Aaron Hiller called Barry and me into his office and made sure we closed the door behind us. "Guys, I just heard from DOJ. They're delivering some kind of a letter today." I accompanied Aaron at 4:00 p.m. to greet a very nervous young assistant from the DOJ office. She met us in the foyer of the House Judiciary Committee suite wearing a large puffy coat, her hands slightly trembling either from the cold or from being tasked with delivering letters of such gravity. There was no need to put the young woman through the ordeal; the letter could just as easily have been emailed. But DOJ had been hand delivering urgent missives since long before the advent of email, and I suppose the formalities had to be observed. At any rate, we were as eager to receive it as she was eager to scurry off. Aaron opened the envelope carefully as we stood in the reception area. I peered over his meaty shoulder, our eyes quickly scanning the one-page document:

> Dear Chairman Graham, Chairman Nadler, Ranking Member Feinstein, and Ranking Member Collins:
>
> I write to notify you . . . that Special Counsel Robert S. Mueller III has concluded his investigation of Russian interference in the 2016 election and related matters . . . The Special Counsel has submitted to me today a

> "confidential report explaining the prosecution or declination decisions" he has reached . . . I am reviewing the report and anticipate that I may be in a position to advise you of the Special Counsel's principal conclusions as soon as this weekend. Separately, I intend to consult with Deputy Attorney General Rosenstein and Special Counsel Mueller to determine what other information from the report can be released to Congress and the public . . . I remain committed to as much transparency as possible, and I will keep you informed as to the status of my review.

"At last!" I thought. But after I made a copy for Barry and the two of us parsed it together, line by line, alarm bells began ringing in my head. Attorney General William Barr planned to advise us on the special counsel's principal conclusions. Why only his conclusions? We had demanded the entire report, as well as the underlying material. We did not want Barr's CliffsNotes. And what about the declaration regarding transparency? If the attorney general was "committed to transparency," why had he not just sent the conclusions he alluded to, or—better still—the whole report? The timing of the delivery was also suspicious. The Friday afternoon news dump was a D.C. tradition; the later undesirable news broke, the better. I ought to know; I had practiced this tactic myself from time to time in my career. We still had no indication of what to expect, yielding a disquieting angst that would soon be felt across the nation.

Despite those concerns, the three people involved in the letter brought my heart rate down to a normal pace. I trusted Rosenstein, whom I had known for years and publicly defended so often. I had tremendous faith in Mueller. I even had some lingering residue of hope for Barr, whose nomination had been greeted with cautious optimism by those I trusted, like my Brookings colleague Ben Wittes. With apprehension and wavering hope, we waited. "As soon as this weekend" was hardly a crumb. What it offered was two more sleepless nights.

Almost immediately, reports started leaking in, each one more certain than the previous drip, regarding Barr's timing for his follow-up letter. It seemed it was going to land in the only zone that is deader than Friday afternoon: a Sunday afternoon—the closest thing to a global Shabbat in the news world. Other than those on the Mueller beat, the media was mostly at rest, or coming home from their weekends away. That meant Barr could deliver his pronouncement with the least amount of noise. Barry and I decided to be together, on duty, side by side, and ready to respond with the rest of the Judiciary staff.

The summary letter arrived on Sunday at 3:45 P.M. Aaron accepted a hard copy—the ritual hand transmission again—then scanned and emailed it around. The first page—quickly skimmed—was a restatement of what we knew already: that Mueller had provided his report to Barr, whose following remarks would summarize his findings. The bold headline on the second page jumped out: "Russian Interference in the 2016 Presidential Election." Despite my desire for the truth and nothing but the truth, hope flared for the briefest sliver of a second, only to be extinguished, harshly: "The Special Counsel's investigation did not find that the Trump campaign or anyone associated with it conspired or coordinated with Russia in its efforts to influence the 2016 U.S. presidential election." Well, I reasoned, we had been braced for that.

My eye flew down the page and onto the top of page 3: "Obstruction of Justice." Surely Mueller had delivered here. Instead it read, "The Special Counsel therefore did not draw a conclusion—one way or the other—as to whether the examined conduct constituted obstruction." What? How? The evidence was so clear! I read the sentence again, then stumbled on. There had to be some explanation. "Instead, for each of the relevant actions investigated, the report sets out evidence on both sides of the question and leaves unresolved what the Special Counsel views as difficult issues of law and fact." Both sides? Unresolved? Difficult issues? I read Barr's words again and again, stunned, struggling to comprehend them.

I sat back in my chair, light-headed. No obstruction? President Trump had ordered Don McGahn to have the special counsel fired, orchestrated bogus statements, commanded false documentation, and—in plain sight—engaged in witness tampering with Cohen and Manafort (and perhaps Flynn) . . . to list just a *sample* of the outrageous acts of which you, the public, were already aware.

When I read, "Deputy Attorney General Rod Rosenstein and I have concluded that the evidence developed during the Special Counsel's investigation is not sufficient to establish that the President committed an obstruction-of-justice offense," my heart plummeted. Mueller had abdicated the duty to justice, leaving her exposed, vulnerable, and Barr and Rosenstein had completely betrayed her.

Et tu, Rod? Dazed and distressed, I talked it through with Barry. As brothers are wont to do, he gave me a knowing glance, followed by a shrug: "I told you so." In fairness, he had indeed told me that he did not share my confidence that Rosenstein would cause Barr to do the right thing, knowing him since they had attended law school together. And unless the attorney general had locked Rosenstein in a basement and compelled his signature under threat of bodily harm, I had to concede Barry was right. Rosenstein was one more victim who had been sucked into Trump's dark vortex.

As Barry and I read and reread the summary, my shock faded into suspicion and then outright disbelief. The questions that had gnawed at me from the first letter resurfaced. Why was Barr cherry-picking the conclusions instead of just giving us the report, or at least sections of it—introductions, summaries, conclusions? If Mueller, after twenty-two months, with over a dozen seasoned prosecutors, more than twenty-eight hundred subpoenas, and his many guilty pleas, convictions, and cooperators could not reach a conclusion, how had Barr done so in the mere forty-eight hours since the report was delivered? And why release the summary at the tail end of a Sunday afternoon if the findings were so great?

Something was not right here, and we would be damned if we would roll over. The chairman and the committee felt the same way.

Nadler had not bothered with shock or suspicion; he saw right through Barr's fabrications and was blunt about it: "He's lying." Barry and I, working furiously with the rest of the team, began work on a draft statement, talking points, and a joint letter for Nadler and his colleagues.

Simultaneously, the whole staff worked the phones with reporters, urging the Sunday afternoon media not to fall for DOJ's attempt to allow the summary to slip under the radar. We explained why they should find the holes in both letters profoundly suspicious and emphasized that these were not Mueller's conclusions, but rather were those of President Trump's handpicked attorney general.

It was to little avail. There was no resisting the gravitational force of this masterful spin job: a curveball whirled perfectly into the catcher's mitt with a loud smack as the hitter flails . . . strike three. Nadler, with our help, put out a fast statement to try to argue the call. His forceful New York and Old Testament style—Brooklyn by way of the Judaean desert—was right on the mark. "These shortcomings in today's letter are the very reason our nation has a system of separation of powers. We cannot simply rely on what may be a partisan interpretation of facts," he insisted to the press in a statement with his congressional colleagues.

Nevertheless, our attempts at media persuasion largely fell on deaf ears. Reporter after reporter responded, "But Barr said he didn't find anything." It was infuriating, how ready they were to accept such a blatant facade. "Mueller Finds No Trump-Russia Conspiracy," said *The New York Times*. Publications across the nation agreed: "Mueller Finds No Collusion Between Trump and Russia" (*Financial Times*); "Mueller Doesn't Find Trump Campaign Conspired with Russia" (*The Wall Street Journal*); "Mueller Report Finds No Trump-Russia Collusion" (NPR); "No Collusion. Key Takeaways from Mueller's Russia Findings" (Associated Press). There were scant exceptions, but not enough.

As a sometime practitioner of the Washington dark arts (though always for the good, I hoped), I had to take my hat off to Barr. From a clinical perspective, the maneuver was perfectly executed: capitalizing on the weekend timing; writing a letter long enough that it seemed substantial, even though it was utterly vapid; and employing a magisterial tone to cover up open, gaping questions. Barr had managed to judo flip the media's sense of fairness, and in one fell swoop the AG had sucked the oxygen away from the biggest scandal of the Trump presidency to date.

My faith in the press, not to mention my belief in the power of my own advocacy, was deeply shaken. Since that day in January 2017 when I had worked with Walt Shaub to reverse Trump's false declarations that he had "no conflicts," I had counted on the media as one of the safeguards of democracy. Much of what we knew about Trump's abuses and obstruction in the Mueller investigation was thanks to them. Perhaps they felt the obligation now to make up for that—to somehow bend in the opposite direction. Or maybe Barr just understood that they would credit what he said.

The media headlines were of course amplified by the president, on air and in his tweets: "No Collusion, No Obstruction, Complete and Total EXONERATION. KEEP AMERICA GREAT!" We would soon see from Barr's smug, smirking demeanor, as he ultimately refused to submit to questions by our committee, that he was aware of the caliber of his propaganda job. Meanwhile, I wanted to open the window and scream to the world, "He's a charlatan!" But—and this frustrated me to no end—I had no proof positive. My *kishkes* told me that the letter was filled with holes. But at that point, I knew only what everybody else did. The most I could ask was for the press to reserve judgment. How could I persuade the media and you, the American people, not to take Barr's bait until we had Mueller's full work?

Hours later, after we had written the last talking point, sent the last text and email, and been hung up on by the last reporter hurrying to meet her deadline, Barry and I finally had a moment to ourselves. There was nothing to say; we just looked at each other, bewildered. Our big bet on justice was not looking so good. We still had the evidence we had gathered from the eighty-one letters. But Mueller had always been the anchor of our strategy. If there was no obstruction of justice, our gamble had failed. Luckily, we were on the same page. "This just can't be right," Barry said.

"I know!" I exploded. "But would Barr really have sacrificed his reputation and his career for the president? How could he distort the underlying report *that* heavily without treading into obstruction himself?"

You know the answer to that question. We would soon find out as well. Lesson learned: in the era of Trump, if you assume the worst of those around him, you are seldom disappointed. The institutions in which I placed so much hope were bending under the pressure.

BARR'S SPIN JOB STARTED TO fall apart shortly after that fateful Sunday, March 24. On March 29, Barr himself issued an odd, backtracking letter claiming that his earlier characterization of the Mueller Report was not intended as a "summary" and emphasizing that he would release a redacted version of the report "by mid-April, if not sooner."

Inside DOJ, rumor had it that Mueller and his team were not happy. We started to hear from reporters and other sources that, like Nadler, some on Team Mueller also thought Barr had corrupted their work. Weeks later, the full story broke. After the March 24 summary was released, none other than Mueller himself had written a short, severe complaint to Barr, claiming that his summary "did not fully capture the context, nature, and substance of this Office's work and conclusions." Mueller resented the response Barr's analysis had provoked: "There is now public confusion about critical aspects of the results of our investigation." Ah. That would explain Barr's backtracking letter.

As the initial evidence of a dispute began emerging in the first week of April, we saw more publications describing the fallacies of Barr's summary. Barry and I enjoyed a session of discussions with the press, trying not to gloat but failing. That Team Mueller too found Barr's summary insufficient and confusing reignited our confidence. Far more satisfying was that we would soon get our hands on the holy grail: Mueller's report itself. DOJ said to expect the report in the second week of April, and then in the third week.

Monday of that third week, word came: the document would land on Thursday, April 18. The report followed a similar means of transmission as the two Barr letters, hand delivered by a DOJ courier, in hard copy and on a CD-ROM. The delivery had something else in common with the letters: it was carefully timed, arriving right before the Passover and Easter holidays, and after Congress had gone out of session. Just as before, the press had started churning rumors of when we would receive it; tensions rose as odd bread crumbs emerged, such as claims that the president's lawyer Rudy Giuliani would be reading the report first.

Our moment of truth, the anchor of countless hours of work over the past years, the document for which we had all been waiting, arrived at the Judiciary Committee offices late on Thursday. If the previous hand deliveries had something of ritual about them, this one required it: two thick volumes clocking in at 448 pages, accompanied by an electronic version too large for email. (The online version that DOJ would shortly post caused its website to labor and then freeze, at least on our clerks' computers.)

What Barry and I saw in those pages vindicated all our suspicions. The portrait presented in volume 1 of Trump's and his campaign's engagement with a hostile foreign actor turned out to be far more damning than the one presented by Barr and Rosenstein. It was true: Mueller had not found conspiracy (or coordination), but he expressly denied that he had made a determination in regards to collusion. He certainly had developed plenty of evidence of it, however.

Volume 1 of the report documented Trump's wrongdoing in spades: inviting Russia to hack his opponent's emails, denying he had economic ties to Russia despite the negotiations for Trump Tower Moscow, his campaign welcoming Russian agents to New

York Trump Tower to get dirt on Hillary Clinton. When you read the entire report (and maybe you have), what emerges is that same definitive pattern that would have infuriated our founders, who had a horror of foreign influence and corrupt elections. Not once, not twice, but again and again and again, the president or those around him engaged with a hostile foreign adversary for personal or political gain during the 2016 election season. In any normal circumstance, that headline would have ruled the day and provided ample grounds to open an investigation of impeachment for abuse of power.

But what Mueller delivered in volume 2 was even more devastating: a 187-page powerful and detailed analysis highlighting ten episodes of obstruction of justice committed by Trump. Any one of those acts would have been sufficient to open impeachment proceedings against a president. Any of them! There were *ten*.

Five of those episodes met every qualifying element of criminal obstruction. Those five most damaging episodes, exhaustively documented in the report, boil down to a very simple tale that bears repeating. On June 17, 2017, the president instructed his White House counsel, Don McGahn, to seek removal of Special Counsel Mueller. When McGahn refused, the president went outside the White House to appeal to one of his henchmen, Corey Lewandowski. When this came out months later, it became apparent that even Lewandowski—as odious a character as you will find in Trump world—would not execute the order. And, incredibly, when the effort to get McGahn to obstruct justice on his behalf came to light, the president told McGahn to make a false statement, to cover it up, and to create a phony document, all while a criminal investigation was ongoing. Finally, the special counsel confirmed the president's open witness tampering with Manafort and Cohen, and backed it with a mountain of evidence (though the president's Twitter feed alone would have largely sufficed). Constitutionally, the contents of volume 2 were as bad as any misconduct ever addressed in a presidential impeachment, Nixon's or otherwise.

"Barr *did* sacrifice his reputation by mischaracterizing the report,"

I told Barry. But the two of us had little time to discuss. We had to get our response out fast to jam our foot in the door of public reaction before Trump, Barr, and their enablers slammed it shut. The team collaborated with Nadler, who was equally disgusted, releasing a fast statement that was a blistering clarion call, urging, "The responsibility now falls to Congress to hold the President accountable for his actions."

With Judiciary's response registered, we all had to dive back into the thoroughly detailed, albeit partially redacted, pages of the report. As we attempted to wrap our brains around what was, to our minds, the most scathing official exposé ever written about an American president, Barry was the first to point out that Mueller likely reached conclusions, at least on those five crimes, only to strip the conclusions out and leave the analysis behind. The report didn't make sense otherwise. But that meant you had to wade through a jungle of legalese to piece everything together. Between the density of the report and the obscurity Barr had implanted with his letter, even the experts could not agree; most concurred that the report showed the elements of multiple crimes, but debates broke out all over the internet and cable about how many and what they were, with dueling "heat maps" showing the crimes and their proof.

By the time the sun rose the next morning, the team had produced a thorough analysis, backed by extensive excerpts, explaining just how bad the report was for the president. Barr had used the past weeks to erect an edifice of falsity around Mueller's work—a thick, deeply hardened wall of lies. Applying our jackhammers to that structure as we argued with reporters made us realize just how much the concrete had hardened. Our pounding, we feared, was creating only more dust and noise. But we furiously drilled nevertheless, and the resulting press coverage was certainly better than that for the Barr letter. It was impossible not to wonder, however, if the public consensus would ever fully recover from Barr's initial spin job.

Our strategy was informed by a Thursday conference call with the full committee to walk them through the report and benefit from their analysis. Jerry and Aaron led the conversation as the members grappled with the damning evidence and with Mueller's mystifying failure to state conclusions. David Cicilline was incredulous as he pointed to particular passages and asked, "How could Mueller not have found a conspiracy?" Dave was an outspoken fighter for justice; we had been friends ever since he led a delegation to Prague to champion human rights and helped me light up the embassy in rainbow colors to celebrate Prague Pride during my ambassadorship. He was a master of the cutting rhetorical question, but on this occasion, he was genuinely baffled and disappointed. Many of us were—Mueller's failure to do the right thing was confounding and had left the door ajar for Barr and Rosenstein to charge through.

A number of members had already come out for impeachment, with that sentiment running strong over the course of the call. Mueller, in his painfully restrained fashion, had actually made an implicit impeachment referral, referencing "constitutional processes for addressing presidential misconduct." The principal such constitutional process was of course impeachment, as Mueller pointed out in a footnote citing the relevant portions of the Constitution. That made the committee even more outraged about Barr's lies. Overnight, the attorney general had completely lost the trust of the committee charged with overseeing him.

It seemed that Barr had fallen victim to Trump's black hole, with its frightening gravitational pull. I had seen the influence of the Oval Office up close. That awesome power, when occupied by a fraudulent and corrupt narcissist, could become a vortex of moral darkness, sucking everything in its proximity into its maw.

Later, I grudgingly admitted to Barry that I had been misguided in my vocal public defense of Rosenstein over the past two years. Though I was truly saddened that both he and Barr had been swallowed up by the Trump vacuum, nothing was as troubling to me as Mueller's failure. As I pored over the Mueller Report that April, my copy becoming dog-eared and coffee-stained and bearing traces of various late-night meals (from vending machines or the 7-Eleven where I would purchase my late-night egg salad sandwiches and spicy pickle packets, one of the few meals available for a kosher diner), a disturbing reality became clear. The same modesty and restraint that had made Mueller such an exemplar for decades—indeed, the same qualities that inspired his tight-lipped, self-mocking advice as we sped through Prague, our nation's flag mounted on my hood and slapping in the wind—were to blame for this lapse in our great hour of need.

He, Rosenstein, and Barr, all of whom had previously held reputations for rectitude, had undone us. It had happened through indecency, or, in Mueller's case, most devastatingly, through decency.

But whatever its imperfections, Mueller's report clearly shifted Nadler's inclination toward impeachment. On April 29, when Congress reconvened, Jerry told me and Barry: "Of course he deserves to be impeached. The question is, how do we get there?" Always a pragmatist, he laid out the obstacles: our committee was not fully on board (although most were and he was confident the rest of them would get there); the caucus was not on board, including leaders like Intel chairman Adam Schiff; the Speaker was not yet on board; and you, the American people, were not entirely with us.

The solution was for Team Judiciary to build the case for impeachment, and fast, by bringing in crucial witnesses: Attorney General Barr and former White House counsel Don McGahn (Mueller's most important witness to many of the episodes in his report), culminating in the appearance of Mueller. That was the most promising route to get to the truth of the special counsel's report.

We started with the attorney general, who had agreed to appear before the committee on May 2. The day before, members voted to allow counsel to question him in addition to their five-minute rounds. That combination would help ensure that the clever, slippery Barr would face maximum accountability. Evidently fearing we would pierce his dissimulations, Barr then canceled his appearance, triggering headlines like "The Lawyers That Barr Was Afraid to Face," referring to Jerry, Barry, and myself. (Flattering as it was to be included, my actual involvement on this occasion would have been limited to sitting behind the two of them and looking perturbed on national television.) The committee was left with no choice but to hold Barr in contempt, with Jerry declaring that his failure to show created a constitutional crisis.

McGahn proved similarly recalcitrant. We had subpoenaed the former White House counsel, who had seen so much of Trump's obstruction of justice firsthand, requesting both his documents and his testimony. On May 7, the White House wrote Nadler: they had directed McGahn not to produce the requested records relating to the Mueller Report, on the grounds that they "remain legally protected from disclosure under longstanding constitutional principles, because they implicate significant Executive Branch confidentiality interests and executive privilege." It was a dubious claim; it was hard to see how documents that McGahn had already shared outside the White House with the special counsel and that Mueller had written about in his now-public report could be privileged. And it certainly did not augur well for McGahn showing up for his deposition on May 21.

This dual defiance ratcheted up the pressure to get Mueller in—and to consider opening a formal impeachment investigation. All day long on the seventh, a stream of members passed through our office making those points, as we and they also huddled individually and collectively with Amy and with the chairman. The most impassioned included Joe Neguse, a skilled legal tactician who cut his teeth as Colorado's chief consumer advocate; David Cicilline, who had been so outspoken on our call to discuss the Mueller Report; Pramila Jayapal, the eloquent head of the Congressional Progressive Caucus; and Jamie Raskin, a constitutional law professor before coming to Congress whom I had known for almost thirty years. Ted Lieu of California and Madeleine Dean of Pennsylvania had similar sentiments. Nadler, not yet ready to publicly break with Pelosi on impeachment, took it under advisement—but we knew where his heart was and I think the members did as well.

When we learned on May 20 that McGahn, following White House orders, would fail to show, that proved the last straw for Jerry. Whatever his personal feelings, he had remained steadfastly unified with the Speaker on impeachment (and she with him, including echoing his proclamation of a constitutional crisis). But, he told the committee members when we met that afternoon, "the president is displaying a monarchal pattern, refusing to allow Congress to do its job, and threatening our republican form of government." He huddled with Pelosi that evening, pressing for her to authorize Judiciary to open a formal impeachment inquiry. At 10:00 P.M. he convened the members by phone to report on her answer: no. She was not ready, in part because the full caucus did not yet support it. She wanted to see how events developed.

Jerry urged the committee to be patient as we pressed forward on the agreed strategy Barry and I had helped formulate, including bringing in the special counsel to testify. Afterward, he was direct with me, Barry, and the other staff: "Get Mueller in here. As quickly as you can." We agreed to make every effort. I allowed myself to hope that this was the solution to the problem of driving impeachment forward. If Mueller appeared before the committee, perhaps I would witness that piercing glint of righteousness once again.

Barry and I had a ritual that we had established in our dreary windowless office. Once we had completed responding to the crises of the day, working hours that at times resembled the triage of an emergency room more than those of a law office, we would break out snacks (typically raw almonds and Trader Joe's rice crackers) accompanied by a glass of our friend Widow Jane bourbon. That night, after I expressed my exuberant support for bringing in Mueller, Barry turned to me and gave me a knowing, warning glance. Nursing his drink, he agreed we should stay the course. But he urged me to remember the adage of that great litigator Mike Tyson: "Everybody has a plan . . . until they get punched in the mouth."

Mueller Time

"We wanted you to hear it directly from us. Special Counsel Mueller will not appear to give *any* testimony."

It was June 17, and I was sitting in the Judiciary Committee conference room across from two of Mueller's top lieutenants: Aaron Zebley and Jim Quarles. I could only stare back at them, dumbstruck.

Zebley had worked for Mueller at the bureau before serving as deputy special counsel and looked every bit the part. He wore the same standard FBI uniform of a blue suit, a dark tie, and a crisp white shirt, even matching his mentor down to their digital Casio watches. He joined the FBI in the terrorism unit and hustled up the ladder to become Director Mueller's right-hand man. His reticence seemed a further reflection of his boss's manner, but Zebley lacked the wry humor that leavened Mueller's severity.

Sitting beside him was another longtime Mueller colleague, Jim Quarles. With thinning hair and a gray soup-catcher mustache, Quarles had endured more high-pressure political situations than his younger colleague. He had been a prosecutor on Watergate and practiced privately at Mueller's law firm, WilmerHale, before joining the special counsel's select team. Also sitting around the table were a handful of others, including top Judiciary and Intelligence Committee aides. Both committees sought Mueller's testimony.

I tried to process Zebley's pronouncement, which—had we accepted it—would have taken a wrecking ball to our mission, now in its fifth month. The Mueller Report made the case for the impeachment of Trump, but too few realized that it did so, including in Congress, because of Barr's obfuscation and Mueller's obscurity. We needed to hear from him directly to cut through the fog. But it was already the middle of June, and just securing this meeting had required two months of intensive effort following the report's release, first with DOJ and then with Mueller's team.

A less aggressive (some might say less obnoxious) group of House investigators might have been deterred by Mueller's May 29 press conference, when he declared, "I do not believe it is appropriate for me to speak further about the investigation or to comment on the actions of the Justice Department or Congress." Ironically, given that my White House nickname was once Mr. No, the word barely registered for me anymore. Besides, Mueller had also alluded to impeachment, stating "the Constitution requires a process other than the criminal justice system to formally accuse a sitting President of wrongdoing." That alone gave us a sense of purpose.

Zebley spoke again, breaking the silence in the wake of his declaration of Mueller's refusal to meet with us. In a slightly nasal tone, he said that Mueller's written work spoke for itself. Doing anything more would undermine their credibility, they felt. Zebley went so far as to imply they would fight a subpoena, saying, "It would be costly, to us and to you," if there was an enforcement battle in court.

Perry Apelbaum, the Judiciary Committee's staff director and chief counsel, politely but quite firmly informed them that we were having none of it. Perry was respected in Congress for his patient, even-handed dedication to finding the compromises that were the lifeblood of the institution. But there could be no flexibility on this point: we had to have Mueller come testify. We needed to address the failure of all our systems at fully communicating the actual content of the report to the public. We would accommodate Mueller however we could, Perry continued, at the hearing. But a no-show simply was not tenable. That message was reinforced in no uncertain terms by Dan Goldman and Maher Bitar, the Intel counsel attending the meeting to represent that committee.

But Mueller's colleagues seemed more concerned about protecting Mueller from questioning than about protecting our democracy. Quarles argued that Mueller's appearance in front of the committee might elicit criticism of the report. That stunned me, given that the attorney general had already distorted its findings in the cultural imagination. I emphasized that after the confusion resulting from Barr's mischaracterization, we had a duty to set the record straight, leaving unsaid Bob's own failures of clarity. Zebley kept up his argument about credibility. What difference does a pristine reputation make when Rome is burning around you? Did he not realize that his toga would go up in flames, too? Aaron Hiller finally leaped in and told them, unequivocally, that we could not move forward without Mueller. The tense meeting broke up, inconclusively.

Afterward, Barry and I retired to our little office. As a lifelong defense lawyer, he remained loyal to the defenders' creed: the prosecution is a suspect too. Zebley's and Quarles's blinders, which prevented them from seeing the big picture, exemplified everything he could not stand about prosecutors and, at times, about D.C.

"Can you believe that!" he exploded. Normally I would try, like a sherpa walking him through the ways of Washington, to provide some counterpoint, but that day it was beyond me. The failure of Mueller and his team to appreciate the gravity of the crisis our democracy was facing stunned me. They had found so much evidence of wrongdoing, including direct attacks *on them* by the president. Was that not enough to warrant a conversation with Congress?

"Sheesh, we're making more progress with Trump's people than we are with those guys," Barry said. We laughed, but both knew there was a sliver of truth to it.

• • •

UNLIKE WITH MUELLER'S TEAM, WE had actually managed to bust through the White House blockade of witnesses. It wasn't easy. The president had proclaimed on April 24 that he would "fight all the subpoenas." To do that, the White House had their own versions of Zebley and Quarles: Mike Purpura and Pat Philbin. Their good-cop/bad-cop routine was almost comical in its adherence to stereotype. Purpura, the shorter and stockier of the two, with dark slicked-back hair, offered the "gee, we can work it out" angle, while Philbin, tall, angular, and pale, resembling a hungry vampire just before dawn, readily landed his fangs into the necks of our negotiations.

They threw every defense they could think of at our subpoenas of the White House counsel, Don McGahn; the communications director, Hope Hicks; and the others who had firsthand evidence of Trump's obstruction. Their main claim: the president's top aides were subject to "absolute immunity" from congressional subpoenas. In other words, lawful subpoenas applied to everyone but them. They were above the law! This fanciful doctrine—more suitable to medieval monarchy than modern constitutional democracy—had been tossed out by a federal court in an earlier case involving Bush White House counsel Harriet Miers. (I had inherited and helped resolve the case when I went to work in the Obama White House, so I knew well the weakness of the doctrine.) No matter; the president's lawyers were as shameless as their client.

But Barry and I had a trick up our sleeves as well. Hicks's lawyer was the longtime D.C. pro Bob Trout. The courtly, white-haired Trout was an old friend and mentor of mine. A straight shooter, he thought little of the concept of absolute immunity and was willing to produce his client. In exchange, he wanted a closed-door hearing. No TV cameras.

We needed a witness, both to bring the Mueller Report to life and to keep the momentum going while we continued pursuing Mueller. Trout's offer was a no-brainer. Members of the committee cross-examined us; they were skeptical about giving up the opportunity to grill Hicks in front of the entire American public on television. But with the chairman's support we persuaded them. The news appeared to incense Purpura and Philbin when they found out, but the deal was done.

That was how I found myself sitting across from Hicks, the president's confidante, on June 19. The committee gathered in the same hearing room where Barry and I had briefed them four months prior.

Hicks sat with Trout at her side, and Purpura and Philbin perched at the edge of their chairs behind her. She was impeccably dressed; not a hair out of place. A court reporter sat at the ready, prepared to record every word. After the chairman and members kicked the questioning off, I alternated queries with them and with my colleague Sarah Istel. With her usual mastery of the intricate facts, she had helped me develop the questions—and now she joined in asking them.

Over a long day, the composed, occasionally confrontational Hicks admitted that the Trump campaign used Russian help in the form of the WikiLeaks releases. She distanced herself from the president's refusal to admit that Russian interference had occurred. And she also broke with Trump's assertion that he would take dirt again if offered by a foreign government. Hicks said she would instead go to the FBI. Purpura and Philbin instructed her not to answer over 150 questions, but their stonewalling only dramatized the president's cover-up.

That was the day I got to like Doug Collins, the ranking member (most senior Republican) on the committee. The tall, lanky, fast-talking Georgian was a capable trial lawyer, and we sparred on the record over various points, each of us giving as good as we got. We also ended up talking off the record, both to facilitate the process and just to trade notes lawyer to lawyer. Barry noticed and whispered to me, "Game recognizes game."

Getting Philbin and Purpura in for the Hicks deposition also seemed to loosen things up a bit in our negotiations for McGahn and the other witnesses. We commenced a series of secret parleys to try to agree on terms, trading proposals. A visibly shocked Kellyanne Conway spotted us slipping out of the White House after one such session and called out, "Norm *Eisen,* what are you doing here?" I evaded her question, genuinely concerned she would put the kibosh on the negotiations. After some not-so-gentle teasing back and forth about which of us was more corrupt, she said she was on her way to see the president. "I'll tell him I saw you!" she said, eyes narrowing slightly as she smiled. Somehow it had the air of a threat, leaving me to imagine the president getting on the loudspeaker system and saying, "If you just met with Eisen and Berke, turn yourself in." Evidently the encounter did no harm, however, because Purpura and Philbin kept talking to us.

WE MOVED FORWARD TO SECURING testimony directly from Mueller. It did not always feel like progress, but we gradually wore them down. At one point we got a suggestion that Mueller would come testify . . . for five minutes. "How can they be so mean?" our colleague Sarah Istel exclaimed. I had to laugh. They were good men who had made enormous sacrifices to do vital work. They just didn't see themselves as bound to do more. At any rate, Mueller's mere willingness to show up represented a crack in the door, one through which we could barge. In retrospect, perhaps it should have given me more pause that anyone would make such a ludicrous offer.

We continued pushing for testimony, and Mueller acquiesced incrementally: first ten minutes, then one hour, and eventually two hours per committee (in each of the Judiciary and Intelligence Committees). Negotiations advanced far enough that by June 25 we felt it was safe to announce that Mueller would be coming in to testify before both committees. Chairmen Nadler and Schiff issued subpoenas to lock in a date of July 17.

Instead of ameliorating the difficulties, fixing a date seemed to intensify them. The amount of time allotted for the hearing became a sticking point for the committee. We had promised them Mueller, and our Democratic members expected us to deliver. On July 10, we presented the members with the two hours—one for us, and one for the Republicans. Because we went down the dais in order of seniority, that meant some of them would not get their five minutes to ask questions. Even if we shaved the time down to shorter blocks, there was just not enough of it to go around. There was a general revolt, nicely summarized by Representative Val Demings: "Everyone asks, or nobody asks."

It was not only the Democrats on the committee who were angry. Nadler, with his characteristic fair-mindedness, insisted on consulting with Republican members that day as well, instead of just telling them how it was going to be, as more high-handed chairmen tended to do. They were livid about getting just an hour for their side as well. With a minority that encompassed some of the most ideological battlers in Congress, they wanted ample time to grill Mueller on various conspiracy theories. The entire committee, Democrats and Republicans alike, had found at least one thing they could agree on.

Mueller raised another issue on the tenth. DOJ had been slow to provide access to his files, and now he decided he needed more time to get ready. The date of July 17 no longer worked for him.

Aaron and Perry, leading negotiations for us, were tearing their hair out. We all were. But we had come too far to have this fall apart now. On July 11, we, Intel, and Mueller's team came up with a bargain. Mueller's emissaries agreed to a third hour for each committee, in exchange for his having another week to prepare. We jumped at it and the date was set: July 24.

I wish I could say that was the end of the drama. It was only the beginning, as constant squabbling continued with a jittery Team Mueller about the details: who would sit where, whether Mueller's aides could speak, and other logistics that might have seemed petty to outsiders but took on monumental significance.

The headbutting between Zebley and Goldman, both high-ranking former prosecutors, and both with strong opinions about how the hearing should be structured, was intense at times, with Aaron and Perry scrambling to find compromises. They were the two calmest among our Judiciary staff and so they were well suited to the diplomatic role. Then, the week before the hearing, DOJ roiled the waters, demanding that they have seats in the front row behind Mueller and giving him instructions that he was not to testify beyond the four corners of his report. This seemed to send Mueller's already nervous team over the edge, but Aaron, for whom negotiating these details had become virtually a full-time job, calmly walked them back. He assured Zebley that Mueller was ultimately in charge of how he answered and agreed that Zebley could sit next to the special counsel in case there were any tough calls. Somehow the hearing remained on track, although an exhausted Aaron proclaimed as he was leaving on Friday, July 19, that it had almost died a thousand times.

Once again, we threw ourselves into intense effort. This would not be a typical congressional hearing. Chairman Nadler did not want that, nor did our members. They wanted something different and spectacular for Mueller. So, with Barry and me as Mickey Rooney and Judy Garland (I will leave it to your discretion to determine who's who), we prepared to put on a show. Our format was not unlike a Broadway production, including the last two weeks of frantic rehearsals. There was nobody better at examining witnesses than Barry, and he and Arya led the staff team and took the pen for the drafting of potential questions. In our run-throughs I acted in the starring role of Bob Mueller. I had the closest relationship with him and was intensely familiar with the material. (I had excelled as an actor in eighth grade, which had also marked the end of my theater career.)

With our actors cast, we got to work on the script with the committee members who would be conducting the actual questioning. Barry, Arya, and I talked through the issues with each member, discussing topics they wanted to tackle, specific questions they wanted to ask, and how that would fit into the larger picture. We went back and forth, developing the script for Judiciary's three-hour share, dividing it among the members, and helping them sharpen their questions. With no sense of how Mueller might respond, we ultimately created two scripts: a direct examination, for if he was cooperative; and a cross-examination, in case he gave us a hard time.

As the chairman, Nadler of course had the critical opening of the first five minutes of questioning, when everyone was watching and the tone was set. We advised that he immediately get Mueller to address the president's lie when he said, "Total Exoneration" and "No Obstruction," after the release of Barr's report summary on March 24. There was some risk in opening with that, because we had no idea how Mueller would respond. We debated over whether to further risk trying to get him to renounce the president's entire mantra by including "No Collusion" as well. I pressed for us to do so, whereas Barry, normally the bigger gambler, felt that treading into collusion was too risky. We yanked it the night before, opting to keep the spotlight on volume 2 of the report.

Nadler and the four most senior members of the majority together had more than a hundred years of experience on the dais. They would set the context and then address McGahn, and the five most egregious obstruction episodes from the report. Member by member, we would tell the captivating story. For the finale of that section, one of our most talented litigators, Hakeem Jeffries, would tie it all together in a bow—explaining that *if* you had this series of episodes and *if* all of them met these elements, then you surely had obstruction of justice by the president of the United States. Not once, not twice, but over and over and over again. We hoped that Jeffries, a lawyer with whom I had worked on a case years before when we were both in private practice, would be able to use his forensic experience and rhetorical gifts to tease out the incriminating language that we believed Mueller and his team had written and then cut from the report. We also hoped that he would get Mueller to admit that the report displayed all of the elements of obstruction, even if he was not willing to draw the ultimate conclusions: that the president had committed crimes and should be impeached.

We needed to question Mueller, of course, but we also wanted to educate the American people. A standard-fare congressional hearing could not accomplish that. Members of Congress are famously independent, each generally using their time to do their own thing without coordination. The discontinuity is even worse for any observer trying to make sense of it because their five-minute blocks alternate between minority and majority. We were going to try to have the members stay in sequence, maintaining a through line. We worked with them beforehand on how to divide up the narrative and synchronize the presentations, and spiced things up by employing video, slides, graphics, and other varieties of media—what we trial lawyers call demonstratives. Barry likes to call them "trial magic." We would offer all of the media materials to the cable networks in advance so that they would know exactly how to caption the examinations and insert the slides as we moved through the topics.

Barry and I lived and died by these explanatory aids when we were in court; they kept judges and juries engaged and helped them learn a case. One of the few times I saw Barry blow up all year (other than at me) was when someone referred to these aids as props.

"No!" he exclaimed. "They are not props, they aren't tricks, they are *demonstratives,* because they demonstrate the evidence and arguments that support our case." Barry's vehement belief in them became an inside joke among us, but the members came to appreciate them as well, and they transformed the way we did high-profile hearings—including, ultimately, the impeachment trial.

The week before Mueller's appearance was jam-packed. We had wall-to-wall meetings with almost all of our members to prepare for the hearing. Meanwhile, information continued pouring in from the eighty-one letters sent out on March 4—much of it relating to the president's campaign finance crimes and emoluments, which we hoped to focus on once we were done with Mueller. We were also negotiating with Purpura and Philbin for additional fact witnesses to (we hoped) follow Mueller, as well as with the personal lawyers for those witnesses, including counsel for the so-far-elusive Don McGahn.

It was during our second wave of member meetings that I played Mueller, enabling the members to get comfortable asking versions of their prepared questions. Barry, Arya, and I started rehearsals with Nadler himself and then worked our way through the halls of Congress to most of the other members, one by one. Naturally, the chairman has earned the largest office. It is adorned with all sorts of memorabilia, including a custom souvenir New York subway sign for his home stop: Ninety-Sixth Street, the red 1, 2, or 3 line. He also has a collection of distinguished photographs: one of him with President Clinton, another with President Obama, and a third (which made it very hard for me to hold my stoic Mueller expression) with Cyndi Lauper.

Starting with Jerry, I would sit in each member's office as they ran through and revised their questions. I demonstrated just how hard it could be to get Mueller to talk by being reticent and reserved. Needless to say, it ran contrary to my voluble nature. Barry interrupted with pointers or demonstrations of how a question could be asked, while I stayed in character and gave the members and him as hard a time as I could.

We covered three House office buildings, dashing to and fro among them to do rewrites of their scripts based on what members had said, done, or edited themselves. Never say that members of Congress don't work hard. Not just the staff, but everybody up to the most senior members was generally awake and available from dawn until midnight. The members worked furiously to familiarize themselves with the ever-evolving material, adjusting the content to suit their voices' distinct pace and rhythm.

For the final dress rehearsal, we gathered in the historic House Judiciary Committee hearing room, with our warren of offices as the backstage. Staring down at us as I assumed the center seat at the witness table were portraits of former House Judiciary Committee chairs. On one side was Peter W. Rodino, who led the Watergate hearings. Near him was Henry Hyde, who held the mantle through the Clinton impeachment. Neither struck me as any less of a lion over his committee than Jerry Nadler.

I took my role in our dress rehearsal seriously, going as far as wearing the same standard blue suit, white shirt, and red tie Mueller favored. Barry stood by as the production's director, ready to coach and critique the members through our moot court session (a practice both of us employed whenever we had an argument or a trial). He also coached me: whispering or passing notes during the performance about being gentler or more aggressive, and generally making sure the rehearsal was as demanding as possible.

As I went through what I thought would be an entertaining practice round in playing Bob, I found—with a start—that it was not so easy to inhabit his mind. I was baffled as to how this American hero suggested but fell shy of saying, "Yes, the president obstructed justice and yes he should be impeached." This man had taken on some of the toughest adversaries that our country had to offer—from organized crime lords to drug traffickers. He had led our nation in defending the homeland against terrorism after the 9/11 attacks. He was such a venerated figure that President Obama secured an act of Congress so that he could stay on for an additional two years beyond his ten-year term. His integrity has been hailed by everyone from Bernie Sanders to Newt Gingrich. Why had *this man* only hinted at criminal behavior, instead of using a megaphone to inform the country that he has served so well?

I wasn't the only one attempting to inhabit a different mindset. Barry and other ringers helped impersonate the Republican members, capturing their quirks and being quick to interject with objections. The team excelled at playing up the ideologues from the other side of the aisle, like the ranking member, Doug Collins, who at times spoke so rapidly with his heavy southern accent that few could understand him. Or the wholly unprincipled Floridian Matt Gaetz, who sported flashy pocket squares and black-and-brown spectator shoes. Or Ohio's archconservative Jim Jordan, against whom I had once filed an ethics complaint for allegedly turning a blind eye to the molestation of wrestlers when he was a coach at Ohio State. We picked a burly individual to play Jordan, sitting in his chair in his trademark shirt and tie, no jacket. When it came his turn to question me, I had some fun by saying in my sternest Bob Mueller voice, "Sir, I won't answer questions from someone so inappropriately attired." Someone in the room was a little too tickled and leaked it to a reporter, and it was up on Twitter in no time, leading to a fusillade of disgruntled Republican social media responses and a firm warning from the chairman, who wanted no more joking and—above all—no more leaking.

At the end of the very long day, Barry and I enjoyed our bourbon and, as was our wont, walked out of the darkened Rayburn building, across the Capitol lawn, and into downtown to our respective homes. That night, July 23, we discussed as we walked how hard the members had worked. As with any production about to open, the rehearsal had its bright spots, but you never know until the curtain actually rises how it will be received. Ours was a onetime-only performance. There would be no encore, no do-overs. The stakes for our country were a lot higher than any show—or any trial that either of us had ever been involved in. We strolled beneath the huge white dome of the Capitol, appearing like a second, larger moon on the horizon looming above us, with nary another pedestrian in sight.

There had to be a breaking point when Trump's uninhibited, unprincipled destruction of the rule of law, of constitutional government, and of democracy, all to suit himself, would catch up to the tyrant. Maybe it will be tomorrow, we mused on our walk. Within hours, the sun would rise on a day that, we hoped, would change everything.

When I came striding onto those same grounds the next morning, the air was thick with tension. There is a particular way that Congress feels on a big day. It's as though the buildings themselves are all leaning in for the occasion, offering a nod of gravitas. On a day like this one, the entire complex—the Mall, the Capitol in the middle, with the Senate wing and the House wing, plus all the surrounding office buildings—was crackling with nervous energy. A massive line of people had queued up outside the building, hoping to get anywhere near our hearing. I passed through security and walked down the hallway, and as I turned the corner and approached the hearing room, I was suddenly blinded by throngs of press with cameras, microphones, and flashing lights. Reporters were spaced out every two feet, facing their respective cameras and attempting to forecast what was about to happen. "Norm, Norm," they cried out, streaming my way and departing just as quickly when I told them, "No comment."

I finally made it to our suite, where staffers and aides bustled around, working out the preparations with the AV team. It was crucial to have all the slides, video, and sound ready to go, given all the unpredictable elements: the inevitable interruptions, members going off script, not to mention the pressure. The team knew that one mistake could embarrass or confuse a member before a global audience. The electricity in the room went up several volts when, after a bit of small talk, a reporter on one of the TVs announced that Bob Mueller had arrived.

He was escorted in by Capitol Police and his own DOJ security. We stowed him in the chairman's conference room, adjacent to the big committee boardroom. Mueller and his team were ensconced in conversation, and we were all careful not to fraternize at any length with him (in fact, one of the first questions he was asked was whether the Democrats had given him any questions in advance).

At one point, he walked out of the room and I went over to greet him. "Good morning, Bob. We're so glad to have you here," I said, extending my hand. I was startled when, in response, he clutched my arm. He had bags under his eyes and appeared more gaunt than I had ever seen him. He said, with hollow eyes, "Norm, I'd rather be anywhere else." I didn't know how to respond. While I searched for an answer, he released his grip and passed through the hallway.

Shortly before 8:30, I took my seat behind the dais with Barry.

The other staff took their places; then the members started filing in. When Nadler entered, the buzz heightened another notch. Everyone knew that once the chairman took his chair, the next person to arrive would be the man we had labored to get into that room for three months. The side door opened, and an assault of camera flashes obscured my vision for a moment, before Mueller appeared. He found his place, then stood, raised his right hand slowly, and was sworn in.

After some prepared remarks, the chairman opened masterfully. In short order, Nadler got Mueller to concede that President Trump was lying when he had said that Mueller had exonerated him. "Director Mueller," Jerry began, "the president has repeatedly claimed that your report found there was no obstruction, and that it completely and totally exonerated him. But that is not what your report said, is it?"

"Correct," Mueller replied. "That is not what the report said." Nadler also got Mueller to acknowledge that the president had refused to meet with him for an interview. *Whoosh,* down went another Trump claim, that he had been exonerated and fully cooperative. Mueller was hardly a voluble witness; he made Jerry work for it, but work Jerry did. I was struck by the contrast—sitting just a few feet behind Jerry and looking right at Mueller—between the two men and the responsibility they no doubt felt in this critical moment in history. Jerry was boldly charging forward, and Mueller was holding back.

Mueller exhibited a profound sense of duty. There was no gainsaying that; he had taken on this role and suffered enormously for it, whether by vilification or just the drainage of soul and self that occurs after spending two years staring into Trump's criminal abyss. However, Mueller was still coloring within the lines, made clear by the seeming discomfort with which he answered questions. As his team had warned he would, Mueller largely stuck to responses that landed within the four corners of the report. He was not going to do us any favors. After engaging with him briefly in the hallway, I couldn't deny that Mueller was changed. He was diminished physically, and it seemed to me he was diminished morally by failing to bring Trump to justice. Like that of so many others, his duty to our country had been interrupted by Trump's sociopathy.

Nadler had rushed into the breach in this critical moment. It was fascinating to watch the expansive constitutional scholar cross-examine the terse lawman, Jerry nimbly rephrasing the questions when he didn't get the answers that he wanted. He juiced every second of advantage out of his five minutes. It was evident that he believed the time had come to impeach this rogue president, but he never said so outright, allowing his listeners to make up their own minds. He did the hard work and expected the members to do the same, with the goal that together they could elicit clear, abundant evidence of the president's wrongdoing so that everyone, including you, the American people, could realize the profound danger Trump presents. After Jerry finished, a TV anchor texted me: "That went about as well as it possibly could."

Next, the microphone passed to the minority. Ranking Member Collins took over the questioning in his machine-gun delivery, which—as expected—was at times incomprehensible to Mueller, who struggled to answer his questions. Despite being a good litigator, Collins proved far less nimble than Jerry when Mueller did not deliver precisely what he wanted. When he waded into the treacherous territory of Trump's possible collusion with Russia, Mueller's mixed set of answers didn't rule out that form of wrongdoing.

Then it was showtime for the rest of the members. Our side of the dais lived up to our hopes, working in synchronicity. They stuck to the scripts and the slides to great advantage. Representative Lofgren set the table, explaining how serious the Russia investigation was (and therefore how dangerous Trump's obstruction had been). Representative Jackson Lee's questioning dealt with the gravity of the ten episodes of obstruction Mueller had laid out, five of which rose to a level that would have gotten anyone else in America indicted. From there, the committee methodically marched through those five one by one, showing why Trump's attempts to get McGahn to have Mueller fired and then to lie about it were chargeable offenses. So was the Trump gambit to have the investigation curtailed using his former aide Corey Lewandowski, and the same was true of the witness tampering with Cohen and Manafort.

Hakeem Jeffries was particularly impressive in walking Mueller through each of the legal elements of obstruction of justice, and coaxing Mueller to concede that Trump's behavior satisfied the individual elements—even if Mueller would not concede the conclusion, that the president had committed the offense itself.

Many members ended with the same tagline: No one is above the law. Nadler had urged us to adopt a simple, binding theme that could serve as the central thrust of the hearing—and the impeachment if we had one. Working with the chairman, Barry, Arya, and I had landed on the idea that anyone else who had done these five acts of obstruction would have been prosecuted. Trump should not get away with it, because "no one is above the law."

Barry and I were kvelling with pride. Even when Mueller stumbled, the members picked up the slack and adjusted, like a sports team reacting in unison on the field. Not a single Democratic member wasted their questioning time to make long speeches. The same could not be said of the Republicans' disjointed assault on the special counsel. They rehashed familiar misstatements and outright lies that we had been hearing from Trump's defenders the past two and a half years. Even capable examiners like Congressman John Ratcliffe, a former U.S. Attorney (and Trump's eventual choice for director of national intelligence), posed one or two questions, but then used them as an excuse to filibuster. Worse still, some of the GOP members walked into obvious traps and blind alleys.

"Can you state with confidence that the Steele dossier was not part of Russia's disinformation campaign?" Matt Gaetz asked, to which Mueller, looking confused and a bit bored, replied, "That part of the building of the case predated me by at least ten months."

Jim Jordan launched into an impassioned diatribe about his outrage that the FBI investigation had "spied on two American citizens associated with a presidential campaign," referring to Papadopoulos and the former Trump campaign aide Carter Page. He then asked, with bombastic self-satisfaction, how Papadopoulos had found out that the Russians "had dirt" on Hillary Clinton. Mueller's look of disdain was a response in itself, but he responded tersely, "I can't get into the evidentiary filings."

Sometimes the GOP's bumbling affirmatively helped us make our case. Colorado's Ken Buck asked Mueller whether Trump could be charged with a crime after he left office, and Mueller responded immediately, with emphasis, "Yes." Perhaps unaware of the favor he was doing us by clarifying the question, Buck repeated the question, more specifically: "You could charge the president of the United States with obstruction of justice after he left office?"

"Yes," Mueller affirmed, unequivocally. It was a great sound bite for the media, unintentionally highlighting the limits that Mueller had faced when it came to a potential indictment.

But after a while, the sheer volume of the Republican onslaught started to have its effect. I could see why Mueller had said he wanted to be anywhere else. He grew tired, becoming overly reliant on his report, often needing to be directed to the page and even the exact line. (Fortunately, our members had prepared for that as part of their incessant drilling.) Mueller didn't take advantage of the openings we offered to describe or expand on his findings. We weren't losing any ground as the morning wore on, but unfortunately, by the end of it, we weren't gaining any. Representative Ted Lieu got Mueller to agree that he didn't charge the president because of the DOJ opinion forbidding it. Lieu had honed his formidable cross-examination skills in the U.S. Air Force Judge Advocate General's Corps, and we all felt good when he secured that admission. It was important because it suggested Mueller might have charged Trump but for that limitation. But (once he was out of Lieu's grasp) Mueller recanted, saying that his response was not framed correctly.

Still, we had scored some important points, even if making some of them had been a struggle. We ended up slightly exceeding our allotted three hours in covering all the material, then broke for lunch.

Mueller retreated to the chairman's small conference room as we prepared to turn over the hearing room to the Intelligence Committee. But there appeared to be a bit of a crisis during the break; the Intelligence counsels Maher Bitar and Dan Goldman were huddled together in the back hallway, Maher looking stricken and Dan downright angry. Barry and I approached them.

"What's wrong, guys?" They told us that Mueller was refusing to come out of the chairman's conference room. His people were claiming that because Judiciary had gone over our time limit, Intelligence should give that time back out of their scheduled three hours. He would not emerge.

It was unheard of. Hearings often went a little over, and everyone understood that. Mueller certainly did, as a veteran of so many of them.

"That's ridiculous, you should insist on having your full scheduled time," we replied (not that they needed to hear it from us). They went back to work, and Mueller eventually emerged for the afternoon session. He sustained several more hours of sharp questioning by the Intelligence Committee Democrats, seeming to pick up his energy even while enduring further meaningless filibustering from the Republicans. Led by Chairman Adam Schiff, the afternoon session ably dissected Mueller's findings of election interference by Russia and the many contacts by Trump and those around him with that adversary.

Immediately following the hearing, we gathered with the Judiciary team. The committee members and staff, under the forceful leadership of Chairman Nadler, had done everything they could to lay out the depth and depravity of the abuses of power made plain in Mueller's report. Pats on the back were shared, along with a round of bourbon and kind words from our colleagues; Perry told us the member and staff preparation was the greatest thing he had ever seen in his almost thirty years working in Congress. But I had been too busy to follow the press reaction. Stepping aside, I scanned the news. The media did not feel the same way that we did. At all.

Reporters and commentators were generous to our members but brutal toward Mueller. The apparent consensus, from *The New York Times* to *The Washington Post,* was that Mueller appeared "confused" and "at a loss for words" and that his testimony was "halting." Many of these reports additionally noted that Mueller's difficulties were not solely in response to combative questioning from the minority, but rather that "even friendly exchanges could cause Mueller to stumble." One of the more somber evaluations came from my former White House colleague, political strategist David Axelrod, who wrote on Twitter, "This is delicate to say, but Mueller, whom I deeply respect, has not publicly testified before Congress in at least six years. And he does not appear as sharp as he was then." The former senator Claire McCaskill (who had joined the CREW board after she left the Senate and I went to work in the House) said that Mueller "frankly wasn't a really good witness." The predominant view was that he had flopped.

The harshest critic, of course, was President Trump. He derided the hearing as a total fiasco and asserted, once again, that "everybody knew it [the Russia investigation] was a hoax, especially the Democrats." The conventional wisdom hardened all the more, aided by the president's malicious mischaracterization from his bully pulpit.

Though it was not Mueller's finest hour, it certainly was not the unmitigated disaster that the press made it out to be. The hearing we read about and saw people discuss on TV did not fully capture the day we had sat through. Might it have been similar to the famous Kennedy-Nixon debate, where the people who listened on the radio thought Nixon had won and those who watched on television thought Kennedy had? Perhaps the television-watching pundits had gotten so caught up in style as to be unable to get past Mueller's demeanor to cover the outrages in his report that he fully confirmed.

They were right about his failure, but for the wrong reasons. Who gave a damn if the fireman stuttered as he pointed to the signs that a conflagration was intentionally set? What mattered was the seriousness of the president's obstruction offenses—and the fact that Mueller had not pursued them all the way. He had given us all the evidence, but he wouldn't draw the conclusion "This was arson!" The refusal to admit there were at least five chargeable crimes was his shortcoming, not his lack of style. I understood his old-fashioned restraint under the special counsel regulations and typical prosecutorial standards. But he had leeway under the rules to do much, much more, and he didn't.

A striking coda to Mueller's failure to go the distance against Trump came when Barry and I later that year met with Rick Gates, Trump's former deputy campaign chair. In one of Trump's written answers to Mueller's questions, the president had said that he did not recall learning of WikiLeaks' 2016 releases of hacked documents in advance. But Gates told us he was with Trump in the summer of 2016 when longtime Trump friend Roger Stone called Trump and apparently told him that WikiLeaks would be releasing additional hacked emails.

Gates was credible and specific when we interviewed him on November 14, providing us with the most detailed accounting of this crucial episode that we had yet heard. With the help of our Judiciary colleague Charlie Gayle, a smart, affable former prosecutor, we were able to establish the likely date of the call: July 25, 2016, just three days after the first WikiLeaks release of hacked DNC documents. Russia's role was already known. Gates described how in the mid-afternoon or early evening, he was riding with Trump in a Chevy Suburban from Trump Tower to LaGuardia Airport to board the campaign plane. They were still in Manhattan when Stone called Trump. Trump held the cellphone far enough away from his ear that Gates could see Roger's number on the screen. Trump listened to Roger, got off the phone, and told Gates, "More information is coming"—clearly a reference to WikiLeaks. Just two days later, Trump would publicly holler, "Russia, if you are listening . . ."

After spending a couple of hours grilling Gates on this and other topics, we had no doubt he was telling the truth. And yet, Mueller had let Trump get away with written answers like: "I have no recollection of the specifics of any conversations I had with Mr. Stone between June 1, 2016, and November 8, 2016. I do not recall discussing WikiLeaks with him." In fact, Trump's written answers to Mueller dealing with WikiLeaks are littered with "do not recalls"—fourteen of them. Maybe Trump had forgotten the Stone call, as implausible as that might seem (and Gates could not rule that out when we pressed him). Either way, Mueller's willingness to accept those answers instead of insisting on an in-person cross-examination was unconscionable.

Mueller brought us so close, and yet left us miles away. By the evening of July 24, it had become clear that his and our work had not moved the public needle materially nearer to presidential accountability. What next? Barry and the Widow Jane—usually a powerful combination for making me feel better—were not consoling me. After everyone else cleared out, Barry told me I was being too hard on myself since our committee could not have been stronger in their questioning and presentation. I snapped back that I graded myself by results. If the press and the commentators had failed to see our overarching argument about the threat our sociopathic president posed to America and democracy, that was our failure.

"Norm, our strategy is sound," Barry insisted. "Remember your Churchill," he added, invoking our shared reading of Sir Winston—and his absolute determination to stay the course. Yes, we had once hoped that the combination of Mueller's report and his appearance would have yielded the knockout punch for the president. It hadn't. But progress had been made. A critical element of our approach was to drive Trump into a corner and constantly pummel him with the truth, until he dropped his guard and showed his real face.

"We don't know how Trump is going to react to this," Barry insisted. "We're going to double down; we're not going to stop! Trust me. He *will* provide the seeds of his own destruction."

You know what he did next.

CHAPTER FIVE

The Highest of High Crimes

As I arrived at the office the next morning and brewed a cup of coffee in our well-used Keurig machine, I mulled over how to implement Jerry's instructions to push impeachment forward. At that very moment, Donald Trump was making it inevitable.

At 9:03 a.m. on Thursday, July 25, our president picked up the phone in the White House residence to talk to the president of Ukraine, Volodymyr Zelensky. Our hearings had concluded less than twenty-four hours prior. Trump had tweeted about them at a rate of about one per hour since, including one at 7:06 that morning, quoting *Fox & Friends:* "Nancy said, Jerry, please sit down. Very bad idea" to impeach.

Trump congratulated Zelensky "on a great victory" in securing a parliamentary snap election. Soon he was onto his infamous demand, "I would like you to do us a favor though." Trump wanted Zelensky to investigate the debunked conspiracy theory that *Ukraine,* not Russia, had attacked the 2016 election, including the hack of the DNC's server:

> Our country has been through a lot and Ukraine knows a lot about it. I would like you to find out what happened with this

> whole situation with Ukraine, they say Crowdstrike . . . I guess you have one of your wealthy people . . . The server, they say Ukraine has it . . . As you saw yesterday, that whole nonsense ended with a very poor performance by a man named Robert Mueller, an incompetent performance, but they say a lot of it started with Ukraine.

The real nonsense was the notion that anyone other than Russia had committed these acts. Mueller had not even been out of the witness chair for a day, and Trump was already attempting to upend his conclusions. But he was also replicating the mistake that he had made after firing both Flynn and Comey: further escalation. If the president had just been able to let go and move on, there would never have been a Ukraine scandal. With time running out before election season, there might never have been an impeachment at all, despite our ongoing efforts.

Trump, however, could not help himself. Indeed, he took his abuse of power to new heights. As you know, he went on to ask Zelensky to investigate his most likely 2020 opponent, Joe Biden, by advancing an unfounded, nutty claim that Biden had interfered with the Ukrainian investigation of a Ukrainian company on whose board Biden's son had served:

> There's a lot of talk about Biden's son, that Biden stopped the prosecution and a lot of people want to find out about that, so whatever you can do with the Attorney General would be great. Biden went around bragging that he stopped the prosecution so if you can look into it . . . It sounds horrible to me.

Of course, I had no idea that this shocking call was happening. But as I went about my business that morning, I agreed with Barry that Trump was not going to stop the pattern of abuse and cover-up that had been unfolding over his entire life. All we could do was move forward with our preparations for impeachment, trusting that it would happen, just not sure exactly *how*. The committee's staff director, Perry Apelbaum, would later say it was like the story of the golden spike, when the Central Pacific and Union Pacific Railroads laid track down from opposite sides of the continent, coming closer and closer until the rails finally met at Promontory Summit, Utah, in 1869. We continued laying down the impeachment track, sure that sooner or later we would meet Trump at our version of Promontory Summit.

As TRUMP WAS WRAPPING UP his call with Zelensky, I was finishing my coffee and moving to the next step in the strategy we had laid out for the committee back in February: drafting lawsuits. We had presumed that sooner or later it would be necessary to sue Trump to get the evidence we needed to decide whether to impeach him. Sure enough, his administration was refusing to give us some of Mueller's documents we needed to understand his investigation's findings, and was also continuing to block our access to Mueller's key witness: the former White House counsel Don McGahn.

We started with the lawsuit for the Mueller documents; as litigators, we always try to get documents first, then use them to examine the witnesses. The papers we craved most were Mueller's grand jury files. Mueller had subpoenaed documents and witnesses before a grand jury to conduct his investigation. As extensive as his report was, we needed that raw evidence if we were going to make independent judgments about the president's conduct. Our committee had asked for these materials, and—no surprise—Barr had refused to provide them, falling back on a federal rule that grand jury documents are secret. Barr was also holding back portions of the Mueller Report that were based on the grand jury findings, so we could not even assess the full extent of what we were missing.

Barr's legal position was a sham. The law allowed grand jury documents to be shared with us if what we were doing was preliminary to a judicial proceeding, and our work was exactly that. We were investigating impeachment, and if the House impeached, a Senate trial would follow. What could be more of a "judicial proceeding" than a trial? Using that logic, courts had routinely granted congressional requests for grand jury information in prior impeachments, and DOJ had routinely cooperated with such requests in the past.

It will come as no surprise that for Donald J. Trump such precedents were evaded or outright ignored. His consigliere Barr broke with tradition and refused to cooperate, claiming—among other excuses—that we were not *actually* investigating impeachment. For months, the chairman had said openly that the committee was considering "whether to recommend articles of impeachment against the President." Everyone from the Speaker on down had approved that statement, sometimes called the "Magic Meltzer" or the "Magic Dick" language. It had that name because it had been painstakingly negotiated in late May and early June with one of Pelosi's top aides, Dick Meltzer, and because, as if by magic, it helped bridge the divide between Nadler's enthusiasm for impeachment and Pelosi's reluctance. Perry and I had helped lead the effort for Judiciary, working with the beloved, grandfatherly Meltzer. When it came to these kinds of compromises, Dick was a wizard (except instead of a magic carpet he drove a baby-blue Thunderbird). The agreed-upon language had been a part of the legislative record since a committee report about Barr's failure to cooperate on June 6 and had been used liberally throughout a series of hearings the committee held later that month and in July to prepare for the possibility of impeachment.

We *were* investigating whether to impeach. We also knew that emphasizing as much in litigation would garner public attention, putting an exclamation point on the impeachable obstruction of justice Mueller had just testified about. Working with House counsel's Doug Letter and his colleagues, we prepared the papers. Shrewd and wickedly funny, Doug had been a DOJ appellate star for decades before coming to the House after the Democrats' midterm success; I had faced off against him in my very first appeal back in the nineties (and I enjoyed tweaking him by occasionally reminding him who had won). The grand jury case had some novel features, and he pressed me—hard—to justify it. With a straight face, I guaranteed success, causing both of us to crack up. Together with Barry and our brilliant Judiciary colleague Sophia Brill, who had helped us develop the arguments, I persuaded Doug and his crew. Doug filed our lawsuit to get the grand jury materials on Friday, July 26, the day after Trump's still-secret Ukraine call, and just two days after Mueller testified. (We also included a demand for those excerpts of the Mueller Report based on the grand jury materials that Barr had held back.)

The impeachment language had its intended impact, leading headlines and dominating the coverage. Although the petition contained a great many more factual and legal arguments, the declaration that we were considering impeachment, on the heels of the Mueller hearing, garnered the lion's share of public attention. Like the Mueller Report and the hearing, the filing of this first action was a landmark in prosecuting our strategy. We were pleased to have as our judge Beryl Howell, the chief judge of the court, who carried a reputation for no-nonsense intellect and fairness.

We followed our petition for the grand jury materials used in the Mueller investigation by drafting a separate complaint to get his and our most important obstruction witness: Don McGahn. McGahn, who was known for his long hair and guitar-playing, was an unlikely hero. He was a champion of dark campaign money, and I had fought his efforts in that regard for years at CREW and in the White House. But it seemed that he had stood up to Trump, refusing to go along with his obstruction of justice and then fully cooperating with the special counsel.

We had subpoenaed the former White House counsel to talk about Trump's obstruction, and the White House had ordered him not to appear. Like the administration's claim that they did not have to produce the grand jury documents, here too they'd advanced spurious legal cover: the so-called absolute immunity of presidential advisers, which claims that the president's men and women are completely shielded from valid subpoenas. This notion—that White

House advisers are above the law—was legal gobbledygook and had already been rejected by the only court ever to consider it.

With a Herculean effort led by Barry and Sarah Istel in our office, and by Doug Letter and his colleagues, we somehow managed to file the complaint to enforce the McGahn subpoena on August 7. We reemphasized that we needed this evidence for impeachment, and again garnered considerable public attention for the *I* word, keeping that topic in the headlines post-Mueller. We were fortunate enough to draw another outstanding jurist, Judge Ketanji Brown Jackson, who had a reputation for brilliance. We were optimistic that we would at least get a fair hearing in both cases. The merits were on our side, which augured well for victory.

We reported back to Jerry and the members before they scattered for August recess. They had seen the headlines and, between those and our judicial draws, seemed pleased. Coupled with those encouragements, a steady stream of House Democrats announced support for an impeachment inquiry post-Mueller—collectively signaling progress on the drive to hold Trump accountable. If we hadn't yet moved public opinion, which remained at just under 40 percent support for impeachment, Jerry felt that as Congress came around, the public would as well. He was fond of pointing out that shortly after congressional Watergate hearings began, just 19 percent of Americans supported impeachment.

So far, so good. The problems started during the August recess, when we were attempting to work out the schedules for the two cases. We had wanted to hear from Mueller before filing them, on the theory that his testimony would establish why we needed the evidence. We had not anticipated how long it would take to get him before the committee. We had also been slowed down by another hurdle: the necessity of going through the "accommodations process" with the White House—required by the courts before suing. Judges do not like to resolve clashes between the other two branches of the federal government: Congress and the executive branch. As a result, the law required us to negotiate with the White House before we filed suit, however futile the exercise might be given Trump's palpable bad faith. That meant interminable, inefficient parleys with Purpura and Philbin, who dragged the back-and-forth out as much as possible before we were able to get to court. Even after both cases were put on expedited tracks, it became clear that we were not going to get our initial district court rulings until October or November. That was before appeal to the circuit and, win or lose, to the Supreme Court. We were looking at matters stretching well into 2020 or beyond before final judgments.

We had promised the committee speed, so when we reported those likely timelines, Nadler and the members were uneasy. Our explanation—that circumstances had changed, but the chance of getting at least initial lower court opinions before the end of 2019 was still pretty good—was not the most warmly received pronouncement of our tenure. The members, some at great political risk, had committed to investigating impeachment as a means of stopping Trump's pattern of abuse. Barry and I had recommended litigation to furnish the documents and witnesses we needed to make a prompt decision, one way or the other. If Trump was as dangerous as we had warned, how could the committee wait as long as this new timeline?

In addition to testing the committee's patience, unfortunately, we also ratcheted up tensions with Speaker Pelosi and her team that August. The Speaker had come a long way from her initial March proclamation that Trump "just wasn't worth" impeachment. She was now open to it, if the evidence merited. While Nadler wanted to accelerate, the Speaker preferred her strategy of "investigate, litigate, legislate," then see what develops. She had rebuffed Jerry's private entreaties for her to announce an impeachment inquiry back on May 20 and since, most recently at a Democratic caucus meeting on July 24 after the Mueller hearing. On the other hand, she had endorsed the "Magic Meltzer" language (that Judiciary was considering "whether to recommend articles of impeachment"). And on August 7, she took her strongest public position yet, writing the entire caucus that we would be filing the litigation to enforce the McGahn subpoena and that it "follows the significant step taken last week when Chairman Jerry Nadler filed a petition to obtain the grand jury testimony underlying the Mueller Report, for the House to 'have access to all the relevant facts and consider whether to exercise its full Article I powers, including a constitutional power of the utmost gravity—approval of articles of impeachment.' No one is above the law."

The clash happened the very next day. Filled with enthusiasm about the McGahn filing and the Speaker's embrace of our litigation strategy, we went beyond the limit of the carefully negotiated Magic Meltzer language. That night, Jerry appeared on Erin Burnett's 7:00 show on CNN, followed by Rachel Maddow's 9:00 show on MSNBC. Burnett, an adept interrogator, pressed him with question after question about the nature of his committee's impeachment work. I had personally prepped with him, and he had deployed the approved language: "We are considering whether to approve articles of impeachment, nothing more and nothing less." But I had underestimated both Burnett's persistence and Jerry's aversion to canned answers. As Burnett drilled down, I could see Nadler growing more impatient with the party line. Finally, when asked by Burnett if we were holding formal impeachment proceedings, he shrugged, and said yes. "This is formal impeachment proceedings." Once he had said it, he felt compelled to repeat the same to Maddow. The dam now broken, he went as far as publicly sharing his prediction when we could have a committee vote on impeachment: by the end of the year.

"'This Is Formal Impeachment Proceedings,'" screamed the headlines the next day. That specific wording had not been approved, and Pelosi's staff was quick to call and ask what the hell was happening. The distinction between "a formal impeachment proceeding" and "having hearings to determine whether to recommend articles of impeachment" may seem blurry, at best. But at that moment in time, when the press and the public were hanging on every word to try to determine how close we were to impeaching the president, there was a gulf of difference between the two. In the Speaker's suite, the interviews were viewed as unsanctioned escalations, and considerable ones. The news coverage fanned the flames.

This was not the first divergence between Jerry and the Speaker on the subject of impeachment—but until now those divergences had been behind closed doors. He had pressed her privately to open an impeachment inquiry, reflecting the wishes of some of his committee members as well as his own views. She had declined, and that had of course leaked out (almost everything does on the Hill). Our two top Judiciary communications colleagues, Danny Schwarz and Shadawn Reddick-Smith, had warned us for months that this day was coming. On May 31, the stylish, sarcastic Schwarz had pointed out that the leaks were creating an untenable situation. I replied that maybe we should just go public with Jerry's real views. That caused the level-headed Reddick-Smith to stare at me as if I had lost my sanity and ask, "Are you saying we should go to war with the Speaker?" I hastily demurred. Now some were reacting as if we had.

Jerry didn't see what the fuss was all about. To him, an impeachment proceeding was an impeachment proceeding. But he genially agreed to be more rigorous in adhering to the Magic Meltzer language as he continued pressing impeachment forward. Maybe I was imagining it, but I thought I saw a twinkle in his eye as he assented to greater caution. Publicly, Pelosi remained gracious, sidestepping the controversy. "Well, I really don't know what the chairman said," she replied when asked. "We are legislating, we are investigating, we are litigating." The incident seemed to blow over. But our obvious push for impeachment had begun to try the Speaker's patience, and we would soon pay a price for that.

Aaron liked to proclaim that "August is one of the best parts of working on the Hill." Congress was in recess for the month, and with the members away, staff was either on vacation or working more normal hours, sometimes in shorts and flip-flops. The buildings had emptied out, my Judiciary colleagues were on staggered work schedules, and Barry was back with his family in New York. Both of our cases were on file, if slightly delayed, and our strategy—with all its ups and downs—had yielded Bob Mueller's report and his testimony. He had in essence confirmed that criminal offenses had occurred and that the president had lied about them, affirming the abuse and the cover-up.

It was time to begin our August homework: drafting articles of impeachment at the instruction of the chairman. He had first raised the task on July 22, as a passing comment when we were preparing for Mueller, and he brought it up repeatedly, including on August 8 when we were preparing for his TV appearances. Barry and I now got cracking in the strictest secrecy, talking on the phone every day and keeping the job of drafting to the two of us, Arya, and our colleague Matt Morgan, a gentle giant in his early thirties who had spent his entire career at Judiciary. Having worked his way up from an intern, he had learned how to be exceptionally good with a secret. After the "formal impeachment proceedings" flap, if it got out that we were drafting articles, it would be . . . well, I didn't even want to think about it.

Neatly lining up the three sets of articles from the prior presidential impeachments on my desk on the morning of Monday, August 12, I paused, allowing myself a moment before plowing into the work. Here before me was the reason I had come to Congress: to help activate the ultimate institutional brake against a president who I believed would be the death of us all, if he remained in office. In the atypical quiet and stillness of my windowless office, my door closed for confidentiality, I scanned the three historical documents and considered the grave responsibility of drafting the fourth one.

I flipped through my copies of the original articles, hoping to draw inspiration. The impeachment articles of President Andrew Johnson were the longest, running twenty pages in beautiful, sloping handwriting on lined foolscap paper. (I also had a printed copy.) The Nixon articles were in the more modern typeset format in which they had been adopted by the House Judiciary Committee in 1974. They had fewer words than Johnson's but were in substance even more voluminous, covering a staggering array of misconduct, including abusing multiple agencies, from the FBI to the CIA to the IRS. To my taste, they were *too* jam-packed, the allegations running together into a laundry list. The Johnson articles, by contrast, took the time to tell a story of a rogue president. It was the wrong story: Johnson merited impeachment for undermining Reconstruction, but Congress did not feel they could address that candidly. Instead, they based his impeachment on a failure to uphold the Tenure of Office Act.

My eye turned to the Clinton articles. They were the first I had dealt with in real time: as a young lawyer, I had worked for a firm that represented witnesses in the case. I had shuttled to and from the Hill to report back to the partners on the proceedings. So I could have the full record, I used the old committee version, which consisted of four articles (two failed on the House floor and never made it to the Senate). The Clinton articles were the worst example of the three, exhibiting numerous technical flaws. The House Republicans were in too much of a rush to string up the president, and so had committed the legal sin of "duplicity." You're not allowed to put different crimes in a single count. This and other flaws led to substantial objections to the articles by the White House (although in the end the Senate decided the case on other grounds).

It struck me that all three sets of articles had been powerfully effective in achieving their drafters' purposes. The Johnson articles had led to his not running for reelection; Nixon resigned, and his party failed in the next election; and even though the Clinton impeachment had lost in the Senate, the hangover contributed to his party's losing. It was a reminder that if we did impeach, even if we failed in the Senate, given its partisan makeup, there would be a higher court, beyond Congress, that would ultimately deliver the verdict that mattered. That, of course, is you.

After letting the historical examples marinate for a few days, Barry and I settled on the Nixon materials as our template. For all their shortcomings, the Nixon articles were the best of the bunch. The Johnson ones were too antiquated, and the Clinton articles didn't quite hit the mark, because they targeted intimate personal failings. "High Crimes and Misdemeanors" were intended by the framers of the Constitution to be offenses against democracy, not personal morality. Impeachment exists for "offenses which proceed from the misconduct of public men, or, in other words, from the abuse or violation of some public trust," Alexander Hamilton explained. "They are of a nature which may with peculiar propriety be denominated political, as they relate chiefly to injuries done immediately to the society itself."

Hamilton had foreseen the Trump presidency to a T. With Jerry, we worked out a list of offenses that constituted the presidential continuation of Trump's lifelong pattern of abuse and cover-up. Here is our never-before-revealed list of possible articles:

I. Collusion: Trump's entanglements with Russia, open and concealed, including inviting the Russian hack of his opponent and negotiating Trump Tower Moscow, even as he disclaimed any connection to that country—all as extensively documented in Volume 1 of the Mueller Report and as elucidated in our conversations with Michael Cohen and others.

II. Obstruction of Justice: his efforts to quash the Russia investigation—particularly the five worst examples we had addressed in the Mueller hearing.

III. Hush Money: the payments Michael Cohen had told us about that were made to Stormy Daniels and Karen McDougal, used to buy their silence and avoid more negative press for then candidate Trump. Ironically, the payments made to avoid scandal were funded by arguably illegal campaign contributions, which helped secure his election.

IV. Obstruction of Congress: his consistent refusal to produce documents and to provide witnesses to us and to other committees in response to lawful subpoenas and requests, such as the ones we were litigating in our two lawsuits.

V. Failure to Protect and Defend the Constitution: his pattern of abusing his government powers to target his adversaries and benefit his purely personal interests. (At the time, we had in mind his targeting of Democrats, in addition to the press, racial and ethnic minorities, and immigrants.)

VI. Emoluments: accepting constitutionally prohibited cash and other things of value from foreign and domestic governments as a result of retaining his business interests and keeping a stake in the Trump Organization, which benefits each time he or other government officials stay at Mar-a-Lago, at his hotel in the capital, or at any of his luxury properties abroad.

VII. Abuse of Power Through Pardon Dangling: suggesting or having his lawyers threaten that he would pardon Manafort, Cohen, and others as a way of protecting himself and effectively ensuring others' silence about his behavior. (The Mueller Report had also raised this issue as to the president's treatment of Flynn.)

VIII. Usurpation of the Appropriations Power for Building the Wall: intruding upon Congress's constitutionally protected power of the purse to reallocate funds for his controversial and costly southern border wall, contrary to congressional directives.

IX. Usurpation of the Appropriations Power for Tariffs: similarly intruding upon Congress's constitutionally protected power of the purse by imposing tariffs as part of his supposed "America First" economic policy, again without congressional approval.

The first time I dug into these nine with Barry, he told me, "You forgot one." I checked my notes, puzzled. No, I told him, that was everything we had discussed. He insisted that I was missing one. "What is it?" I asked.

"What he will do next," Barry replied. He intended it as a tongue-in-cheek reflection on the length of the list, but he made a good point. With Trump, there is always a tenth article. I duly jotted "X. The Next High Crime" on my list.

We asked Arya to work with us on the first article, and Matt on the second. We held on to the others ourselves and began researching and drafting. That included diving back into issues that had been sidelined during the furious activity of the year so far, like hush money and emoluments (we even planned hearings on both for the fall as part of reviving them). Did we imagine that we would ever get all of these articles passed? Absolutely not. But Trump had done these wrongs, and we were resolved to keep on. Few people would compare seventy-two-year-old Jerry Nadler to Wayne Gretzky, famous for skating not to where the puck was but to where he *knew* it was going. And yet Nadler, with his deep background battling Trump and defending the Constitution, knew where we were headed, right down to predicting—on national television, no less—the timing of impeaching Trump before the end of the year. Having given the instruction to draft articles—along with incessant advocacy and encouragement for impeachment—he was making sure we were where we needed to be.

ON AUGUST 20, WE GOT the first whiff of the matter that would enable a pair of those articles to see the light of day. Together with Aaron, Barry and I attended a meeting with Pelosi's staff and representatives of other committees in the Speaker's formal conference room. Atop a tall cabinet was a stuffed bald eagle soaring in place for all time. On the wall next to it was a portrait of young Lincoln from his days in Congress. And unlike the side rooms where we usually met in the Capitol, there were windows offering an expansive view of the National Mall. We called these "deconflict" meetings; the objective was to avoid clashes among the overlapping investigations of the six principal committees investigating Trump: Judiciary and Intel, plus Oversight (a.k.a. COR, the Committee on Oversight and Reform), Foreign Affairs, Financial Services, and Ways and Means.

We discussed pending litigation—Judiciary's two new cases, plus ones Intel and Financial Services had going for Trump's financial information, and the Ways and Means suit for his tax returns. All faced the same delays that confronted us; indeed, we were moving briskly by comparison. The committees traded notes on continuing lines of investigation, including hush money and emoluments (our private third and sixth articles of impeachment).

Intel reported that, together with COR and Foreign Affairs, they were investigating the president's lawyer, the former New York City mayor Rudy Giuliani. We were glad to hear it. We knew Giuliani was roaming the planet, but whether he was representing his own interests, the president's, or some unholy blend, no one could tell. I had been struck by an episode a few months earlier in May. After being the subject of an unflattering exposé in *The New York Times,* Giuliani had canceled a trip to Ukraine to meet with the new president-elect, Volodymyr Zelensky, to urge him to investigate Joe Biden's activities in that country. Giuliani had been pushing a crazy Rube Goldberg construction. He claimed Biden had gotten a Ukrainian prosecutor fired to block an investigation of the Ukrainian energy company Burisma—supposedly to protect the financial interests of his son Hunter, who sat on its board. In fact, Joe Biden had been advocating the agreed position of the State Department, the U.K., and the EU. Had Hunter hypnotized all of them too? As if that foolishness weren't bad enough, Giuliani was apparently trying to cook up a story about Ukraine's interference in the 2016 election, with the evident goal of coming up with a competing narrative to Mueller's tale of Russian interference. Back in May, I had emailed my Judiciary colleagues that "I don't think Congress should let this behavior pass," but we were overtaken by other concerns, and the story faded away.

Now the *Times* was working on an update, and the committees were evidently tracking. The day after our deconflict meeting, on August 21, the paper reported that Giuliani was back at it, pressing on both his alternative 2016 election theory and constructing one for 2020 to drag down Biden right in the areas where Trump himself was vulnerable: foreign entanglements and corruption. Barry, Arya, and I added Ukraine to our watchlist of simmering Trump scandals that could trigger impeachment. Our interest bubbled up again after another press report at the end of August that mentioned that American military aid to Ukraine was being held up. But after more than three years of following Trump's scandals, we didn't get too excited. The likelihood was that the Ukraine flap would take its place alongside the thousands of other stories that had exploded and evaporated over Trump's campaign and presidency. We would just have to wait and see.

SEPTEMBER STARTED OFF ON A high note. As of the Mueller hearing, we had 95 members who supported impeachment or at least an investigation. Despite the press's post-Mueller-hearing kvetching, that number had grown to 135 by the time Congress returned to start work on September 9—now a majority-plus of the caucus. They had seen the substance for what it was, and our litigation filings had helped demonstrate forward movement within our committee.

If anything, we had been *too* successful in driving impeachment forward, in that we were provoking resistance. On September 11, Pelosi hosted her regular "Crescendo" meeting, bringing together the heads of the various groups within the Democratic caucus, from the more moderate "Blue Dogs" to the Progressive Caucus. One of the heads of the Blue Dogs, Representative Anthony Brindisi, complained that impeachment chatter was getting out of hand and that some in the caucus did not want to go down that route. At first, the Speaker defended Judiciary, saying that we had a duty to investigate. One of our members, Karen Bass, urged a clearer message on impeachment. The carefully nuanced Magic Meltzer language was starting to confuse people. Why did we have to use that formula?

The Speaker refused. She would not budge from the agreed-upon language. For good measure, she added, "Judiciary staff may think it is impeachment, but it is not. They may think they run the place, but they do not. That's a caucus decision, not theirs. And you can tell them that." Some of the attendees hastened to do so, chilling me and my colleagues to our marrow. It is never a pleasant feeling to defy the most powerful person in Congress, especially not when you work there. Amy Rutkin absorbed the brunt of it as the most senior staff member on our team; Barry and I were just tourists. But impeachment proceedings would never move forward without Pelosi's support. As strongly as we felt her reproach, we also appreciated that she was in a difficult spot, having to keep the caucus unified while balancing their competing desires.

Jerry's direction was to stick to the approved language but to keep pressing forward with impeachment-related actions, within the parameters of what the Speaker would allow: investigate, litigate, legislate. The growing caucus numbers were evidence of momentum, but we needed to keep it going to help convince Pelosi and more of the Democratic members—not to mention the American people—that impeachment was warranted. We started with some low-hanging fruit for Pelosi's "legislate" basket: a hearing to mark up and adopt impeachment procedures. They would govern the use of sensitive grand jury materials in our impeachment inquiry, if we won that case. The procedures also spoke to our second case, for McGahn's testimony. They authorized counsel (that is, Barry and me) to question McGahn, or any witnesses, in impeachment hearings, a privilege not otherwise available in the full committee. The Speaker agreed that Nadler could go forward with a hearing on adopting those and other impeachment procedures, which we scheduled for September 12.

The markup elicited howls of outrage from the GOP members of our committee. The Republicans claimed that you could not have impeachment without a full vote of the House, and so the consideration of "impeachment procedures" was not yet ripe. The DOJ used the same argument to counter our claims that we urgently needed documents and witnesses to decide on impeachment. There is no consideration of impeachment, they said, because there has been no House vote.

Nadler dismissed that and other GOP arguments. As we told the courts, such claims were not true. The Judiciary Committee had often considered impeachment before a full House vote. In the

Nixon case, for example, the committee had begun its inquiry in October 1973, but the full House did not pass a resolution endorsing the inquiry until February 1974. The procedures eventually passed along party lines after considerable, agitated debate.

That was when we hit a wall. We had filed our two impeachment-related cases. More members had signed on. We had adopted impeachment procedures. Now what? Barry and I had asked ourselves and the team that question incessantly, from when we arrived in the office, through to our chats with the Widow Jane and our late-night walks home.

We recommended to Jerry and the committee that we schedule a public hearing with additional witnesses. It was risky, because the most important remaining witnesses were allied with Trump. But we had the Mueller Report and were confident in the committee's and our own abilities to use it to good advantage. After a great deal of staff and member discussion, a panel of three witnesses was agreed upon: Rob Porter, the former White House staff secretary (a golden boy who had been ousted from the administration after two ex-wives alleged he had abused them); Rick Dearborn, former White House deputy chief of staff for policy implementation; and Corey Lewandowski, President Trump's former campaign manager. All three had witnessed important aspects of the five worst obstruction of justice episodes. The more voices we could get to confirm such episodes, the more we could bring the Mueller Report's revelations to life for Congress and the American people.

Lewandowski was the most important of the three, despite his penchant for acting out (as shown by public footage of his manhandling a reporter from no less a right-wing outlet than Breitbart). As the Trump campaign evolved, the volatile Lewandowski had been ejected in favor of the seemingly more mainstream establishment Republican Paul Manafort. The danger with Lewandowski was that we would be exposing ourselves—and, more important, the members—to a fringe right-wing provocateur.

But Lewandowski had remained a planet in Trump's orbit. The

president had repeatedly instructed him to tell Jeff Sessions to make the Mueller investigation for future elections only. That would have effectively immunized all of Trump's past conduct and that of those who worked on his campaign. If Sessions refused, Trump wanted Lewandowski to fire him. Even Lewandowski, with his notorious reputation, apparently was not comfortable acting on such orders, but just because he never carried them out does not mean there was no obstruction. If you shoot at somebody and happen to miss, the police are still going to charge you. Our goal was to get Lewandowski to tell us what happened. Porter and Dearborn had lesser, but still important, pieces to add, and our hopes were that the three together would make a substantial panel.

Our attention to Ukraine had perked up again after a *Washington Post* editorial on September 5 suggested that the aid suspension and Giuliani's shenanigans were linked. "Not only has Mr. Trump refused to grant the Ukrainian leader a White House visit, but also he has suspended the delivery of $250 million in U.S. military aid to a country still fighting Russian aggression in its eastern provinces . . . [W]e're reliably told that the president . . . is attempting to force Mr. Zelensky to intervene in the 2020 U.S. presidential election by launching an investigation of the leading Democratic candidate, Joe Biden," the *Post* stated.

Arya immediately forwarded the article to me and Barry with a note that neatly summarized the scandal that would come to dominate our lives for the next six months: "Trump withholding WH visit and funds to force 2020 election interference." Arya followed her message with one of her patented hair-on-fire visits to our office (perhaps that's why she wears it short: controlled burn). She was up in arms about the pattern. Once again, it looked as if Trump were sacrificing our national interest for his own personal and political gain. If anything, this episode had a sharper point on it because he was extorting a vulnerable foreign ally mired in a shooting war on

Russia's border—one in which Ukraine was doing America's heavy lifting by fighting our adversary.

Occasionally these visits from a worked-up Arya led to closed-door shouting matches. But in this case, Barry and I readily agreed. We talked about where to locate it on our secret list of potential articles of impeachment. I favored jotting it in as the evergreen tenth article that Barry had inspired when we were first going over the list. As the keeper of Article I, collusion, Arya made the case for putting it there, as part of the pattern. Ultimately, we plugged the Ukraine misconduct into Article V of the secret impeachment articles: "Failure to Protect and Defend the Constitution." At that point, it leapfrogged many of the issues we had been investigating for months. Why didn't we rank it even higher? Because the top four—collusion, obstruction of justice, obstruction of Congress, and the hush money scheme—had been well established and had passed the test of time. In this case, the evidence was just starting to come in. Many a Trump scandal had been editorialized about, only to somehow dissolve into the ether.

I had been in nudge mode with Intel's Dan Goldman that week, asking that they release their transcript of an earlier deposition they had done with Lewandowski before our hearing so we could use it to prepare. I asked him about the *Post* story, and he assured me they were on top of it. On Monday, September 9, Intel publicly announced their Giuliani investigation, to be conducted jointly with the Foreign Affairs and Oversight Committees. The three committees' joint release laid out the core case that Trump and Giuliani "appear to have acted outside legitimate law enforcement and diplomatic channels to coerce the Ukrainian government into pursuing two politically-motivated investigations under the guise of anti-corruption activity." It accused the two men of pressuring the Ukrainian government to assist with Trump's reelection campaign and noted the possibility that "the White House and the State Department may be abetting this scheme." The committees sent letters to the White House and State asking for the preservation of all records relating to Trump's and Giuliani's interactions with Ukraine, and that key records be turned over by September 16.

I talked to Goldman again on September 12 to ask what the status was with the Lewandowski transcript. He apologized for the delay and explained that there was a fight going on in the committee and the GOP members were going crazy. "So what else is new?" I answered. No, he said, you don't understand—"this is big." The next day, the story broke. The Intelligence Committee revealed there was a whistleblower who had filed a complaint with his inspector general (IG) "regarding a serious or flagrant problem, abuse, violation of law, or deficiency within the responsibility or authority of the Director of National Intelligence." The inspector general had, in turn, deemed this complaint a matter of "urgent concern." The complaint did not, however, say specifically against *whom* the whistle was being blown.

"Dude, this is Ukraine," Barry speculated. He pointed to places in the press release that hinted as much. Notable among them was Schiff's conclusion that "the serious misconduct at issue involves the President of the United States and/or other senior White House or Administration officials." But beyond texting my congratulations to Intel on the progress they were making, I stayed out of it and I urged the Judiciary team to do the same. We had our hands full getting ready for Lewandowski, Porter, and Dearborn. Everyone had grown accustomed to, and therefore numbed by, the sheer volume of the scandals that had exploded only to sputter out or settle to a low flame. So the gravity *still* did not fully register: Trump had succeeded in lowering any standard of expectation for how a president is supposed to behave. We didn't elevate Ukraine from number 5 on our impeachment hit parade—but we didn't downgrade it either.

THE PERSON WHO EXPRESSED THE most serious misgivings about the upcoming hearing, and in particular about calling Lewandowski as a witness, was the normally fierce Arya. She signed on to the strategy but continued to worry that Lewandowski was too volatile and that we were being too reckless. It's difficult to control an obnoxious blowhard like Lewandowski who thrives on the limelight, no matter how low he stoops to get it. But thanks to the rule change that had been adopted, Barry—perhaps the most formidable cross-examiner in America—would be standing by to take his licks after the members finished. (I would do the same for the other two witnesses.)

Arya had a fair point about the risks, and we had a series of consultations with Amy and Aaron on the twelfth and the thirteenth. Should we come up with an excuse to cancel the hearing? Barry and I strongly recommended against it. All of us would work with the members on writing and rewriting their questions, just like with Mueller. And I would play Lewandowski in rehearsals so the members would be ready for what was coming. We agreed to push on, hoping that the hearing would represent another step toward persuading the Speaker, the full caucus, and America.

Having played a hero in my last role, I found it almost cathartic to play a villain as we rehearsed with the members—like Hollywood actors who relish being cast in the occasional dark role. I was crude, disrespectful, and snarling. It was an eye-opener for the members to see what they were in for. This was not the normal course of their experience in Congress—and for good reason. It would have been unusual in previous administrations to permit somebody with a temperament as disrespectful as Lewandowski's to appear before such a distinguished body. But he was a perfect model for the new normal in Trump world. Barry and I were fine with that: we wanted the world to see the obstruction we were facing.

As before, we practiced with the members, then broke, offering suggestions and tips, rewriting scripts on the spot. In between meetings, Barry immersed himself in preparing his cross-examination, studying Lewandowski's prior public appearances. He would have the final half hour to mop the floor with him, if necessary. Some of the members were dubious, asking Barry, "Are you really going to be able to do anything with this guy that we cannot do?" Very modestly, he said, "Well, we'll see how it goes, but thirty minutes can be a long time . . ."

On the morning of September 17, Lewandowski appeared before us. The other two subpoenaed witnesses—arguably less important but still valuable in terms of what they might have witnessed—did not show. The night before the hearing the White House released a statement that "the president has directed Mr. Dearborn and Mr. Porter not to appear at the hearing." It was absolute immunity again—the same bogus doctrine that was at issue in the McGahn litigation. True, other administrations of both parties had from time to time pushed immunity, but never so aggressively, or with such relish, or for officials as junior as Dearborn. The president had reached the stage of flaunting the notion that he was above the law. We pointedly left name tags and empty chairs for the two absent colleagues.

The president had also claimed the night before the hearing the right to limit Lewandowski's testimony under a legal doctrine known as executive privilege. It allows some communications involving the president and executive branch officials to be protected from disclosure. But this was an absurd stretch: Lewandowski had never even held a White House job title or office. The administration asserted that he was an adviser nonetheless. It was a preposterous claim—made slightly less so by the concession that the president would allow Lewandowski to speak about what the Mueller Report had already documented. Philbin and Purpura were seated behind him in the front row of the gallery, the good cop and the bad cop, ready to leap up at a moment's notice to defend the president's obstruction.

Lewandowski kicked off the hearing by kvetching that we had designated his testimony as part of our impeachment inquiry. He began his prepared remarks by gushing about the Trump campaign as the greatest political movement in our nation's history. He went on to praise Trump's decision to "ride down a golden escalator and seek the Republican nomination." He made scathing attacks on our committee's efforts at holding the president accountable, suggesting that "the American people continue to be sold a false narrative with the purpose of undermining the legitimacy of the 2016 election results," echoing Trump on "the fake Russia collusion narrative," and deriding the investigation as being "populated by many Trump haters who had their own agenda: to take down a duly elected president."

As the chairman and the members questioned him, Lewandowski was openly contemptuous, asking for a copy of the Mueller Report and even demanding he be read the exact language. He refused to answer questions until he was provided with a copy of the report, then delayed all proceedings by repeatedly asking for the paragraph and the line that the questioners referenced. When he was asked about the instructions that he'd received from the White House, instead of answering, he offered to share the letter that the White House had already provided to the committee, then proceeded to read from it. In the middle of the hearing he launched a super PAC (Stand with Corey) on social media for his prospective Senate run. Zero scruples. He was transparently doing everything possible to evade questions and advance his contempt for the committee, for our process, and for our purpose of bringing to the surface President Trump's shocking obstruction of justice.

Lewandowski wasn't the only one misbehaving. Ranking Member Collins was furious about being forced along on Nadler's impeachment ride and waded in with points of order the entire time. He and the Republicans used every tactic in the parliamentary bag of tricks that a minority party can draw from to disrupt a hearing. Many of their disruptive maneuvers required a full vote of the committee, dragging out a hearing that grew chaotic.

To their credit, the members fought through it. Point by point, they extracted every concession we needed. Did the president order Lewandowski to talk to Sessions? Check. Was the message to curtail the Mueller investigation? Check. Did Trump tell him to fire Sessions if he did not go along? Check. Had Lewandowski been so concerned he locked his notes in his safe? Check (though he answered the question with a sneering reference to the guns he kept next to them, taunting our pro-gun-control majority). Yes, Lewandowski's repeated refusals to answer questions were maddening. So was his disrespectful behavior and that of the minority. But (through an ever so slightly rose-colored lens), I saw an upside: Lewandowski put a face to the infuriating Trumpian obstruction we had to deal with on a regular basis.

And all that was before we deployed our secret weapon.

AFTER THE MEMBERS HAD FINISHED examining Lewandowski, it was Barry's turn. He was sitting beside the chairman in the counsel chair, with me sitting directly behind, passing notes and making sure his slides and his video operated seamlessly. Before he could begin, there was another eruption of Republican anger as they again objected to counsel's being allowed to question Lewandowski. Nadler explained repeatedly that this was the first hearing under impeachment inquiry rules, which permitted such cross-examination. After heated argument (one photograph of which was later published by *The New York Times* as a "Renaissance tableau" illustrating the difficulties of partisanship surrounding impeachment), Nadler put an end to it, declaring, "You don't interpret our rules. Counsel has the floor."

At last, Barry was given the opportunity to do what he does best. He snapped the witness to order just with his tone of voice. "Mr. Lewandowski," Barry began, "did you ever become concerned that the president of the United States had asked you to do something that could expose you to criminal liability?" A tipster had told us that Lewandowski had taken the Fifth on a prior occasion, and he squirmed as he began his fruitless attempts at evading Barry's questions. Barry, way ahead of him, relentlessly bore down on Lewandowski with his opening series of questions. I cast a look at the members, who were rapt and clearly loving the confrontation, and then I made eye contact with Purpura and Philbin, who looked slightly queasy. They were pros and knew what was coming.

As the questions ramped up—"Were you ever concerned that the president had asked you to do something that put you in harm's way?"—a visibly rattled witness started stumbling. "I think I've actually answered that question," was all he could come back with. He knew he was dissembling, and he was badly shaken up, like a prizefighter wobbling at the end of the first round.

Barry pivoted to a second line of questions, about false statements Lewandowski had made to the press. As news clips appeared on the screens, showing Lewandowski repeatedly contradicting himself, his eyes grew large, beginning to resemble those of a raccoon trapped in a garbage can. Barry played a Fox News video revealing a Lewandowski misrepresentation, again about self-incrimination. Lewandowski tried to parry, using the ploys he'd been relying on all day. But Barry didn't fall for it, instead harnessing all the force of his personality to make Lewandowski feel as small as he is. As Barry bore down, Lewandowski started to crack. "I don't think I was under any obligation . . . when speaking to Fox News to not engage in hyperbole if I so chose."

Word had spread that something notable was going on, and staff from all over began coming back into the chamber; reporters who had been slouched over were sitting up in their chairs again, furiously typing. Had he been a normal witness, I would have felt sympathy. But this man had been so outrageously rude all day, as contemptuous and baselessly pompous as any witness I had encountered in my three decades of attending hearings on the Hill.

"Have you ever been untruthful about being asked to answer a question by the special counsel?"

Lewandowski attempted to evade Barry's query, then stated that he'd always been honest. Then qualified himself: "to the best of my ability."

"Sir," Barry punched back, "let me show you another clip." He ran one from *Meet the Press*. A lie, of course. Barry turned to Lewandowski, unrelenting. "*Sir,* is that truthful? Is it accurate what you said on national television?"

Helpless, Lewandowski struck out with his default tone of sarcasm. "Oh, I'm sorry nobody in front of Congress has ever lied to the public before."

Barry pounced. "Is that an admission that you *did* lie?"

"What I'm saying is that when under oath I . . . I've always told the truth," Lewandowski stuttered.

"That's not my question to you, sir. My question to you is, on national television did you lie about your relationship with the special counsel?"

There was dead silence in the room, making it only more excruciating for the trapped raccoon. Finally, after a series of ten questions, with Lewandowski trying every possible method to slither through the bars, Barry showed him an interview with Ari Melber of MSNBC in which Lewandowski claimed, "I don't ever remember the president ever asking me to get involved with Jeff Sessions or the Department of Justice in any way, shape, or form, ever." There it was: the culmination of our hearing.

"That wasn't true, was it, *sir*?" Barry said, his voice full of disdain.

"I heard that," was the only thing Lewandowski could say. With all his defenses used up, Lewandowski finally uttered the words that would dominate our press coverage: "I have no obligation to be honest with the media because they are just as dishonest as anybody else."

There was an audible gasp in the room. Never in the history of congressional testimony had a witness successfully advanced a Senate bid during his testimony, only to see it absorb such a devastating blow before he even left the witness chair. I wanted to leap out of my seat and pump my fist; instead, I leaned back, crossed my legs, and settled in for more.

Lewandowski grew increasingly desperate, with flailing responses like "Well, I didn't get to go to an Ivy League school, or Harvard Law," as Barry had. His attitude only sharpened Barry's questioning. Everybody in the immediate vicinity started showing up to see Barry work his magic, just as they did when he worked in New York courtrooms. This was Cross-Examination 101, exposing what *Slate* would call "next-level gaslighting" on Lewandowski's part.

After Jerry mercifully gaveled the hearing closed, we returned to the members' conference room, and the committee gave Barry a round of applause. He returned the compliment: they had wrung out concession after concession, however painful.

As pleased as the members were with Barry, however, they were furious with Lewandowski. During the brief interval before we scattered, it became clear that they did not think their point-scoring, or the spanking Barry had administered, was a sufficient response to Lewandowski's outrageous behavior. We agreed to all gather again the following day to continue the discussion.

Barry and I genuinely believed that the hearing had accomplished its purposes, including driving continued attention to impeachment. But the press was lacerating. The coverage focused on Lewandowski's shenanigans at the expense of the presidential crimes he had confirmed. While Barry's performance was praised, reporters and analysts felt that the hearing had been chaotic—and that we should have done more to control the witness. Even Michael Cohen got into the act, sending me a message from prison: "I watched yesterday's debacle and as an American, am embarrassed."

THE NEXT DAY, AS THE committee reconvened in our Judiciary conference room, Barry and I tried to explain that there was a lot to like about the hearing. We had confirmed more of the abuses in the Mueller Report. The hearing had validated the proposition that counsel questioning had an important role to play in advancing our investigation. We had put a face on the administration's refusal to cooperate and garnered widespread attention to impeachment, even if some of that attention was less than flattering. "All press is good press," I proclaimed.

But the members were not having it—at all. They were frustrated, both because the hearing had not won many converts to impeachment, and because of Lewandowski's behavior. "It was a shitshow," one said, speaking for many in the room. They had never seen a witness act out like that and were determined to respond forcefully. They were getting grief from their colleagues, including the Speaker. Pelosi had said the committee should have held Lewandowski in contempt on the spot. (It was a move that we had researched in advance and that, regrettably, our rules did not allow.)

Barry and I pointed out that the committee's work up to that point had taken impeachment all the way down the investigative runway. When the next scandal hit, the House would have nowhere else to go other than to take off and impeach. Given Trump's history and pattern, we knew he was going to continue to engage in wrongdoing; the only question was whether he got caught.

But the conversation kept coming back to Lewandowski. We had intentionally left the hearing open, which meant we could still hold him in contempt. We discussed the different forms of that remedy and potential timetables. No single approach commanded a consensus, and there were a lot of technicalities to work through. The team agreed to dig in, look at all the permutations, and report back.

Afterward, I told Barry that was not quite the client reaction that I was used to. "Good, maybe I can go home early!" he joked, then saw my distressed expression. He insisted I was overreacting. It was one hearing. We hadn't been in a courtroom, where the judge could enforce contempt right on the spot. We would explore all the options for punishing Lewandowski's bad behavior. And now that we were past Lewandowski, we could start having hearings on other issues that we had long wanted to pursue, like emoluments and the illegal hush money payments.

"That's all well and good," I replied. "But in the meantime, Trump's misconduct is ongoing!" Our job security was getting worse, and his was getting better. How could we stop him before he high-crimed again?

Like clockwork, we'd have an answer to that question within twenty-four hours.

CHAPTER SIX

A Whistle Is Blown

"AMY. HAVE YOU SEEN *THE WASHINGTON POST*?"

"No, what is it?"

"Take a look. The whistleblower complaint is about the *president*. This changes everything."

It was a little after 9:00 P.M. on September 18, the day after the Lewandowski hearing. The *Post* had just reported that President Trump's interaction with an as-yet-unspecified foreign leader "included a 'promise' that was regarded as so troubling that it prompted an official in the U.S. intelligence community to file a formal whistleblower complaint with the inspector general." The intelligence community inspector general (ICIG), Michael Atkinson, had determined that the complaint not only was credible but met the threshold to be considered a matter of "urgent concern," thereby setting up notification of congressional oversight committees. That clicked like a key in a lock with the bits and pieces about Ukraine that had been heating up for the past several weeks. The whistleblower complaint was surely about Trump and Ukraine, and the administration was refusing to turn it over. Trump was once more welcoming foreign intrusion into an election to corruptly benefit himself, then trying to interfere with its investigation, just as we'd seen in the Mueller investigation. Indeed, it was worse; this time, he was encouraging the election attack from the

White House and dangling privileges granted by the awesome powers of that office.

On my phone call with Amy, I assured her that this was going to blot everything else out. "If it's about the president and Ukraine, Amy, no one is going to *care* about Corey Lewandowski anymore; just give this a couple of days. Trust me."

That's fine, Norm, she responded. But our entire committee was focused on the Lewandowski fallout. We had to keep pushing on the issues they had raised earlier that day. Of course, I replied, but ended our call with a guarantee that, within a week, Lewandowski would be overshadowed.

Things would move even faster than I had imagined.

THE NEXT DAY, THURSDAY, SEPTEMBER 19, the *Post* confirmed that the whistleblower complaint concerned Ukraine. Intel held a closed-door briefing with the inspector general and released correspondence about the whistleblower complaint being withheld by the director of national intelligence (DNI). They made clear that they did not know if the press reports were true about the president's involvement: "We do not have the complaint; we do not know whether the press reports are accurate or inaccurate about the contents of that complaint." The details of the cover-up were also clarified: the ICIG wanted the complaint to be released, as required by law, but that was being blocked. The ICIG was clearly the good guy in this fray: he had notified Congress and gotten the ball rolling. The bad guy was clear as well. "We do know that the Department of Justice has been involved in the decision to withhold that information from Congress," Chairman Schiff stated. "Barr strikes again," I told Barry.

He, Aaron, and I convened with top staff from Intel and the other committees on Friday, the twentieth, in the large conference room in Pelosi's suite, the stuffed eagle and young Lincoln looking down on us expectantly. The Speaker liked to point to Lincoln and remind visitors of his adage that "public sentiment is everything." Whatever had come before, we had a new shot at boosting that sentiment for impeachment—especially if we could get our hands on the whistleblower complaint. A majority of the Democratic caucus and about 40 percent of Americans were already persuaded of the wisdom of an impeachment investigation. Now I hoped we could increase both (depending on what the whistleblower said, of course).

We went through DOJ's arguments one by one, trying to figure out what to do. As someone who had worked on whistleblower cases and legislation for decades, including inside the White House and at CREW, I agreed with the group that the department's position reeked to high heaven. The law mandates that complaints be turned over to Congress if they urgently concern an intelligence activity within the DNI's jurisdiction. *All* intelligence activities were within his jurisdiction! But DOJ was claiming that the law didn't require a turnover to the committee, because it didn't involve misconduct by a member of the intelligence community or "an intelligence activity under the DNI's supervision." They said executive privilege applied—that bugaboo again, DOJ's all-purpose shield for presidential wrongdoing. Just as Trump had his playbook, Barr and DOJ had theirs.

I pointed out that this was what we had seen during the fight over the Mueller Report and what we were attacking in our grand jury materials and McGahn cases: floating fanciful legal theories to hold back damaging information and protect the president. Every administration did it to some degree of course, but we had never seen anything like the scope and scale of obscurantism that Trump and Barr were engineering. It was also grist for impeachment for obstruction of Congress (our Article IV—though I didn't let on that the drafting had already begun).

Maher Bitar and Dan Goldman noted that DOJ's position had a chilling implication: if the complaint fell outside the terms of the statute, the legal protections for those who blew the whistle might be inapplicable, and this individual could therefore be exposed to potential retaliation. On DOJ's twisting of the plain language of the statute, the whistleblower was not a whistleblower at all. The statutory doublespeak reminded me of Humpty Dumpty's statement from *Through the Looking-Glass:* "When I use a word, it means just what I choose it to mean—neither more nor less."

The president had been relatively silent on the whistleblower thus far, but Intel expected him to lash out forcefully at any minute. In the meantime, they warned, the GOP minority was quietly developing conspiracy theories to explain away this latest scandal. The commander in chief and his congressional enablers were now well practiced at spinning away any consequences for Trump's obstruction, and abuse. Elisabeth Kübler-Ross described five stages of grief upon the death of a loved one; we identified Trump's five stages of grievance that kill the truth. We knew them well from the Mueller investigation, and have seen the exact same reaction to the devastating COVID-19 crisis that has occurred since:

1. Blanket denial.
2. Attack those who reported on the issue, and accuse *them* of wrongdoing.
3. Slowly admit what happened.
4. Test rationalizations until you find one that sticks while maintaining the attack and charging hypocrisy.
5. Fully embrace the wrongdoing and claim perfection.

Conflating the terrible thing Trump did (which he characterized as fine) and the benign or even noble thing that his opponent did (which he characterized as terrible) creates a constant stance of unfairness and victimization. It's a highly distracting formula that had worked to spin the Mueller Report. As the meeting broke up, we agreed that—unless we moved briskly on Ukraine—Trump and his enablers would run the same play to similar effect.

It didn't take long for them to try. When the president later that day derided the whistleblower as a "partisan person" whose complaint was "a political hack job," we were ready to punch back. Judiciary joined the three investigative committees in leaping to the whistleblower's defense. The four chairs issued a joint statement: "The President's brazen effort to intimidate this whistleblower risks a chilling effect on future whistleblowers, with grave consequences for our democracy and national security."

Hours later, we met with the full Judiciary Committee to discuss the rapidly evolving state of play, as well as any lingering post-Lewandowski issues. We were eager for the world to see what a creep he is, one who received his comeuppance from Barry and the committee. *The Washington Post*'s Jennifer Rubin named Barry "distinguished person of the week" for his examination, while law professors said that his examination should be taught in law schools across the country. But Lewandowski had shamelessly acted out, and while he left the building with a drubbing to his reputation and to his Senate run, he had not received any official reprimand. Members were continuing to grapple with how best to handle that, including through holding him in contempt.

The conversation inevitably turned to the Ukraine scandal. The Colorado congressman Joe Neguse's words resonated: the paradigm was shifting, and we had to shift with it. He appreciated how Jerry and staff had kept the impeachment lane open. Then he pivoted to the same problem that we had discussed that morning with Intel and the other committees: "Say the whistleblower is telling the truth. By the time we get the actual complaint it will be normalized. We will miss the moment, as we did with the Mueller Report. We are in constant crises and if we wait we will lose the moment again." I assured him that we got the message.

After the meeting, one of my favorite representatives, an early impeachment adopter, Veronica Escobar, took me aside. She was one of the *tres comadres* (godmothers), three new members of the committee who had bonded with one another and with me and Barry. Veronica and the other two, Debbie Murcarsel-Powell of Florida and Sylvia Garcia of Texas, had helped us understand how to communicate Trump's wrongdoing through the lens of the diverse communities of their respective home states. Veronica had also endeared herself to us at the end of a long working dinner by pulling out a large bottle of top-shelf tequila to rival our Widow Jane and toasting our shared work.

Now she was distraught. She looked at me and, with real anguish in her voice, said, "Norm, if these new allegations are not enough for impeachment, what is?" I explained that we had been speaking with leadership and the other committees and we were moving as fast as possible. She warned that while we were gathering facts, the president would run the same play: selectively deny, spin, normalize, and target his opponents until the accusation wilted away.

Afterward, we sat with Nadler in his vast office. He was calm, as steady as ever. Clinton, Obama, and Cyndi Lauper looked out from their stately posts. He counseled us to stick to the strategy. Yes, prioritize the new evidence, but keep all our lines of inquiry moving. Think about a simple persuasive narrative. Connect the dots. Be ready for hearings. And focus on the endgame: impeachment and trial. "We *have* kept the impeachment lane open," he said. "Let's wait and see what happens." Pelosi was rightly concerned about the whole caucus, including the forty or so front-liners and new members who represented districts that Trump had won and who had given her the majority. She had been annoyed with our pushing, which Jerry accepted. We had a job to do, and she had a job to do. That dynamic was about to change.

ON SUNDAY MORNING, I SPOKE to Barry's and my counterparts on the Intelligence Committee, Dan Goldman and Maher Bitar. Like Barry, Dan was a leader in the New York bar (the two were friends from trying a high-profile criminal case against each other just two years before). Maher and I were both D.C. insiders (we had worked together at the State Department, and he had even visited me when I was ambassador in Prague). By this stage, the four of us deeply trusted one another, and those bonds would prove essential through the turbulent months ahead. That is not to say that we always saw eye to eye. When we disagreed, Maher and I resolved our differences with the Foggy Bottom diplomatic skills in which we had both been steeped, and Dan and Barry did so with what passed for diplomacy among New York litigators.

Our conversation that morning was focused on how to secure the release of the whistleblower complaint. It was outrageous that the DOJ was blocking the DNI from turning over the complaint on bogus executive privilege grounds. This had never happened in the twenty-year history of this statute, and—having served as the lawyer who advised Obama on whistleblower issues—I knew it never would have happened in his or any other administration. Among the more drastic remedies discussed, we debated a mandamus case: asking a court to order a government official (who was flagrantly violating a statute) to comply.

But even if the courts eventually agreed, timing remained the problem. Look at Judiciary's situation: we wouldn't have the initial decisions on the grand jury and McGahn cases until the latter part of 2019. They could get held up for a year or more on appeal. Friday's talk about not letting Trump run out the clock rang in my ears. Our president had spent a lifetime abusing the legal system to his own ends. He knew the power of delay and that it generally worked in his favor. There was simply no time for litigation, particularly if these allegations were true. Whatever we did, it had to be fast. We had to move at the speed of Trump if we wanted to hold him accountable. That was particularly so here, where he was engaged in behavior that was a threat to the rapidly approaching election.

The conversation turned to impeachment. The Constitution provides for that remedy in cases of "Treason, Bribery, or other high Crimes and Misdemeanors." Before assessing bribery, we needed more evidence. (This was before the record of Trump's call with Zelensky was released.) It certainly felt like bribery; the president was offering badly needed aid in exchange for personal benefit: investigations of his rivals.

Maher rightly sounded a note of caution: What if the facts don't end up clearly proving an explicit quid pro quo? "Even if it wasn't bribery," I said, "it would still be a high crime and misdemeanor: abuse of power." When the framers wrote the words "or other high Crimes and Misdemeanors," their preeminent concern was, as Hamilton had put it, "the abuse or violation of some public trust." That was the highest of high crimes, and certainly included a president abusing his office for purely personal or political goals. The Ukraine allegations seemed to be a textbook case.

In what would become a familiar cadence over the next six months, I agreed that Judiciary would delve into these and other legal questions while Intel and the other two committees plowed ahead on the facts. I briefed Barry after the call, and we started by sending them the research we had on executive privilege, demonstrating that the president's basis for withholding the whistleblower complaint was nonsense.

Then, in an unusual move for a weekend, Pelosi sent a "Dear Colleague" letter to the full caucus and shared it with the press. It warned, "If the Administration persists in blocking this whistleblower from disclosing to Congress a serious possible breach of constitutional duties by the President, they will be entering a grave new chapter of lawlessness which will take us into a whole new stage of investigation." Schiff made it even more explicit, telling CNN that he had been resistant but "the president is pushing us down" the road toward impeachment. "And if," Schiff continued, "after having sought foreign assistance and welcomed foreign assistance in the last presidential campaign as a candidate, he is now doing the same thing again, but now using the power of the presidency, then he may force us to go down this road."

That same day, Trump admitted discussing Biden with Zelensky on July 25. "The conversation I had was largely congratulatory, with largely corruption, all of the corruption taking place and largely the fact that we don't want our people like Vice President Biden and his son creating to [*sic*] the corruption already in the Ukraine," he said to the press. He also declared there was "no quid pro quo, there was nothing. It was a perfect conversation."

We would have to dance faster than he did. I called the Judiciary team, parceled out assignments, and redoubled my own efforts to be ready for the week ahead.

When we checked in with Nadler on Monday morning, he told us he'd talked to the Speaker. She had probed his thinking on next steps. While she hadn't made up her mind, it was a cordial conversation, and she seemed to be open to impeachment at last. Nadler let Pelosi know that he was comfortable with Schiff's committee taking on a lead role in the next phase provided that—if impeachable conduct was revealed—the case would be referred back to Judiciary for the drafting of articles and conducting hearings to determine whether to recommend them to the full Congress. Having pushed the boulder to the top of the hill, he was willing to let others roll it down the other side.

I asked how he thought our own House front-liners and the Republican-dominated Senate would greet our efforts. His eyes darted to the pocket Constitution on his desk. It did not matter if the Senate failed to fulfill its responsibility, he said, or if we had challenges within our own caucus. We had *our* constitutional duty to guide us, and we had all sworn an oath to protect it. "Or an affirmation," I chimed in, a private joke between us. Chairman Nadler knew that as an observant Jew I'm forbidden by the Torah to swear any oath; instead, we affirm. It was time, he said, for us to live up to the duty required by that oath—"or affirmation," he added with a smile.

I was bolstered when I clicked on *The Washington Post* that evening to read a clear and powerful piece by seven freshman Democrats, asserting that the allegations against the president in the Ukraine affair "are a threat to all we have sworn to protect." All of them had military or national security backgrounds: Representatives

Jason Crow, Gil Cisneros, Chrissy Houlahan, Elaine Luria, Mikie Sherrill, Elissa Slotkin, and Abigail Spanberger. The last four of the group represent Trump-voting districts, but clearly believed that the threat he posed was so dire for the country that they would risk their political futures to make this public declaration.

WE AWOKE THE NEXT MORNING to confront a dreadful idea that was circulating through the caucus and in the blogosphere: creating a select committee to investigate the Ukraine affair, like the one that targeted Benghazi. A newly formed select committee would take time to organize, staff, and get working. It would fit right into Trump's five *D*s: delay, delegitimize, distract, deflect, and—ultimately—destruct. It was exactly the wrong thing to do. Plus, Intel and the other two committees were well under way with the fact investigation, and Judiciary was well suited to handle the articles and impeachment hearings if it came to that.

We immediately started talking to everybody, from the anti-Trump neocon right to the progressive left, to try to put the kibosh on the select committee idea. Amy and I furiously worked our Rolodexes, as did the entire staff. Among my contacts was Bill Kristol, who had been pushing the idea of the select committee. After our discussion, Kristol tweeted, "I've mentioned a possible select committee on Trump-Ukraine. But I'm now advised by people who know the Hill well that this could mean complexity and delay. If so, let House Judiciary handle the inquiry (with help from other committees). A fair, fast, and focused inquiry is key." Alexandria Ocasio-Cortez, at Amy's urging, retweeted her ideological opposite Kristol, adding, "Yes, this is an emergency. We don't have the luxury of time w/ another committee. Judiciary has been investigating and putting the pieces together for months. Impeachment belongs there. We must honor jurisdiction, historical precedent, and work done and allow Judiciary to move forward."

That afternoon, the Speaker called the six chairs together for a meeting. These were the heads of the same six committees investigating Trump whom we had been meeting with at the staff level all year long: Judiciary, Intel, Oversight, Foreign Affairs, Financial Services, and Ways and Means. The agenda was unclear, so we prepared with Jerry for every contingency. Barry, Amy, Aaron, and I walked with the chairman across the Capitol to the Speaker's suite for the 3:00 P.M. gathering, to be held in Pelosi's personal office—airy and Californian, decorated in tones of pink and peach, filled with bouquets of flowers, framed by large windows. They looked out at the magnificent front yard of our nation: the Capitol grounds, the Mall, the Washington Monument, the Reflecting Pool, and, at the far end of the vista, the Lincoln Memorial. I was still chatting with Jerry when the Speaker walked in to greet the committee chairs. My anxiety rose, but was instantly assuaged as she greeted the group. "Hello, hello. Well, here we are. The day has come," she said.

There they were: the words we'd been waiting to hear since the Mueller Report had dropped. I said a silent thank-you to the heavens as I slipped out of the members-only gathering. The Speaker went on to inform the group that she would announce her support for the ongoing impeachment inquiry to the entire caucus and then at a press conference. She talked about the exact words to use to introduce this momentous step forward, then asked Nadler about Judiciary's role. He foresaw Schiff and Intelligence, along with any other committees that had information to contribute, finishing their investigations and handing the facts over to Judiciary to evaluate and analyze. We would then perform our historic role of holding hearings and considering and drafting the articles of impeachment. (He did not add that we had been researching and writing them for more than a month.) The key was to move as quickly as possible.

Speaker Pelosi voiced no objection, and Jerry emerged from the meeting satisfied. If our long list of possible articles had gone by the boards, he felt, so be it. We would focus on Ukraine for now and see how things developed. It would still take time and work for him and Pelosi to restore their relationship to its former level of personal warmth—a process he expedited by later telling reporters (who by now were well aware that something was cooking) that he would support whatever Speaker Pelosi announced. Barry, Amy, and I walked with him to the caucus meeting. After having pushed so long, you might think there would be some sort of exultation. It was the moment that we had slaved and sweated and sleep deprived ourselves for, dining out of vending machines and grabbing catnaps on sofas for seven arduous months. In reality, it felt as if the decision had been made to drop the atom bomb; it was indeed "solemn" and "prayerful." The *Times* captured a photograph of us en route to the meeting looking as serious as we felt.

By the time we arrived at the caucus, practically every one of the 235 Democratic representatives was packed into a basement meeting room. The meeting was slightly delayed while aides scrambled to find more chairs for all the members. Pelosi often looked to Lincoln for inspiration, and a long quote from him was shown on the screens that ringed the room. It read: "Our Safety, Our Liberty, Depends upon Preserving the Constitution of the United States. . . . The People of the United States are the Rightful Masters of both Congress and the Courts, not to overthrow the Constitution, but to overthrow the men who pervert the Constitution."

Hakeem Jeffries, in his capacity as the chair of the House Democratic Caucus, began the meeting by telling the room that the conversations they were about to have were "some of the most important we will ever have as elected officials." Pelosi told the group, "Here we are: a moment of truth. Truth is what this has been about all along. *Alea iacta est*"—the die is cast. Schiff noted that when the president tells a foreign leader who is dependent on the United States what he wants, doing it is not optional. "We have gone from bad, to worse, to even worse," he said (an augur of what lay ahead if Trump's escalating misconduct was not responded to). When it was his turn to speak, Jerry explained that we needed to move quickly, stating "we don't want to waste time while they normalize the conduct." The lessons of the Mueller investigation—indeed, of decades of dealing with Trump—had not been lost on Nadler.

Then Speaker Pelosi returned to the hallway outside her office and made her public announcement standing before a wall of American flags lined up like sentries:

> For the past several months, we have been investigating in our committees and litigating in the courts, so the House can gather all the relevant facts and consider whether to exercise its full Article I powers, including a constitutional power of the utmost gravity: approval of articles of impeachment. And this week the president has admitted to asking the president of Ukraine to take actions which would benefit him politically . . .
>
> Therefore, today I'm announcing the House of Representatives moving forward with an official impeachment inquiry. I'm directing our six committees to proceed with their investigations under that umbrella of impeachment inquiry.
>
> The president must be held accountable. No one is above the law.

She thanked the six chairs one by one, starting with Jerry. And she quoted Thomas Paine, "The times have found us." We had come to our Promontory Summit, driving the golden spike at last.

Barry and I returned to our office, with most of our team squeezed into every available inch of space waiting for us. "Hey, hey, hey!" he proclaimed, breaking the tension and triggering a round of applause, followed by a flurry of questions. I understood the enthusiastic sentiment, but was surprised to find that my own feelings remained mixed. Of course there was gratification; the president would finally face accountability, and we all knew it was called for. We had beaten back the counterproductive idea of a special committee and preserved Judiciary's role. But the nation was looking down the barrel of a traumatic reckoning. We had a president who was a high criminal; that is a sobering truth.

At least we would get to do something about it. And so can you.

THE NEXT DAY, THE WHITE House released the record of Trump's July 25 call. As Barry and I read it together, we literally could not believe what was on the page in front of us. We read the lines out to each other, with increasing astonishment in our voices:

> I would like you to do us a favor though because our country has been through a lot and Ukraine knows a lot about it. I would like you to find out what happened with this whole situation with Ukraine . . . The server, they say Ukraine has it . . . As you saw yesterday, that whole nonsense ended with a very poor performance by a man named Robert Mueller, an incompetent performance, but they say a lot of it started with Ukraine . . .
>
> The other thing, [t]here's a lot of talk about Biden's son, that Biden stopped the prosecution and a lot of people want to find out about that, so whatever you can do with the Attorney General would be great. Biden went around bragging that he stopped the prosecution so if you can look into it . . . It sounds horrible to me.

"Barry," I said, "I *never* would have advised President Obama to release a transcript like this. And I was in charge of transparency!"

"Obama would never have said anything like this," he replied. Even Nixon, we noted, hadn't sunk to this level.

Trump's request for "a favor though" came right after Zelensky thanked him for the guns and money he had sent so far, and asked for more: "We are ready to continue to cooperate for the next steps specifically we are almost ready to buy more Javelins from the United

States for defense purposes." But the quid pro quo was not quite spelled out: again, Trump adeptly walked the edge of criminality without toppling over. He had an uncanny skill for it, honed over a lifetime of practice. The call record would only get us 85 percent of the way to impeachment, and given Trump's propensity for obstruction, proving up that last 15 percent was going to be a challenge.

On Thursday, September 26, the long march began. The acting director of national intelligence, Joseph Maguire, was set to testify before Intel about the Ukraine allegations. It seemed like months since his appearance had been announced, though it had been only eight days. That morning, in advance of his appearance, the whistleblower complaint was finally released. It began by stating, "I have received information from multiple U.S. Government officials that the President of the United States is using the power of his office to solicit interference from a foreign country in the 2020 U.S. election. This interference includes, among other things, pressuring a foreign country to investigate one of the President's main domestic political rivals."

The hearing was a chance to highlight the whistleblower's revelations. In his opening statement, Chairman Schiff likened Trump's call with the Ukrainian president to "a classic organized crime shakedown" and delivered a parody of Trump's statements in Mafia-like language. Trump, in response, tweeted that Schiff had "illegally made up a fake and terrible statement" at the hearing, asking his followers whether the congressman should be arrested for treason. Afterward, Barry and I bumped into Schiff and the team in the cafeteria. We congratulated them on an effective launch. The chairman was in a good mood despite Trump's tweet. He told us that we had set a high bar with the Lewandowski cross-examination. Still smarting from the public criticism of the hearing, I jokingly asked if he would be willing to issue a press release to that effect.

The Judiciary team met one more time before we left for the weekend. Chairman Nadler addressed the whole staff, reminding us once again not to get overexcited. "Stay the course. Keep on doing what you are doing. It's working," he said. Barry and I retreated to our small office afterward, discussing how the past seven days were a surreal dream. Was Trump finally going to get his due? "Bro," he said, "a week ago after the Lewandowski hearing you thought we could be out of here. Now . . . we're doing what we came for!" It was a remarkable turn of fortune. For only the fourth time in American history, the House would be moving toward impeachment of the president.

CHAPTER SEVEN

The Pendulum Swings

SILENCE FILLED THE CHAMBER AS THE FORMER PROSECUTOR consulted his notes. A lock of his brown hair fell over his brow as he looked up, staring at me with cold blue eyes and readying his first question. I stared back—but not as Norm Eisen. Instead, it was the latest of my moot court performances. I was playing my former ambassadorial colleague Bill Taylor, currently our envoy to Ukraine and an important witness against the president.

It was Monday, November 11, shortly after 6:00 P.M., and I was the first State Department veteran to experience what a stream of my diplomatic colleagues would soon face: sitting in the witness chair of a congressional hearing room, about to be grilled by the Intelligence Committee counsel Dan Goldman. The hearing room was not a public one, but Intel's SCIF (Sensitive Compartmented Information Facility), a windowless space hidden in the Capitol's basement where the nation's most secret testimony is taken. The audience comprised about a dozen elite congressional operatives—lawyers, analysts, press secretaries, and other seasoned pros from Intel, COR, Foreign Affairs, and the Speaker's office, all working together as one to drive the impeachment investigation forward.

As Dan wound up to throw his first fastball, the observers had pens poised above their notepads like scouts at spring training. They were there to gauge how his approach would play on opening day: the actual interrogation of Taylor in room 1100 of the Longworth House Office Building, one of the largest and most ornate of the House's public hearing rooms. Normally the home of the Ways and Means Committee, it had been made available for the hearing. Just over thirty-six hours away, it was expected to be standing room only, and to be watched by more than ten million TV viewers. Taylor's interrogation would kick off what Barry and I privately called impeachment month: two weeks of fact hearings in Intel followed by two weeks of applying the law to those facts in Judiciary, passing articles (or not), as the evidence warranted. If impeachment month succeeded, we would pass articles through the House and head to the Senate trial with a burst of momentum. If it failed, the reckoning that Trump so richly deserved would as well.

The stakes were even higher for this dry run than with the Mueller or Lewandowski prep. Barry was seated next to me, playing the other witness slated to testify side by side with Taylor, the State Department anticorruption and Ukraine expert George Kent, who was also expected to publicly denounce Trump's machinations. We had been quick to accept when, a couple of days earlier, Goldman and Maher Bitar, our equivalents on Intel, had asked us to play the witnesses.

We took our roles seriously, reading the deposition transcripts of the two men, studying exhibits, and using our chronologies that we had been building. For the mock testimony, I distilled Taylor's story down to a list of sixty key dates and events that covered two sides of a single page, now centered on the table in front of me. As with my previous cameos, I did everything I could to channel the man, so was dressed for the part, wearing the crisp blue blazer and white shirt of a longtime State Department official, regarded highly for his military service and forthright nature. I had attempted to get Barry similarly attired, suggesting that he go as far as wearing Kent's trademark bow tie. I even offered to provide one from the substantial number in my own wardrobe. He looked at me, brow raised. "Norm, I am not a geek," he replied.

Goldman was directly across from us, seated on the elevated dais. He launched his questioning, bearing down on me with the intensity that all of America would soon get to know. He began with the most shocking detail anticipated from Taylor's hearing. On September 9, Taylor had sent a text to two other ambassadors who had been pushing Trump's scheme. It read, "As I said on the phone, I think it's crazy to withhold security assistance for help with a political campaign." The message crystallized what was strongly implicit in the record of the infamous July 25 phone call: our president's attempt to trade U.S. military aid in exchange for Ukraine's investigating Trump's U.S. political opponents. Or, as Trump referred to it, a perfect call.

"Ambassador Taylor," Dan asked me, "you sent a text that is on the screen now. Can you read it please?" I read the text aloud. When he asked me precisely what was meant by it, I explained the elements of the quid pro quo that were reflected in the text. Quid: $391 million of U.S. taxpayer money that Ukraine urgently needed to buy weapons to fight Russia on our behalf; money that was being dangled and withheld. Pro: "The United States has been very, very good to Ukraine. I wouldn't say that it's been reciprocal." Quo: "I would like you to do us a favor, though." The favor was presumed dirt from 2016 and an investigation of Trump's likely 2020 opponent, Joe Biden.

As I articulated Taylor's realization of the "crazy" quid pro quo, the enormity of Trump's misconduct hit me anew. A president of the United States had pressed a foreign ally—a fragile one, fighting a hot war on its border against our adversary Russia—to meddle in American elections. He had backed up that ask by withholding taxpayer dollars, as well as a White House meeting that was a vital signal of our support. You can understand why I felt confident that, surely, *this* would be the breaking point for the American people.

Goldman carried on, testing specific factual questions that he would ask two days later. The real Bill Taylor would be one of the most important witnesses in the case for impeachment: proving once and for all that this is a president who had abused, distorted, and bent as far as possible all authority, rules, and norms, and would continue to do so. He will do anything in pursuit of his selfish interests, including crossing heretofore sacrosanct red lines. We had seen this since the days of his campaign, we saw it again with Ukraine, and if we did not stop him now, his pattern of sacrificing America and Americans for his own gain would go on.

Dan kept at it, firing direct questions, one after another: "Who directed the security assistance for Ukraine?" "Should it have been frozen?" "When did you learn about it?" "Did any other part of the United States government agree with that?" I had the answers at my fingertips; all the names and dates were on my cheat sheet. I'd been worried that Dan would stump me in front of this audience of a handful of my most outstanding peers, so I was determined not to let a single relevant fact that might have been percolating in Taylor's mind evade me. Maher sidled over at one point, whispering in my ear, "Norm, you're *too* good. Give shorter answers. Make Dan work harder."

Dan turned his attention to Barry, who did not relish the amateur theatrics quite as much as I did, but played a creditable Kent nonetheless. When we broke, everyone in the room launched into a vigorous critique of Dan's performance. We were as unsparing as the Judiciary team had been when they brutally mooted Barry's and my strategy months prior. Nothing less was required if we were to break through to the American people. We were all striving for the same headline, as simple as it was shocking: President Trump invited a foreign government to attack our elections for purely selfish reasons, again.

THE ROAD I HAD TRAVELED to get to that witness chair had been an up-and-down one. On September 25, the day after Pelosi announced her support for impeachment, Nadler had gathered the Judiciary Committee and senior staff together in the members' conference room and congratulated everybody. He told us we were on the cusp of achieving presidential accountability and would not have been here without the incredible work of everyone in the room. We had blazed the path for the 135 impeachment adopters pre-Ukraine. For now, Intel, Foreign Affairs, and Oversight would lead the way. This was a time for unity, not turf battles.

Some of my friends in the press advanced a different theory. They put forth the notion that the disappointments with the Lewandowski hearing, compounded with escalating friction between the Speaker's and the chairman's stance on impeachment, had caused Pelosi to take the responsibility out of Judiciary's control. I did not believe it, I told our members. Intel's investigation together with the other two committees had started in August, well before the Lewandowski hearing. The complaint at hand was within the other committees' jurisdictions: Intel and Foreign Relations covered Ukraine, while Oversight was the main stop for whistleblower issues. The Speaker was not going to wrest it out of their grasp at this stage, and we were not going to try to grab it. Jerry explained that if the investigation ripened further in the direction of articles, it would eventually come back to us, and that would be the time to press our jurisdiction. That was quite similar to what had happened in the Clinton impeachment, where an independent counsel (Judge Ken Starr) had sent a report to House Judiciary, and somewhat analogous to the Nixon one, where the special prosecutor had sent a "road map" of his investigation to Judiciary. Yes, there had been real tensions between Pelosi and Judiciary over impeachment. But on this issue, the press was connecting one dot too many when they concluded that impeachment was somehow being taken away from us.

The members, arrayed around the long conference table, accepted the circumstances with grace. The consensus was that it was a good thing to have the spotlight elsewhere for a while. "You guys have taken more than your share of the heat," Amy Rutkin pointed out. The tone was a dramatic contrast to the alarm that had predominated at our last committee meeting in this room, in the wake of the Lewandowski hearing. Judiciary had led the way on holding the president accountable, and now that was happening. The members felt good about it.

Jerry offered the same message to the full Democratic caucus by phone the following Sunday, September 29. He urged everyone to embrace the narrowly focused Ukraine probe and to stick to the Speaker's plan. As the voice of the progressives who had supported impeachment even before the Ukraine revelations, Jerry might have pushed for a broader inquiry, at least to encompass the Mueller allegations. But he reiterated his strong emphasis on unity. He reminded the caucus that they were all in this together now. Both the Speaker and Chairman Schiff made a point of thanking Nadler and noting that impeachment would come back to Judiciary.

When Barry and I conferred with Jerry privately, he was philosophical about the pendulum swinging to Intel and the other two committees. It would return to us, he said, and we needed to be ready for that. We should worry less about media speculation over turf battles and more about getting ready. He had experienced the Clinton impeachment, as well as numerous judicial ones; he knew how much work we would have to do.

For some on our Judiciary impeachment crew, taking a backseat was like withdrawing from drugs. Arya stormed into our office after the committee meeting and declared, "I am a wartime consigliere, not a peacetime one!" She asked why we were not considering hauling Giuliani before our members for public testimony. That would have led to war all right—with the other committees. We urged her to be patient, work on her piece of the draft articles, and go home early for once. Later that day I passed her at her desk, staring into space. Not everyone is good at taking a break.

Barry and I used the hiatus to forward plan. If Jerry's predictions were accurate, we would indeed have a lot to do. By the end of the year we were going to have to work on the articles of impeachment, develop the underlying legal analysis, apply that law to the facts of the case, substantially draft one or more major reports (likely one focusing on the law and one applying the law to the facts), have hearings with experts and a presentation of the facts, mark up the articles, vote the articles out of committee, and if they passed in the House, prepare to try the case in the Senate. Barry said to me, "Dude, imagine if you were trying the biggest case of your life in January. It is the end of September, and we haven't prepared for it at all!"

By the first week of October, the team was working overtime again. Arya was once more staggering under her customary load. (Never have I seen someone so thrilled to be working every night until 2:00 A.M.) If we were this busy now, what would it be like when the center of gravity returned to our committee?

If I could have asked the chairman and his senior staff to recruit an army, I would have. But unlike during previous impeachments, we were not going to get a large supplemental budget. Nor did we have time to find and assimilate a large cadre of helpers. If there was one lesson we had learned, it was that we needed to move faster than Trump. If we let him, he would run out the clock before the election and use the Trump toolbox of distraction to completely flatten and redirect accountability. Still, some reinforcements would be necessary.

The first new hire was Joshua Matz. We had written and litigated together since the beginning of my three-year Trump opposition campaign. Joshua was a former Larry Tribe student and had clerked for Justice Anthony Kennedy on the Supreme Court. We had worked together on the emoluments cases, he had since written the definitive book on impeachment with Tribe, and he jumped at the opportunity to join us full-time.

Joshua's expertise on impeachment law complemented another hire—a specialist in organizing complex facts. We'd previously reached out to one of America's best firms, Sullivan & Cromwell, and recruited one of its top young lawyers who had a gift for managing large, fact-intensive cases, Kerry Tirrell. A young mom, she was so dedicated to our mission that she relocated from New York City to

D.C. with her husband and infant child, working eighteen-hour days to help coordinate this massive undertaking.

We still needed somebody who knew the Senate, because that was where we were headed, and somebody with foreign policy chops. We found the perfect person in Maggie Goodlander. A former foreign policy aide for Joe Lieberman and John McCain, she had gone to law school mid-career, had just finished a clerkship on the Supreme Court, and was in her first year at another top firm, Skadden, Arps. She was at work within seventy-two hours of accepting our offer. With that, our Judiciary impeachment Delta Force was complete: we had twenty lawyers and clerks to do the work that had been done by a House Judiciary team of more than forty-eight people on Watergate.

STARTING IN OCTOBER, INTEL AND the other two committees drove the fact investigation forward at a blistering pace. A series of witnesses—first a trickle, then a flood—appeared for closed-door depositions in the Intel SCIF to provide the full context for the July 25 call. The first was someone I knew well, Ambassador Kurt Volker, the president's former special Ukraine envoy, on October 3. To his credit, he showed up despite the typical Trumpian efforts to block him from doing so—obstruction thinly veiled.

His testimony, and the texts that he produced, illuminated every phase of Trump's plot. Volker had not been on the July 25 call, but he had helped advance Trump's scheme by meeting with Giuliani, the president's personal lawyer, plugging him into Ukraine's top leadership, and facilitating the planned announcement of the bogus investigations. He had told Giuliani that Biden was not corrupt, but he nonetheless had forwarded to the Ukrainians Giuliani's language for the announcement of the two smear campaigns.

I had known and liked Volker for years and was flabbergasted when I read his testimony. Graying, soft-spoken, and incisive, he had visited me in Prague as a distinguished ex-NATO ambassador. He had dined in my home; I had sought his advice about fighting corruption; we had sat on panels together. Though he tended toward the conservative and I toward the liberal, we were part of a broad consensus that I thought transcended parties—indeed that made party irrelevant—upholding the importance of principled transatlantic democracy. Why had he not categorically refused to go along with pushing the two bogus investigations, refused to forward the language at all, quit sooner, and sounded the alarm? He was the head of the John McCain Institute, for heaven's sake, its founder the epitome of outspoken courage! (Volker and the institute had a parting of the ways after his testimony.) It was tragic to see Volker, for all his principles, fall into the Trump trap.

That only sharpened my admiration for the next deponent, my friend and former colleague Ambassador Masha Yovanovitch. Trump tried to block her too, but she was having none of it. The committees served her with a subpoena, and she honored it promptly on October 11. Her testimony focused on the origins of the scheme in 2018 and the first part of 2019: how she had signaled her independence to Giuliani and Trump, including not granting a visa for a corrupt actor who wanted to come to the United States to advance the bogus Biden narrative, declining a suggestion to tweet praise for the president, and fighting actual corruption in Kiev as opposed to the imaginary Trump-Giuliani variety. With Yovanovitch in the ambassador's chair, Giuliani had little hope of getting Ukraine to announce his client's sham investigations, so he and Trump slandered and smeared her.

Masha had been my primary liaison at Main State in D.C. when I was ambassador in Prague. We emailed or spoke constantly back then and worked together on regional anticorruption policy. I was the former ethics czar, and she put me to shame in her determination to fight official misconduct; I could only imagine the emotions she had inspired in bent souls like Giuliani's and the president's.

After Masha came a torrent of other depositions. Fifteen more current and former official government deponents, predominantly from the State Department, all deflected the president's efforts to obstruct them from appearing—a first in the Democratic House's nine-month effort to collect evidence. Trump had run into the ultimate immovable force in the U.S. government. It was not the prosecutors of the Department of Justice, who had ultimately been unable to stop his onslaught against the rule of law—with help from his handmaiden, Bill Barr. It was not the special counsel apparatus, which provided for independence but allowed Trump to steamroll past Robert Mueller's damning report, again with Barr's aid. It was not even the military, whose generals had taken high White House and cabinet jobs to hold Trump in check but were driven from the administration battlefield.

It was the State Department. The career cadre of their nearly fourteen thousand foreign service officers represents a true elite of the U.S. government. An entire vast bureaucracy that has been handpicked, like our tiny Judiciary band of impeachers. Every year America's top undergrads (and some graduates with advanced degrees) compete for a handful of slots to become foreign service officers. It is as rigorous an admissions process as anything in the government or indeed in our wider meritocracy.

Then, like the Jesuits or some other religious order, they are toughened and trained by being sent around the world, often to the most inhospitable and dangerous countries on the planet. They endure long separations from the United States, and in "hardship postings" are also separated from their partners and children. Then there is a further winnowing that takes place as the State Department officers are culled at every level; it is an up-or-out bureaucracy.

By the time one gets to the very top, the career ambassadors like Masha Yovanovitch and Bill Taylor, what remains is the crème de la crème. State Department foreign service officers know every nook and cranny of the system and are probably the single smartest group within the government. What's more, there is a strong culture of resisting the worst impulses of political appointees, who come and go with every administration, sometimes bringing bad ideas with them (as I was occasionally and none-too-gently reminded during my ambassadorial tenure). So ingrained is State's attitude of defiance that the department offers an annual award to the foreign service officer who most effectively exhibits dissent.

Trump had, finally, picked the wrong folks to mess with. Theirs was a culture of outspoken moral courage, and it turns out that courage is what immunizes you against the Trump toxicity. Of course, that culture did not explain it all. Some of the problem, for Trump, came from the exceptional moral fiber of individual career ambassadors and foreign service officers like Yovanovitch and Taylor to be sure, or more junior ones like the bow-tie-wearing George Kent. Some from within State failed, like Volker and my friend David Hale (whom I knew from shared Middle East peace efforts and who did not defend Yovanovitch as fully as he should have). And others outside State, like my former Brookings colleague Dr. Fiona Hill and her co-worker Lieutenant Colonel Alexander Vindman, showed incredible spine.

But the courage of Yovanovitch, Taylor, and their outspoken peers was all the more remarkable because many of them currently worked for the president and showed up despite a stream of spurious efforts to stop them, phony legal claims, and threats made by the State Department and then by the White House itself in a series of letters, each more absurd than the last. Adam Schiff would later quote Bobby Kennedy on the floor of the Senate, to try to inspire the senators to rise to the ethical level of those heroic witnesses who honored the subpoenas: "Moral courage is a rarer commodity than bravery in battle or great intelligence." Of course, that also matters to this ultimate trial, in which you, the American people, are now engaged. In a democracy, the most fundamental act of moral courage is voting.

On October 17, the impeachment investigation also got some help from an unlikely source: the president's acting chief of staff, Mick Mulvaney. At a White House press conference he declared that *of course* an investigation into the 2016 election interference was one of the reasons why aid to Ukraine was held up. "Did he also mention to me in passing the corruption related to the D.N.C. server?" Mr.

Mulvaney said, referring to Mr. Trump. "Absolutely. No question about that." He added, "That's why we held up the money." When a reporter pointed out to him that what he had described was the very definition of a quid pro quo, Mulvaney told him, "We do that all the time with foreign policy . . . Get over it. There's going to be political influence in foreign policy." After the press conference he tried to walk it back, claiming "the media has decided to misconstrue my comments," but the confession was right there on video for the world to see.

The press conference riveted our attention in Judiciary for a second reason: Mulvaney also announced that the president would be holding the 2020 G7, a gathering of the leaders of the world's top economies, at his Doral property in Florida. This would be the mother of all emoluments, with millions flowing into Trump's business, and so into his own pockets, from the United States and six other governments as they paid for lodging, meals, golf carts, everything down to individual-serving-size water bottles emblazoned with the Trump Doral logo. When Trump first floated the idea in August, Judiciary had immediately thrown down the gauntlet to the administration, launching an investigation and declaring that the proposal was grossly unconstitutional.

Mulvaney's announcement set off a firestorm that temporarily equaled the Ukraine scandal. If Trump had followed through, it might well have resuscitated our dormant secret sixth article of impeachment for emoluments violations. But all good things must come to an end, and so too with bad ones. The heat became too intense even for Trump. Two days after Mulvaney's press conference, the Doral proposal was off. The G7 would be held elsewhere. It was another one of those wins for the Constitution that have also characterized the era of Trump—albeit one that was soon forgotten.

As the three committee depositions were proceeding in October, Barry and I set up a parallel operation for the core team on Judiciary to process the facts—to learn them just as well as our Intel colleagues, or at least as well as we could. In addition, we began analyzing how these facts supported the potential grounds to impeach the president. On the extremely abbreviated schedule that Jerry had predicted, ending with a floor vote in December, we were looking at Judiciary hearings starting in early December. If so, there would be no chance for us to master the evidence from scratch *after* the Intelligence Committee had completed their investigation and transmitted their report, presumably at the end of November.

There would also be no time on that schedule for Intel and the other two committees to independently master the intricate law and lore of impeachment, an arcane body of authorities dating back to fourteenth-century England. But their factual report and our legal one would need to fit together like a key in a lock, snugly meeting each of the elements of eighteenth-century "high Crimes and Misdemeanors" (assuming the evidence played out as expected, that is).

The Judiciary Committee impeachment staff commenced working on two parallel tracks: the law and the facts. On the law side, with me and Joshua in the lead, we very quietly continued evolving the articles of impeachment, started drafting the update of the 1974 Nixon report on the meaning of high crimes and misdemeanors, and thought through our magnum opus, the eventual two-hundred-page impeachment report, prewriting as much as we could. On the fact side, with Barry, Sarah, and Kerry taking point, we prepared a lengthy day-by-day, hour-by-hour chronology that ultimately ran to thousands of entries, as well as lists of major and minor witnesses, collections of relevant documents, and summaries of deposition transcripts as Intel released them.

We kept Judiciary management (the chairman and senior staff) apprised but otherwise strictly siloed our activities because of the fear of leaks. The team working the facts didn't talk to that working the law, and neither group talked to anyone else in the office. Barry and I were the only ones who crossed the silos. We were insanely busy, but it was all below the surface. Someone analogized the operation to a duck, seeming to placidly glide on top of the water when below it his feet were rapidly churning.

In the meantime, our communication and coordination were ramping up with the Intel team and with the tight group of aides from the Speaker's office who were overseeing the impeachment process. My mission was to do everything possible to help impeachment to succeed while accelerating the investigation coming back to Judiciary as quickly as possible. I had an infinite appetite for subtly tilting the table so the marbles would roll in our direction—what Barry laughingly called my dark arts. One day I was sitting in the Speaker's conference room helping draft press talking points. I made a passing reference to the way we used to do these when I worked at the State Department. A young comms aide asked me what I had done there. When I told her that I was a former ambassador, she looked stunned. Barry, never one to pass up a free swing at the piñata of my ego, loudly proclaimed, "How the mighty have fallen!" It *was* a bit humbling at times.

A key moment came on the afternoon of October 25, when I was sitting in with aides from the other committees in the ornate Rules Committee offices on the third floor of the Capitol. We were meeting to address the impeachment process, including the president's and the GOP's claims it was not fair. That whining had reached a climax earlier that week, when a gang of dozens of Republican members stormed an Intelligence Committee deposition in an act of (barely) civil disobedience, complete with the obligatory angry press conference. They argued that impeachment was illegitimate because there had been no formal vote to open an inquiry. I was familiar with the issue because it was at the center of our grand jury case, in which Judiciary had argued we needed Mueller's files for impeachment and that no House vote was necessary.

As we were discussing legislative responses to the Republican kvetching that Friday afternoon, my phone buzzed with an incoming alert. I looked down at the screen to read, "Federal judge rules that impeachment inquiry is valid." My brain froze for a moment, slowly thawing while I processed it: we had won the grand jury case! Better still, the judge had ruled on the precise issue that the Republicans had been making the most fuss about, knocking down their legal tent pole. I broke into the conversation and shared the good news. We were a step closer to getting our hands on the evidence of Trump's prior wrongdoing—a pattern that continued with Ukraine. It also gave momentum to Jerry's ongoing push to include that pattern in the articles I was helping to draft.

It didn't take long for the press to figure out that Judiciary was fully back in the mix. On Tuesday, October 29, Barry and I were spotted heading with Jerry, Aaron, and Joshua into the Intel SCIF. A throng of media spied us ducking into an elevator to make the ride down to the basement. They were there when the doors closed and then sprinted down two flights of stairs and were waiting when the doors opened again at the bottom. Kyle Cheney of *Politico* snapped a quick iPhone shot, immediately tweeting it out with the caption "Judiciary Committee lawyers Barry Berke and Norm Eisen (Nadler is behind them) make their way down to the SCIF. Won't say what for."

The Twitter furor that ensued put forth a torrent of speculations about the imminent resurgence of Judiciary. All the reporters who had let me be for the past four weeks converged at once in a text flash mob, my phone buzzing incessantly in my pocket. I had not anticipated the fuss, but I did not mind it either, which might have explained the slight smile on my face (characterized with some accuracy by the right-wing media as a disgraceful smirk).

We were there to help finalize the legislative package that had been the subject of the Friday meeting. By now, only one major sticking point remained: what due process we would afford the president when impeachment came back to the Judiciary Committee. Nixon and Clinton had the right to call witnesses and to submit or seek documents. But they had cooperated, whereas Trump was completely stonewalling. The witnesses who had thus far appeared had done so despite his orders, and many others had refused to appear because of them. He had not produced a single document in response to the impeachment subpoenas. When he declared, "We will fight all the subpoenas," he was for once true to his word. To those who knew his pattern, this came as no surprise: Trump's abuses are always served with a side of cover-up.

Given that he had made a mockery of his own legal obligations, should we guarantee Trump the same rights to present evidence as his predecessors? Schiff thought it was absurd, as a matter of principle. But Nadler insisted on it, also as a matter of principle. The rules package was about to head for the floor, we were running out of time, and so we journeyed to the SCIF to settle things once and for all. On our way in, I spotted Lieutenant Colonel Vindman, the White House Ukraine specialist who had listened in on the president's July 25 call. On a break from his deposition, he looked a little uneasy. Who wouldn't, when he was accusing his boss of severe misconduct—particularly when that boss happens to be the president of the United States?

We made our way to Schiff's nondescript office. SCIFs are not known for high style, in part because everything that enters them has to pass through an X-ray machine. The bookcase, desk, and mismatched guest chairs were generic. A stack of yet-to-be-hung art had made it through and was leaning against the wall: posters from James Bond movies and one from the spy cartoon *Archer*. Doug Letter was there, together with Maher and Dan and other Intel staff.

Schiff and Nadler launched right into a vigorous debate. Schiff and I were both protégés of Larry Tribe, as was Joshua. He and I had taken the precaution of asking Tribe for his view. He came down emphatically on the side of extending many of the same protections as in the past. I said as much, and Schiff countered that he had to wonder about the neutrality of our presentation to the professor. Touché. The disagreement raged on until Schiff had to return to the Vindman deposition, and Nadler to Judiciary business. Staff for both committees stayed behind to try to come up with a solution.

Maher broke the impasse in his typical diplomatic style. He

and his colleague Wells Bennett (with whom I had worked at Brookings) proposed compromise language. It afforded Trump his rights—but provided that Nadler would have the discretion to limit them if the president continued his obstructive behavior. That power of the chairman had existed in previous impeachments but had not before been expressed in the rules. We negotiated the language right then and there, with Maher shuttling to and from his workstation to draft and redraft. When it was completed, we showed it to our principals, who thankfully agreed. As much as they respected each other, I don't think either relished continuing that particular debate.

The procedural bill was introduced later that day, making Judiciary's forthcoming return official. It stated expressly that we would take the handoff from Intel and the other committees. We would accept their reports, hold hearings of our own to assess if the facts merited impeachment, and vote out articles if merited. We had secretly worked out a time split for the public hearings: Intel would have two weeks, wrapping up at the end of November, followed by two weeks for Judiciary and then a full House vote on articles before the holiday break in December. The bill contained Jerry's due process protections for the president and another important Judiciary-inspired feature: allowing extensive questioning at each hearing by counsel, a legacy of Barry's good work on Lewandowski. It was all working out just as Jerry had predicted, right down to an impeachment vote before the end of the year. "*Du bist a novi,*" I told him in Yiddish—you were prophetic! He looked embarrassed, shrugged, and said, "It wasn't that complicated." "*Halevi,*" I responded, meaning roughly, "As if!"

INTEL'S TWO WEEKS OF PUBLIC testimony launched on Wednesday, November 13, with Taylor and Kent. Barry and I, watching together, thought our portrayals held up pretty well. Whenever the originals scored a particular point, we would say to each other, "Good job,

Ambassador Taylor," or "Good job, Mr. Kent." They and those who followed—including Volker, Yovanovitch, Lieutenant Colonel Vindman (who looked a little less green around the gills than when I had spotted him previously), and seven others—filled in that missing 15 percent or so needed to fully comprehend the high criminality of Trump's shakedown call.

Schiff and the Intel committee members, with Dan as the staff questioner, were brilliant in eliciting the facts that we would need to judge whether high crimes and misdemeanors had occurred. We had sketched out and shared with Intel the legal elements that we would need to prove; if anything, they responded with too much evidence. The biggest challenge for us was how to structure the gusher of information that was daily pouring out of the hearings. As we prepared for our Judiciary hearings, we needed a succinct narrative to fit below the simple headline that Trump did it again, abusing the public interest to promote his own. Working in parallel as Intel had their hearings, the Judiciary staff organized the facts into five simple chapters (initially proposed by the indefatigable Maggie Goodlander) that ended up framing our work.

The Scheme

Starting in 2018, as his reelection campaign loomed, President Trump and Rudy Giuliani began taking steps to coerce Ukraine to do two things. First, to offer a false narrative that would shift blame for 2016 election interference off Russia and onto Ukraine. That would prove the Mueller investigation, which Trump hated, was indeed a "hoax" and remove the lingering taint from his prior campaign. Second, and even more urgent, they also wanted Ukraine to announce bogus investigations into Trump's chief political rival, Joe Biden, to give the president a leg up in 2020. For Trump's scheme to succeed, he and Giuliani first needed to remove the American ambassador to Ukraine, Masha Yovanovitch, who they knew would never go along with their plan. So in the spring of 2019 they did.

The Solicitation

When President Trump called to congratulate President Zelensky on his successful election on April 21, he agreed that someone at a "very, very high level" would attend the inauguration. Vice President Pence was slated to go. But after Giuliani was denied the meeting he wanted with Zelensky to push the scheme, Trump ordered a lower-level delegation to take Pence's place instead. It consisted of Volker, Secretary of Energy Rick Perry, and Ambassador to the EU Gordon Sondland, who termed themselves the Three Amigos. They became entangled in Trump's scheme, with Sondland conveying to Zelensky that Trump was expecting to hear support for the sham investigations. This chapter culminated in the July 25 call and Trump's demand of Zelensky: "I would like you to do us a favor."

The Pressure

Ukraine initially resisted pursuing the investigations Trump demanded, so he turned up the heat by ordering a hold of $391 million in military assistance. The president's agents also conveyed that a White House meeting would be scheduled only if Ukraine announced investigations. Trump's freeze on the military aid undermined our national security, and by August his entire cabinet wanted it released. On September 7, President Trump told Sondland that Ukraine must make the announcement of the two sham investigations. Having received direct confirmation from Trump, Sondland relayed his corrupt message to Zelensky himself.

The Bust

President Zelensky finally cracked under the pressure, agreeing to announce the investigations and scheduling an appearance on CNN for September 13. But a whistleblower had reported Trump's misconduct to the intelligence community inspector general, and the House announced that it would be looking into Trump and Giuliani's corrupt scheme. On September 11, the president finally ordered the aid released. On September 25 the detailed record of the July 25 call was released. The same day, Trump met with Zelensky on the sidelines of the annual UN General Assembly. The White House meeting was never scheduled.

The Cover-Up

Once he had been caught, Trump engaged in a systematic obstruction of any investigation into his wrongdoing. He ordered every government agency and every official to defy the House's impeachment inquiry. A sizable number complied, and the administration failed to produce even one single document that was demanded pursuant to subpoena. Put aside Trump's lies, or his claims that the July 25 call was perfect, or his threats against the whistleblower. This obstruction of Congress, like his abuse of power, was unlawful, unprecedented, and entirely in keeping with the pattern of behavior he has exhibited for his entire adult life.

If some complained that at times the hearings were dull, with NBC lamenting in its headline that they contained "little drama," I and millions of others found them riveting. Step-by-step, they told the story of a president who thought nothing of sacrificing America's national interest or of hurting all Americans for the sake of his own personal and political gain. A few months later, on the heels of the Senate trial, when our nation faced an even greater threat, we'd hear eerie echoes of what was revealed in the hearings.

The Intel hearings were closed out on November 21 by the appearance of my friend and former Brookings colleague Fiona Hill, Trump's Russia adviser, who resigned that post in July, a week before the Trump-Zelensky call. She testified alongside David Holmes, a senior diplomat who served at the U.S. embassy in Ukraine. She reinforced key elements of what had occurred, testifying that the Ukraine election interference theory was flat-out wrong, not to mention dangerous. "This is a fictional narrative that has been perpetrated and propagated by the Russian security services themselves." She confirmed the shakedown of Ukraine that the White House had tried so hard to deny: "It became very clear that the White House meeting itself was being predicated on other issues. Namely, investigations and the questions about the election interference in 2016." She also stated that it was clear to her that Sondland, working on Trump's order, was more committed to carrying out the president's "domestic political errand" than the "national security foreign policy" of the country.

Bogus claims about Ukraine interference in the 2016 election, she said, were doing Putin's work for him. She directly targeted the minority on the committee, saying, "Some of you on this committee appear to believe that Russia and its security services did not conduct a campaign against our country—and that perhaps, somehow, for some reason, Ukraine did." She was also clearly addressing Giuliani, the president's other enablers, and the president himself. On the break, TV commentators marveled at the intensity of her response. I told Barry it was a typical encounter with Hill. That's what you get every time you pass her in the hallway.

It was damn impressive. Schiff and his members, plus Dan and the entire staff who had attended that moot in the SCIF, had set a high bar for Nadler and the rest of us associated with Judiciary as we prepared to open our proceedings. It would be our first high-stakes convening since Lewandowski. The American people would be watching to see whether we caught the baton seamlessly and even accelerated for the anchor leg or whether we ignominiously stumbled and dropped it. We weren't hoping for a medal; instead, we were seeking ample votes in the House to impeach the president.

No one felt that pressure more keenly than I did. In a matter of days, I would be leading the counsel questioning in our opening session.

CHAPTER EIGHT

"If This Is Not Impeachable . . ."

WHAT WOULD YOU THINK IF, WHEN YOUR GOVERNOR ASKED the federal government for the disaster assistance that Congress has provided, the President responded, 'I would like you to do us a favor?'"

This question about Trump's propensity to abuse power did not come from Governor Gretchen Whitmer of Michigan after he threatened her during the COVID crisis, saying at a press briefing: "If they don't treat you right, I don't call." Nor was it from other governors, like Jay Inslee of Washington, who Trump said ought to be more grateful if they wanted help. Nor was it a query from a journalist reporting on Trump's hints that he might deprive states of crucial assistance unless they "showed sufficient appreciation"—or unless he can "get something for it."

No, it was House Judiciary Committee expert witness Professor Pamela Karlan, on December 4, 2019—weeks before doctors in China started raising alarms about a deadly new disease. She was giving her opening statement at 10:59 A.M. on the very first day of the long-awaited Judiciary Committee impeachment hearings, explaining the danger of Trump's actions to a packed room and an audience of millions watching on television. Professor Karlan was seated at the center of the witness table in the magnificent chamber, normally used by the House Ways and Means Committee. Facing her on the elevated dais were the forty-one members of the Judiciary Committee and me. Chairman Jerry Nadler sat center stage. I sat to Nadler's right, about to launch my questioning of the expert panel, which in addition to Karlan included Harvard's Noah Feldman and the University of North Carolina's Michael Gerhardt. (A fourth witness selected by the GOP, George Washington University's Jonathan Turley, completed the group.) We had painstakingly selected the majority witnesses from a list of twenty-eight experts based on their ability to bring the hearing to life, grabbing those watching around the country by the lapels, pulling them through the TV screens and into the room, and warning of the consequences of Trump's abuse of office.

The Intelligence Committee's two weeks of hearings had offered a vast abundance of detail about the Ukraine scandal. They confirmed that the fateful July 25 call in which Trump asked for the investigation of his U.S. political adversaries was not a spontaneous request but rather part of an elaborate scheme that had stretched back to Giuliani's contacts with Ukraine at the end of 2018, a scheme that was stopped only when Trump was caught red-handed in September and that then morphed into a cover-up. Trump had still not provided a single document in response to the subpoenas, and clearly wasn't going to.

Our job now was to answer three core questions for the American people: what Trump had done; why it was an impeachable high crime and misdemeanor; and why they should care. The amount of detail the Intel hearings had accumulated was overwhelming, in every sense of the word. Judiciary's role would include reminding America of the simplicity of what had happened—an old-fashioned shakedown of Ukraine—and explaining and emphasizing why it mattered so much. Ergo the Karlan example of a corrupt governor. Eerily prescient? Yes and no: the pattern of Trump's abuse and cover-up has been plain for years.

Her testimony, and that of all our witnesses, was part of

explaining why this misconduct rose to the level of an impeachable high crime and misdemeanor. The intricate, antique nature of impeachment law, coupled with the infrequency with which it had been tested, meant that even members of Congress needed a refresher. And of course, we also had you—the American people—in mind.

Karlan was a veteran Supreme Court advocate who specialized in the law of democracy and would press the case that Trump's pattern of behavior threatened the foundation of America itself. Feldman was a recent convert to the impeachment cause, having been driven over the edge by the Ukraine scandal. No one was better at explaining the framework of constitutional law and interpreting some of the more arcane constitutional impeachment language than he, and his prior skepticism gave him credibility. Gerhardt was the cleanup hitter. While his cohorts studied impeachment together with other subjects, Gerhardt was an impeachment specialist who could handle any issue that arose, no matter how abstruse, expounding it in plain, powerful language.

I would lead off by questioning them for forty-five minutes, followed by five-minute blocks from each of the members. We at Judiciary had prepared intensely for hearings throughout the year, but our members and staff took things to a new level for the impeachment launch. In the ten days leading up to the hearing, we spoke with our experts on an almost-daily basis. Not to prepare them to testify—these were some of the greatest authorities in the world and hardly needed it—but to prepare ourselves. What *had* happened here? How *did* it violate the Constitution? Why *should* it matter to all of us?

During a session over the phone on November 26, Karlan came up with the (as it turns out, not so) hypothetical example of the president's extorting a governor. The team and I were discussing how to animate the concerns of the framers for the American people. "Why not bring it close to home?" she suggested. "If I talk about a governor seeking disaster relief, that rings the bell for everyone." This was what we wanted the American people to understand: that Trump's radical selfishness makes him a threat to every American, no less than it was to the Ukrainian soldiers fighting a war against Russia. His pattern of behavior would never stop on its own.

The preparations for the hearing extended beyond our conversations with the witnesses. The chairman wanted to forcefully deploy parliamentary procedure to avoid another scene like the GOP-driven chaos we had dealt with for Lewandowski. We gathered the most brilliant parliamentary experts from inside and outside the committee to privately drill with Jerry in the small upstairs hearing room. The committee had even hired a new parliamentarian, John Williams, a Hill veteran whose genial manner belied his ferocious application of the rules. Aaron Hiller presided as he, John, and the other experts put the chairman through his paces.

"Point of order, Mr. Chairman: you had a conflict with Trump on his New York real estate; you should recuse!"

"Point of order: you hired the impeachment experts Eisen and Berke even *before* the impeachment; has that happened in any prior impeachment?"

"Point of order: you already made up your mind to impeach; this hearing is a charade."

"Point of order: Why won't you bring in Hunter Biden to testify? Joe Biden? The whistleblower? Will you at least say who it is? How do you sleep at night?"

Jerry's instinct was actually to respond to the questions, prompting the parliamentary pros to jump in: "No! Mr. Chairman, those are not points of order. You should refuse to recognize them. Please do not take the bait." Jerry encouraged them and us to push him, then retooled everything from his posture to the timbre of his voice to how rapidly and loudly he banged the gavel. It was a testament to the chairman that after his decades of experience and his superior knowledge of all things constitutional, he was humble enough to put in the work to meet the stakes of the occasion. By the third practice session, Jerry was wielding his gavel like the hammer of Thor.

Our preparation was complicated by the fact that the report from Intel and the other two committees, which our committee and our experts would be reacting to, wasn't going to be published until December 3, the day before our hearing. I fought all suggestions to postpone our hearing, consistent with my philosophy that we needed to move at the speed of Trump, or faster, to hold him to account. Not to mention that the president had a proclivity for encouraging foreign attacks on our elections, and one was approaching. There was no time to lose. Aaron concurred, telling the staff, "Thanksgiving break is canceled this year. If anybody needs a meal, my house is a couple blocks away."

Early Thursday morning, I dropped my wife and daughter at the train to Philadelphia to enjoy my mother-in-law's cooking. I continued on to the office, for a day of digesting our experts' three lifetimes' worth of scholarship. Eight hours later, I pushed my three huge piles of paper aside and took a break to walk to Aaron's with Arya and Joshua. We ate a delicious Thanksgiving feast far too quickly, thanked his family, and raced back across Capitol Hill and into the darkened Rayburn House Office Building. Perhaps as a result of missing my own family, I ate an entire pumpkin pie at my desk that night. Barry could only laugh, telling me he feared I would be discovered the next morning sleeping beneath my desk with a pie pan for a pillow.

The following Tuesday, the day before the expert hearing, the Intelligence Committee report was released in the early afternoon. We blasted it out to our three experts and dropped everything to inhale it. Though I had been working with Intel, and had seen and commented on sections of the draft, I had yet to review the entire report. I spent the rest of the day rejiggering my examination to take account of its precise wording, including having slides made up with notable quotations. By 9:00 p.m., I was able to send a revised outline of my questioning for a second opinion to Barry, who replied with a thumbs-up.

We lived and died by the moot court, and so, before heading home that night, I gathered the troops to do one last practice run of my examination in the cavernous hearing room. Ten of us were present, including colleagues to play the witnesses and the full tech team to run the slides. My two previous moots had been fine—loose, conversational, and lively. This one felt different—tight and forced. My colleagues agreed. After I finished, they took turns critiquing me, some offering gentle suggestions (perhaps taking into account that I would be doing this for real in less than twelve hours), some quite direct. Barry fell into the latter group, taking me aside to offer his candid opinion: "Norm, that sucked." Somehow, in my last-minute wrangling of the Intel report, I had lost the magic.

Instead of heading straight home to sleep, as I had planned, I slogged back to my office at 11:30, conscious of the ticking clock. I closed the door, sat down at my desk, and turned to Barry, sitting across from me. "You said it was good!" I shouted.

"It *was* good, on paper," he replied. "It just didn't work in real life."

What could I say? I had only myself to blame, including for insisting that we have the hearing immediately after the Intel report came out. I went back to work. Barry stayed there to brainstorm with me as I figured out how I was going to recut the whole thing again. Periodically, he would say, "Don't procrastinate! Are you looking at Twitter?" (He knew me too well.) I forced myself to revise. Finally, and I'm still not sure how, the thing just clicked into place. Barry and I did one last run-through, and he agreed: "Norm, you got it. Now let's get out of here." At 1:30 A.M., I sent a long email to the team reordering the slides and video and asking for some new ones to be made up. I headed home and managed to get about four hours of sleep before waking to check the final slides that were to be sent to the networks at 8:00 A.M.

Then I put on my best ambassadorial finery—blue suit, white shirt, blue tie—and made my usual morning stop at the neighborhood 7-Eleven for a cup of coffee. Far more potent than the caffeine, however, was the buzz that hit my bloodstream the moment I reached the Hill. I stepped out of my Uber and made my way through the halls, past a long line of spectators waiting for seats, and into the grand Ways and Means hearing room. It seemed I had burned off whatever anxiety I might have had the night before. The committee was gathering in the room behind the dais, helping themselves to Dunkin' Donuts and coffee on a side table as they reviewed their scripts. They too seemed calm and ready. It had been much more nerve-racking to push for impeachment all those months when leadership and many voters in their districts were opposed to it. Nadler, who would get the closest scrutiny, appeared to be the most nonchalant of the bunch. Amy Rutkin eventually poked her head into the little anteroom. "It's time," she said.

First the staff entered and took their seats behind the dais, then the members, and finally I accompanied Jerry to his place at the center. The packed room was crackling with anticipation as Jerry and I took our chairs and he gaveled the hearing in. Table after table of reporters were jotting down every word, while viewers across America tuned in from home. As is customary, Nadler began by recognizing himself for his opening statement, which would hit our three key questions over a sharp, punchy ten minutes (timed to the second).

But before he could even begin, the GOP congressman Andy Biggs—evidently occupying a role as leadoff provocateur—piped up, attempting to re-create the chaos of the Lewandowski hearing. "Mr. Chairman, I have a parliamentary inquiry." Nadler cut him off at the knees: "I have the time for an opening statement. The parliamentary inquiry is not in order at this time." While Biggs appeared uncertain about how to respond, Nadler launched directly into his statement. We all maintained a decorous silence, but I could sense the members up and down the dais and my colleagues arrayed behind me exclaiming, "Way to go, Jerry!" without saying a word or moving a muscle. The minority did not dare to interrupt his opening remarks, though as soon as he finished Biggs tried to cut in again. Jerry was too fast for him. Without pausing to take a breath, Nadler had immediately recognized the ranking member, shutting down Biggs and once again leaving the minority flummoxed. Where was the amicable Jerry Nadler, willing to go back and forth, patiently debating the finer points of parliamentary inquiries? He wasn't here today, instead replaced by a laser-focused man with one objective: to determine if we were going to impeach the president.

After Doug Collins's opening remarks for the minority (including criticizing the majority for our speed) and some other preliminaries, Jerry passed the microphone to me. Every lawyer has his or her own gold standard for questioning witnesses. My role model for a direct examination was not Perry Mason, not Atticus Finch. It was Johnny Carson. We used to watch *The Tonight Show* when I was growing up, and I was always transfixed by Johnny. He was genuinely interested in what people had to say. Though always in control, he asked his guests thoughtful, open-ended questions, he listened to them, and he responded accordingly. Half of the value of the question comes from believing that the person asking it really cares about the answer. When it came to impeachment, I certainly did.

I began by putting up a slide of the articles of impeachment that were under consideration: abuse of power for Ukraine; obstruction of Congress in that scandal; and obstruction of justice as uncovered by Mueller. Turning to the first, I asked the experts to unpack what it was. When the framers of the Constitution determined a president could be impeached for "other high Crimes and Misdemeanors," they above all had in mind, as Hamilton put it, "the abuse or violation of some public trust." That included, as our experts confirmed, a president using his office for purely personal political goals, instead of to promote our shared public interest. Our country was founded to overthrow monarchy, not to promote it. The evidence in the Intel report showed there was no legitimate basis for Trump's demand—only the desire to get a leg up on his political opponent in the coming election (and rewrite the story of the last one). This was a classic abuse of power case.

But, the scholars continued, it was even worse than that. Beyond abuse of power, two "other high Crimes and Misdemeanors" that worried the framers greatly were betrayal of the national interest and corruption, particularly of our democracy. Together with abuse, they literally constituted the ABCs of other high crimes and misdemeanors. Here, we had both betrayal of the national interest (Trump had harmed our ally Ukraine and hampered it in taking on our adversary Russia) and corruption (Trump's misuse of taxpayers' dollars to try to extort a personal benefit). Trump had hit the trifecta, for the first time in presidential history. Professor Gerhardt delivered the line of the day when he said, "If what we're talking about is not impeachable, then nothing is impeachable."

At one point I gave the GOP witness, Jonathan Turley, the opportunity to join in; he himself had previously written that the kind of behavior Trump had exhibited would be sufficient to constitute an impeachable abuse of power. He admitted he had written that but then attempted to filibuster by qualifying his statement. I was having none of it; just as ruthlessly as Johnny Carson would cut off a guest because of a commercial break, but perhaps with a bit more relish, I stopped Professor Turley by saying, "Sir, it's a yes or no question." With palpable annoyance he acknowledged that yes, he had.

Abuse of power was our main topic, but we also covered in shorter form the other two potential articles, obstruction of Congress and obstruction of justice. All, the witnesses explained, were variations of abuse of power; all were well-recognized impeachable offenses. Before I knew it, I was on my very last question, about what the framers of the Constitution would do if presented with Trump's conduct. It was answered in dramatic form by Professor Feldman. He declared that this was "precisely the situation that the framers anticipated. It's very unusual for the framers' predictions to come true that precisely. And when they do, we have to ask ourselves: someday, we will no longer be alive, and we'll go wherever it is we go, the good place or the other place. And, you know, we may meet there Madison and Hamilton, and they will ask us, 'When the president of the United States acted to corrupt the structure of the Republic, what did you do?' And our answer to that question must be that we followed the guidance of the framers, and it must be that if the evidence supports that conclusion, the House of Representatives moves to impeach him." Exactly at the forty-five-minute mark, to the second, I yielded back to the chairman.

The committee members gave me silent nods and looks of approbation as Collins handled the initial questioning for the GOP side (principally gratifying Turley's desire to filibuster by giving him open-ended questions, the first of which he answered for thirteen minutes straight). Barry passed me a note that said, simply, "Norm, that was perfect." I jotted down a couple of things I felt I could have done better and passed it back. He scribbled again and handed it to me: "Do you know what's better than perfection? Nothing." Knowing how tough he was on himself, and how harshly he'd criticized me the night before, I knew he wouldn't pay the compliment lightly.

Our members were at their best in the four hours that followed, their collective 151 years of congressional experience shining. Zoe Lofgren led off by talking about the fact that this was her third presidential impeachment; she had been involved as a staffer on the Nixon matter, as a young member on the Clinton case, and now as a senior member on the Trump proceedings. Her questioning built off her history by eliciting important testimony about how Trump's conduct compared with Nixon's wrongdoings ("not favorably"). Sylvia Garcia addressed obstruction of justice, noting, "As a former judge and as a member of Congress, I've raised my right hand and put my left hand on the Bible more than once, and I've sworn to uphold the Constitution and laws of this country. This hearing is about that, but it's also about the core of the heart of our American values: the values of duty, honor, and loyalty."

Val Demings delved into the obstruction of Congress, eliciting testimony that Trump, by preventing key witnesses from testifying, was "denying the power of Congress under the Constitution to oversee him and to exercise its capacity to impeach." She was a former police chief, and one of the high points came when she spoke about the same question that had so riveted us when we had first pressed

Karlan: Why does this matter? "As a former law enforcement official," Demings said, "I know firsthand that the rule of law is the strength of our democracy, and no one is above it—not our neighbors and our various communities, not our co-workers, and not the president of the United States."

Turley came in for rough handling by one of the most talented cross-examiners among the members, California's Eric Swalwell. He dug through the GOP expert's history and made a discovery. Turley had advanced similar arguments before when defending a federal judge on impeachment charges. They were ones that Swalwell pointed out had been rejected by a bipartisan super-majority in the Senate, since it voted to convict. "And respectfully, Professor, we don't buy it either," he said, finishing with Turley with a flourish. Homework is a key to the litigator's art, and Swalwell always did his.

On the witnesses' side, Gerhardt and Feldman were both familiar TV faces (at least to impeachment junkies), and their excellence was expected. Karlan's revelatory contribution was her knack for relatable scenarios, coupled with clever turns of phrase. At one point it got her into a spot of trouble. When explaining limitations on Trump's constitutional powers, she said, "So while the president can name his son Barron, he cannot make him a baron." Barry immediately passed me a note: "uh oh." One of the inviolable rules of D.C. is never to mention a minor child. The White House whipped up a social media frenzy, including a critical tweet from the first lady. Trump didn't hold back either. It is always the inveterate bully who can't take what he dishes out. Professor Karlan realized her error on her own and later in her testimony apologized for mentioning the president's son—it was intended as a figure of speech.

The fleeting episode did not overshadow the hearing, however. The press greeted us with comments like "By Wednesday afternoon the committee had presided over something almost unheard of in the 116th Congress: measured, substantive and relatively orderly debate about impeachment." The story's headline was a bit more of a backhanded compliment, "Dems Exhale as They Dodge Impeachment

Debacle," but we gladly took it. The most important verdict of all came from the Speaker's office: her staff told me, and then she told Jerry directly, "Well done."

We were back in business, and our most important business lay just ahead.

NORMALLY, AFTER AN ENDEAVOR LIKE the expert hearings, I would at least take the rest of the day off to recuperate. I was not afforded that luxury on this occasion: we had articles of impeachment to work on. I got back to my desk, desperate for a nap, but settled instead for a strong cup of coffee from the office Keurig (by now as overworked as we were and wheezing as it filled my mug). A small, leakproof crew from the House Office of General Counsel, Intel, and Judiciary had been laboring intensely together, trading ideas, drafts, and other materials. A tremendous amount of good work had been done. But the effort hadn't been able to go beyond hypothetical drafts of the first two articles (abuse of power and obstruction of Congress regarding Ukraine) until we had the Intel report, with its final judgments and exact language. Those choices would in turn affect how we phrased Article III—obstruction of justice regarding Mueller—if we even had one. That remained undecided. We had danced around that and other open questions in the hearing, eliciting testimony on those subjects without making commitments.

Toward the end of the day, the Speaker asked to see the current draft articles. That night she gave Jerry her reaction. "There are too many words," she said. She felt they needed more clarity and simplicity—and fast. She was about to take the next public step and call for them. I told Doug Letter that Judiciary would take the pen back for the final drafting push. He readily concurred.

At 9:04 the next morning, December 5, framed by the same phalanx of six American flags as when she proclaimed her support for the inquiry, Speaker Pelosi appeared before a league of reporters and TV cameras. She stated that the House would be drafting impeachment articles against President Trump. I was still at home in my pajamas. I had been up since 6:00 A.M. working with Joshua, attempting to wrangle the articles into the pithy, tight shape that Pelosi had requested.

As the Speaker was making her announcement, Joshua and I were in the middle of revising Article I, on abuse of power with regard to Ukraine. The Speaker was right: it had too much detail for a good article of impeachment. We organized the facts using our five-chapter approach, focusing in Article I only on the first three chapters—the scheme, the solicitation, and the pressure. (We left the last two chapters, the bust and the cover-up, for Article II.) Joshua and I talked through how to simplify and keep the article to a single page, in plain prose. We drew upon our shared study of the Nixon and Clinton articles (mostly the former) to frame the charges against Trump. We took pains to distill the centuries-long history of the offense of abuse of power into plain language that the American people would recognize. We finished with why it matters, inserting language about the pattern of abuse from which we continue to suffer as a nation today as Trump compulsively demonstrates the threat he represents to our national security. Once Joshua and I were satisfied, we shipped it off to Barry for his edits. He called and asked me if he should turn on tracked changes. I said, "Barry, love means never having to red-line." He cracked up, and it became a recurring catchphrase of ours (although on this occasion he did choose to mark his edits). Then it went off for internal circulation and comment among Judiciary staff before clearing it with Jerry, and then outside the office (with Schiff and Pelosi and their teams).

While the first article circulated, we turned to the second and third, for the obstruction of Congress's Ukraine investigation and of Mueller's Russia investigation, respectively. They were further along and more easily lent themselves to being simplified down to a single page. Trump's obstructive responses when Congress investigated Ukraine and when Mueller investigated Russia were two of a kind.

While we were laboring over the final articles, Trump was busy too—slapping aside the due process rights that Jerry had fought so hard for back in October. In November, Nadler had cordially written to Trump, to invite him to send his lawyers to our hearings, to cross-examine our witnesses, or to call any of his own. The White House had replied on December 1, declining to take part in our first hearing with the experts but saying they would let us know more going forward. That Thursday morning, Trump took Jerry's olive branch and pummeled him with it on Twitter, proclaiming, "If you are going to impeach me, do it now, fast, so we can have a fair trial in the Senate, and so that our Country can get back to business."

"I *think* he doesn't want due process," I joked with Jerry. He urged me and Barry to find out for sure. Later in the day, we spoke to Philbin and Purpura, the good-cop/bad-cop team at the Office of the White House Counsel. Barry reaffirmed that the door was still open for the president to participate fully in the Judiciary Committee as Nixon and Clinton had done. The White House lawyers asked questions but were noncommittal. The president's formal answer followed in a letter from the White House counsel, Pat Cipollone, rejecting all cooperation, declaring that "House Democrats have wasted enough of America's time with this charade" and quoting the president's demand to "do it now, fast." So much for Trump's claim that he was being denied the right to participate; in his world, no good deed goes unpunished.

Jerry did not take that—or anything else Trump did—personally. Maybe that is because he knows Trump secretly respects him. Nadler's calm reaction made me think back to a phone call between the two earlier in the year. On May 24, Jerry had become dehydrated at a public event, felt faint, and been briefly hospitalized. None other than Donald Trump had been quick to call, reaching out from Air Force One to ask how Jerry was feeling. Jerry explained what had happened and assured Trump that he was fine. The president seemed genuinely glad to hear it, and went on to praise Jerry's toughness, not once, but over and over again. Jerry thanked him, and the president lavished praise on his adversary—telling him he was a fighter, and adding that the first lady was with him and also sent her best wishes.

Shortly after the call, I asked Jerry if he thought Trump was doing it to rub it in or to lord it over him after he felt ill. "Absolutely not," he said without hesitation. Jerry said that Trump sounded lonely and that it was an opportunity for him to make a connection—yes, with an adversary, but nonetheless one who had known him the longest of all of his current primary antagonists. Their knowledge of the other was reciprocal. Jerry explained to me, "He knows I'm not giving up until he's impeached." Now that was about to happen.

THAT NIGHT, A SIX-CHAIRS MEETING was called to make a final decision on whether there would be one, two, or three articles of impeachment. The Ukraine article would be safe no matter what; that was the baseline, and we had been able to boil it down into a simple, one-page story. The obstruction of Congress article was almost equally secure; if we allowed a president to behave like this and get away with it, it would be the end of congressional oversight. When we sat with Jerry to discuss what lay ahead in the evening meeting, he mostly focused on doing battle to argue for obstruction of justice. In his office, among the subway signs, awards, celebrity pictures, and the little ornate silver face of the *pushka,* we brainstormed about how to interdict Trump's pattern of misconduct. That was the point of impeachment; the founders created it not to punish past wrongdoing but to protect the nation by stopping an ongoing risk. Jerry prepared to argue that the third article was necessary to establish the perilous cycle and thereby stop it.

Barry, Aaron, and I accompanied Jerry to the meeting. We sat with the other staff in a side room while the chairs met with the Speaker. We talked with Maher and Dan, taking advantage of the moment to discuss details of the articles and make a plan to meet with them and Schiff the next day to do some wordsmithing on them—however they emerged. After what seemed like an inordinately long amount of time, the meeting broke and Jerry came ambling out. We slipped into a side room to learn what they had concluded, and were joined by another of the six chairs, Eliot Engel—chairman of the Foreign Affairs Committee and also a venerable New York congressman. He and Jerry were of a similar vintage; they had been friends and close colleagues for decades.

Engel explained that while Jerry had then advocated eloquently for obstruction of justice, the Speaker had been persuaded otherwise before the meeting. That included the majority makers—those members seeking reelection from vulnerable purple or red districts—who wanted to avoid the Mueller angle. Her decision was to go with two articles of impeachment. Poof—just like that—the obstruction of justice article based on the Mueller Report was gone.

Engel turned to Nadler and said, "You did everything you could, Jerry; it was *bashert,*" a Yiddish term meaning predestined. Jerry paused for a moment before responding. "Predetermined? Yes. *Bashert*? No," Jerry answered, to laughter from the five of us. That is, yes, it had been fated. But *bashert* also meant finding one's true love, and Jerry had been denied his true love of at least that third article. The five of us understood enough Yiddish to get the joke. But Jerry went on to inform us that there was a consolation prize: he had convinced his colleagues of the importance of arguing the pattern of Trump's behavior. He instructed us to try to get as much of it as possible into the text of the two articles.

I hustled back to the office, where Matz and I crafted language for each article, designed to highlight and reference the recurrence of both abuse and obstruction. For Article I: "These actions were consistent with President Trump's previous invitations of foreign interference in United States elections." For Article II: "These actions were consistent with President Trump's previous efforts to undermine United States Government investigations into foreign interference in United States elections."

THE NEXT MORNING, CHAIRMAN SCHIFF received a group of us (Doug Letter, Dan, Maher, Barry, Joshua, and me) in the SCIF to work through the remaining issues, the largest of which was whether to charge bribery together with abuse of power. Schiff had clearly been working hard: the movie posters all remained stacked against the wall. He was cordial, funny, and quite deferential to Jerry about the articles. His two cents were that they should be simple, brief, and to the point—echoing the Speaker.

We then debated the bribery issue. The Constitution speaks of "Treason, Bribery, or other high Crimes and Misdemeanors" as the reasons for removal by impeachment. The problem was that "Bribery" alone did not quite capture what had happened here. Trump wasn't exactly demanding a payment from Ukraine. Abuse of his public power for personal, political ends was a better fit and a high crime and misdemeanor of its own. I had been quizzed a lot of late about whether we should charge for bribery, including by one of the Intel Committee's leading lights, the savvy, persistent Representative Jackie Speier. As I had told her and anyone else who would listen, abuse was the *highest* of high crimes, incorporating all the rest including bribery. We also feared that if we pleaded bribery, it would send people scurrying to modern criminal bribery cases and bog us down in quibbling about whether they applied, requiring us to prove a quid pro quo beyond a reasonable doubt. These standards *didn't* apply—the Constitution was written long before they were adopted—but the whole thing was complicated enough already without having to fight about those side issues too.

Virtually everyone in that room was a grizzled trial or appellate lawyer, and among us we had handled thousands of cases. Schiff himself had been a very successful federal prosecutor. We all knew that you can't peddle multiple theories in your case. It's imperative to keep a central focus. What was at risk, we agreed, was the very idea of America: that we are a nation of laws, not of men. But to drive that forward, which claim would it be, abuse or bribery? We went back and forth. I advocated for abuse of power, which was ultimately Schiff's position as well. But we did agree that we would mention bribery by quoting the constitutional impeachment text to lead off the article (a clever suggestion by Doug). And Judiciary would discuss in our report why the misconduct was bribery too; we just wouldn't lead with that as our theory of the case. Schiff ended the meeting by saying, "We've given you our feedback; now it's your problem." He also quoted one of his senior colleagues, who had once said to him, "We're all behind you unless it fails . . . in which case, you're on your own." Everyone laughed, and I quickly riposted with Franklin's adage "We must, indeed, all hang together or, most assuredly, we shall all hang separately." As we left Schiff's office in the SCIF, we felt good; we were hanging together. We had come a long way from our tense October debate in that same room over Jerry's insistence that Trump get due process rights.

Over the weekend, Joshua and I refined and stress-tested the text of the articles, ensuring they could withstand the scrutiny that was coming their way. We measured them against the factual record compiled by Intel and the legal framework developed in Judiciary. We compared them to prior articles and reread the records of the Johnson, Nixon, and Clinton proceedings to anticipate every legal attack that might be mounted against an article of impeachment. At one point, Maher called to raise a question about Article II: Should we remove the names of the nine Trump administration officials who had defied congressional subpoenas? After all, they were just following orders, and it was the president, not his subordinates, whom we were impeaching. In the end, we all agreed on including the names. These men had made their own decision to put loyalty to Trump over loyalty to the country and the Constitution. They had been corrupted by Trump and chosen to participate in his cover-up of high crimes and misdemeanors. We would let posterity know their choice.

By Sunday night all the Judiciary members had weighed in with suggestions as well (Amy and Joshua had met with them and solicited their views). Joshua and I reworked the language extensively based upon the committee's sharp and insightful questions and comments. Then we got Nadler and Schiff's final agreement, shipped the consensus draft off to the Speaker for her review, and held our breath for her approval.

WHILE I'D PIVOTED MY FULL attention to the articles, Barry was getting ready for his central role in the committee's next hearing, on Monday, December 9. The chair and members would examine the majority and minority counsel of Intel, Dan Goldman and Steve Castor, who would formally present their two very different versions of what happened in the Ukraine scandal. Barry would have the leadoff counsel spot for Judiciary, providing an overview of the facts and the argument for impeachment in his opening statement, then questioning the two men before the committee did. It was a critical day to keep the momentum from the last hearing going, and Barry had been consumed by it, occasionally surfacing to comment on and edit the draft articles.

As soon as the articles were off to the Speaker's office that Sunday night, I joined the frenetic prep. It was in a state of high dudgeon due to the volume and complexity of the multimedia that would be used in the presentations and questioning. The problem with using so many visuals is that if you change the script, the timing and content of the media has to be adjusted as well.

At around 2:00 A.M., Barry's final instructions were issued, the night shift was cranking away on the slide deck, and I headed home to get some sleep. On my way back in the next morning at 7:30, my phone rang. It was the wonderful Sarah Istel, who had guided us through so many complex factual excavations and now was working around the clock helping run Barry's fact operation for our impeachment hearings. She was distraught, so much so that I could barely decipher her words. "What's wrong?" I asked, alarmed. I was able to discern that wires had crossed and Barry's slides had not all been prepared for the hearing that was now ninety minutes away. It was no fault of her own, or anyone's, just the result of an overnight email misunderstanding. "Sarah, don't stress," I told her. "I'll help you take care of it. Be right there."

On the ground floor of Rayburn, I found Sarah and the panicked and sleep-deprived production team. We went through Barry's opening presentation together, providing slides on the fly and getting the deck together. The gang—led by our digital director, Jessica Presley—did incredible work and somehow the deck was ready by 8:45. I sprinted ahead to Longworth before the public was admitted and proofread the slides one by one on a laptop. I was still going when the hearing began.

Jerry once again got us off to a strong start, hammering the need for impeachment in his opening remarks:

> The integrity of our next election is at stake. Nothing could be more urgent. The President welcomed foreign interference in our elections in 2016. He demanded it for 2020. Then he got caught. If you do not believe that he will do it again, let me remind you that the President's personal lawyer spent last week back in Ukraine meeting with government officials in an apparent attempt to gin up the same so-called favors that brought us here today and forced Congress to consider the impeachment of a sitting President.
>
> This pattern of conduct represents a continuing risk to the country. The evidence shows that Donald J. Trump, the President of the United States, has put himself before his country. He has violated his most basic responsibilities to the people. He has broken his oath.
>
> I will honor mine.

Collins lowered the bar by using his time to further complain about the Democrats' process. His final comment, as Barry was given the floor, was to holler, "The steamroll continues!"

As Barry began his opening statement from the witness table,

Sarah and I sat behind Jerry on the edge of our seats. When the first slide went up, our stomachs clenched. But it worked perfectly, as did all the visuals. Other than a slight tremble in the hands of the tech team that was operating the computer, there was no indication that about ninety minutes earlier that visual presentation had not existed.

Barry humanized the problem before us by quoting a question from his son: "Dad, does the president have to be a good person?" The answer was no, but the president did have limitations. He was not somebody who could flagrantly abuse his power, betray the national trust, or corrupt our elections (our ABCs of impeachment). After summarizing the overwhelming evidence that Goldman would shortly detail, Barry offered a prophetic warning if Congress did not hold the president accountable: "Our imagination is the only limit to what President Trump may do next or what a future president may do next to try to abuse his or her power to serve his own personal interests over the nation's interest."

Next the floor was turned over to the Republican counsel Steve Castor to present thirty minutes on the GOP's alternative, fact-free version of reality, in which the president was innocent of any wrongdoing and had merely been pursuing corruption (although why he never mentioned corruption in his conversation of July 25 was left unexplained). Castor showed up with his papers in a Fresh Market bag, causing a social media flurry (including a tweet from the grocery chain itself, despite the fact that some of its kale-munching customers were unlikely to be thrilled by this right-wing bag model). Castor and I exchanged nods; he had been in the middle of Republican conspiracy-mongering for years, and we had crossed swords when I was Obama's ethics czar and he had investigated me! I bore him no grudge but must admit I was looking forward to Barry's cross-examination.

After Castor came Goldman, who was there to present the facts of what happened, which was the core of what the hearing was about. As damning as the facts were, he presented them neutrally—leaving the impeachment implications to the committee. He was every inch the lawman, reminding me of Jack Webb in *Dragnet*: "The facts, ma'am, just the facts." As we listened, I leaned over and commented to Arya how much ground Intel and the other two committees had covered, and in so short a time. An investigation like this would normally take years. It is much harder than it looks to examine a succession of witnesses in such close proximity to one another—as Goldman, Schiff, and the Intel members did—and to carry it off seamlessly. In the private sector, any one of those examinations could have entailed weeks or even months of preparations. As Dan sat before us sharing the results, it was a testament to Intel's work, but also to the dozens of staff at COR, at Foreign Affairs, and in the Speaker's office who had worked together nonstop behind the scenes to make it all possible. They had done just what we talked about at the outset: moving at the speed of Trump. It was the only way to hold him to account. It represented the best of the best of law and politics . . . as opposed to the schlock show the Republicans had put on. I wondered, not for the first time, how it was that such mediocre talent had been able to rise to such prominence in the years of Trump, starting with the president himself.

After a rebuttal from Castor, Barry kicked off the questioning by examining both of the witnesses, using Goldman to poke holes in Castor's preposterous narrative and drawing yelps from the GOP lawyer ("Barry . . . *Barry!*"). Once Doug Collins and his counsel got forty-five minutes to attempt to tear down Goldman and rehabilitate Castor, we were on to the five-minute member rounds, coordinated and incisive, blending hard-hitting questioning and clever use of visual demonstratives. I found it entertaining, and the day sped by in a blur. A bit of history was made, too. After the minority counsel, Ashley Callen, took her turn, she proudly told me that she had just become the first female staffer to examine a witness at a presidential impeachment hearing.

Only one moment marred the day for me. When his turn came, Congressman Greg Steube of Florida referred to Barry as a "New York lawyer" with a demeaning affect that caused me to stiffen. That can be a common code word, as in New York *Jewish* lawyer. I shrugged it off the first time, but when he did it again my temper flared up. So did Twitter, with some commentators feeling that it was an anti-Semitic dog whistle. To his credit, my friend Congressman Ted Deutch, a leader in the Jewish-American community, did not let it go. He challenged Steube to explain what he meant by his choice of words. Parliamentary procedure did not provide for the query, and the debate moved along—but everyone got Ted's point. Afterward, staff for the minority apologized to Aaron for Steube's comment and assured us he did not mean anything by it.

When it was all over, I congratulated Barry and his family; his wife and daughter had come down from New York and were in the audience. I told him to go with them to enjoy a meal. Barry adores his family but looked at me as if I were nuts. "Norm, we have too much to do." I tried arguing with him, but he had a point: it was time to finalize the articles of impeachment.

I HAD GOTTEN A HEAD start as the hearing was still going on: midway through, I received a note from Doug Letter, saying he had the Speaker's comments. I grabbed Joshua and we raced down to a side room to meet the House counsel. The news was good: the Speaker liked the articles, though she wanted a series of edits, particularly emphasizing the national security issues that loomed so large for the front-liners. Joshua sat at a computer inputting and modifying the changes as the rest of us stood behind him yelling out conflicting instructions on what to write. We were joined by two top Oversight staffers, Dave Rapallo and Susanne Grooms, who jumped into the cacophony.

After the hearing we sat down with Jerry and the core Judiciary staff to review the Speaker's edits. We munched on an Indian take-out feast of vindaloos and kormas as Jerry perused the latest versions of the articles. His green pen hovered over the page, occasionally dropping down to change a "thereby" to an "in so doing." Flipping to page 2, he altered the title of the second article from "obstruction of the impeachment inquiry" to "obstruction of Congress." He noted with approval our added mention of the pattern in both articles. Following up on our conversation after the Speaker put the kibosh on the obstruction of justice article, we had included a statement in each of the remaining articles pointing out that Trump's Ukraine behavior was a continuation of his prior misconduct. His collusion with Russia predicted his misconduct with Ukraine, and his obstruction of the Mueller investigation forecast his attempt to block Congress's work here. Before long, Jerry had come to the end, and he pronounced judgment: "This is very good."

He had once hoped for nine or more; then he had fought for three; now we were down to two. "Well," he said, "better than none." After the meeting, I stopped in his office to ask him to decipher one of his edits. After explaining what it meant, he asked me for the paper back. Taking up his green pen, he inscribed it, "To Norm, one of the real authors," and he signed it Jerrold Nadler. It is a keepsake I will always cherish, complete with its stains from the Indian food in the margins. By the time I went home that night, we had final sign-off from all of the principal parties concerned.

AFTER JOINING ARYA AND JOSHUA to present the final articles to Judiciary members early the next morning, Tuesday, December 10, Barry, Aaron, and I raced to the Speaker's conference room. The six chairs and the Speaker were gathering as she prepared to release the final articles at a 9:00 A.M. press conference. How many battles we had fought in this room over the past ten months beneath the painting of young Lincoln and the stuffed bald eagle atop the cabinet. Now the eagle seemed to be stretching its wings wider, soaring aloft with a satisfied glint in its eye.

The Speaker was seated at the head of the table. She told the group what a sad, historic day this was for her and talked about how faith had guided her. I had known her for a long time, seen her with her guard down and her guard up. As a religious person myself, I knew she meant it when she said that this was a prayerful time, and I believed her when she said that she prayed for the president. After addressing the entire room, she stood and walked around thanking the lawyers and other staff who were present. "Thank you, Norm," she said, taking my hand and looking me in the eye. "Thank *you,* Madam Speaker," I replied sincerely. After the tensions of the year gone by, it was a relief to be back in the good graces of perhaps the most powerful woman in the world.

At the press conference, the Speaker, Nadler, Schiff, and the rest of the six chairs presented the two articles to a mob of reporters and TV cameras. As networks broke into their programming, they described what would happen next. Starting the next day, each article would be debated and then voted on by the Judiciary Committee in a multiday proceeding. Every member would have a chance to address both articles and to offer amendments as they saw fit. It was only the fourth presidential impeachment to reach that stage in American history, a milestone that caught the attention of a global audience.

We spent most of that day working with any members who wanted help on their opening statements. This wasn't like examining Hicks, Mueller, or Lewandowski, where tricky technical problems required us to work closely together to prepare. There was a different art to these openings: combining the personal and the political, the members humanizing what was at stake by connecting it to their own lives. Our role included helping the members tease out the best stories from their backgrounds. For example, Judiciary's wonderful vice-chair, Mary Gay Scanlon, wanted to connect the impeachment to the civics lessons she had imparted when she once taught at a high school. She was concerned that it lacked enough color to be interesting. We asked her probing questions until we discovered that the name of the school was . . . Constitution High! As soon as she said it, her face lit up and it made for a great presentation the next day.

Others were just as good in their opening statements that Wednesday, December 11. Val Demings said, "I am the youngest of seven children. My mother cleaned houses for a living, and my father was a janitor, but he also mowed lawns and picked oranges . . . I grew up poor, but my parents were good, decent, honest people who taught me to be decent and respectful. They taught me to work hard and play by the rules . . . but the law means nothing if the accused, whether the man who breaks into your house or the president, can destroy evidence, stop witnesses from testifying, and blatantly refuse to cooperate in the investigation." The freshman Sylvia Garcia spoke about the weight of impeachment on her personally. "I take no pleasure in the work of this committee today. I grew up poor in rural south Texas, one of ten children. I know the taste of commodity cheese and butter. I know what it is like to stand in line at a welfare clinic to get a shot. And I know what it is like to pick cotton in the hot, blistering Texas sun . . . I never imagined that I would be a member of Congress. Even less, I never imagined I would be in a position where I would need to consider impeaching a president." Lucy McBath, of Georgia, literally brought the Judiciary staff to tears by speaking about her son, whose death had impelled her into Congress. "I believe the president abused the power of his office, putting his own interests above the needs of our nation, above the needs of the people I love and serve—and for that, I must vote my conscience," McBath said. "And I do so with a heavy heart and a grieving soul." She concluded by saying she wanted to fight for an America that "I pray that my son Jordan would be proud of." Zoe Lofgren focused on her history with impeachment, stating at the hearing, "I have worked on presidential impeachments as part of this committee twice before, and a third time brings me no joy," she said somberly. But, she emphasized, Trump "is not contrite. He poses an ongoing threat."

How right she proved to be.

The Republicans were unusually substantive in their remarks as well. Perhaps it was the gravity of the moment, the weight of history, or Jerry's continuing firm grip on the gavel. Whatever the explanation, a profound sense of importance—of bearing witness to history in the making—filled the room by the time the debate on the articles of impeachment commenced the next morning, Thursday, the twelfth.

The GOP had the power, theoretically, to propose an infinite number of amendments to the articles and then to have a full debate (five minutes per member times forty-one members) on each of those amendments. The whole thing was a charade, because they didn't have the votes to move any of the amendments and they knew it. But Jerry was unwilling to cut the minority off on a matter of such grave importance as impeachment, so he let them offer amendments until they ran out of steam.

The clock was ticking: the Republicans were angling to keep us late but didn't want to keep us there all night. Moreover, the president was hosting a holiday party at 6:00 that night, to which they had all been invited. Some of their spouses had even come from around the country to attend and were sitting near the front of the cavernous chamber. Doug Collins's wife had flown in from Georgia and was dressed in her Christmas finery to attend the reception. We hoped they might wind up in time for them to attend their party, if not at 6:00 sharp, perhaps by 7:00 or 8:00.

No such luck. The amendments kept coming as the debate wore on, using regurgitated Trump-inspired arguments. This is where Arya was at her finest. As she zoomed around behind the dais, preparing our members to rebut each claim, Barry and I could sit back and relax. The counterarguments had been prepared in a thick notebook containing thirty-eight rebuttal arguments, with topics preassigned to different folks on the dais. Arya, aided by Sarah Istel and Kerry Tirrell, passed members individual rebuttal sheets. We were even able to use slides and video in some of the rebuttals.

The Republicans showed no signs of letting up. At about 5:00, I saw Collins go and whisper in his wife's ear. As he planted a kiss on her head, my heart sank with hers (for different reasons). They were not planning on making the White House holiday party. As the marathon session continued well into the evening, the GOP goal became obvious. They were going to run the clock out and force us to take this most consequential vote in the middle of the night, when the fewest Americans were watching. We attempted to negotiate with the Republicans to have the vote no later than 10:00 P.M. They refused.

At 10:00, the GOP informed us that their last amendment was at the desk for the final debate of the day. The venerable representative Jim Sensenbrenner, who had been a distinguished chair of the committee, uttered words that I never thought I would hear after the year's chaos: "I would like to start out by commending the chairman for following the rules. I think that this markup has been a lot better than it could have been . . . I think the chairman has been probably very evenhanded on that." Jerry appreciated (and for his patience deserved) the kind words. But he had no intention of being rolled.

When the debate on this last of the amendments was completed (which we anticipated to be a little after 11:00 P.M.), Jerry held the procedural power to gavel the hearing over to the next morning, without telling the minority in advance. Normally he would consult Collins, but if he did that here, they would just drag it out more. We knew a unilateral move would infuriate the Republicans to no end, but it would enable the vote to be held when it should be: in the light of day, for the country and the world to witness. Jerry did not want to exercise this nuclear option without passing it by the Speaker. A message was sent to her. While the debate raged on, Pelosi called Jerry back. He handed his phone to Amy, and I trailed her into the anteroom.

"Hello, Madam Speaker," she said. She explained the situation and presented the two options neutrally: we could finish in the dark of night and miss our opportunity to talk to the American people; or Jerry could gavel out, and likely enrage the Republicans. The Speaker asked her what the chairman felt, then asked Amy, "What is your wisdom?" Amy took a deep breath and answered.

"It would be better in the morning."

"Okay. I trust you and the chairman."

With the green light, Amy and I rushed back to the chamber, and she whispered in Jerry's ear. He nodded.

At 11:14, once the debates had ended, instead of calling the vote on the two articles—as would have happened 999 times out of 1,000—Nadler announced, "It has been a long two days of consideration of these articles and it is now very late at night. I want the members on both sides of the aisle to think about what has happened . . . and to search their consciences before we cast our final votes. Therefore the committee will now stand in recess until tomorrow morning at 10:00 A.M. . . . [E]ach of us may have the opportunity to cast up or down votes on each of the articles of impeachment and to let history be our judge. The committee is in recess," he finished, and gaveled us closed. The Republicans literally leaped out of their chairs. Collins started yelling, almost incoherently: "Mr. Chairman, there was *no* consulting for the ranking member on your schedule for tomorrow, in which you have just blown up schedules for everyone??! . . . This is—this is the kangaroo court that we are talking about!"

"It's Stalinesque," Louie Gohmert chimed in. "Let's have a dictator!"

Nadler gathered his papers calmly. "Ten A.M. tomorrow." The members and staff followed him back into the anteroom, except for Aaron, who stayed behind to attempt (without success) to apply oil on the roiling waters. In any other situation Jerry would have told them what we were doing; that was the normal rule of collegiality on the committee. But they had intentionally dragged it out, belaboring the proceedings until after 11:00 P.M.

"As they would have said back in the Crown Heights yeshiva, baller move!" I said to Jerry.

He peered at me over his glasses. "Norm, that is *not* what they would have said at the Crown Heights yeshiva."

• • •

SHORTLY BEFORE 10:00 THE NEXT morning, the committee gathered in the anteroom. Lucy McBath led an impromptu prayer, with members and staff of all denominations gathering and bowing our heads. She asked for the Lord to guide us, to protect us, and to help us to do the right thing. Congressman Jamie Raskin, the co-founder of the Congressional Freethought Caucus, added a coda quoting Thomas Paine from 1776: "The summer soldier and the sunshine patriot will, in this crisis, shrink from the service of their country; but he that stands by it now, deserves the love and thanks of man and woman." Jerry thanked the members for their "intelligence, fortitude, and gumption," and then the members filed onto the dais for the last moments of our historic journey as a committee. The Republicans were still on a high-boil rage, furious at having been dragged back into the full light of day for the vote.

They refused to speak to us but also made no effort to slow things down; the quicker they got it over with, the better. Jerry gaveled the hearing to order at 10:03 and called for the vote. As each of our members cast his or her vote, I felt a sense of passage and of immense gratitude. These strong-willed, strongly opinionated leaders had welcomed us. And we'd delivered what we had promised, even if there had been some surprising detours along the way. First Article I and then Article II passed along party lines, by votes of 23 ayes and 17 nays. By 10:10, House Judiciary had voted through two articles of impeachment.

Barry and I savored the moment. Walking back afterward, I said to him, "Our strategy . . ." I paused, searching for the right words.

"Yeah," he said, then completed my thought: "I can't believe it worked."

We were off to the floor of the House for the vote on impeachment, followed soon after by the Senate for the trial.

Or so we thought.

CHAPTER NINE

Uncivil War

Impeachment has occurred once per century: Johnson in the nineteenth, Clinton in the twentieth, and now Trump in the twenty-first. Our president was about to be branded with the scarlet letter *I,* a reckoning that would be written in indelible ink in the history books.

But instead of satisfaction that Trump was finally facing accountability, on December 18, the morning of the impeachment vote in the House, I was full of anxiety as soon as I lifted my head from the pillow. My eyes popped open: we were not prepared for the day *after* the day of reckoning. Not just a mountain of work lay ahead, but a range of mountains. Judiciary needed to produce a formal trial record to be used in the Senate, consisting of every piece of evidence we had relied upon in passing the articles. In the Clinton case, the record ran to more than fifteen thousand pages. Ours would likely be close to double that number. We'd also have to help the House managers—the members who would actually prosecute the case in the Senate—shepherd hundreds of pages of trial briefs and other filings to kick off the proceedings, not to mention preparation for the trial itself. The House managers in the Clinton impeachment trial had made twenty-four hours of presentations on the floor of the Senate just to *open* the case, with many trial days beyond that.

As I picked out a tie suitable for television (I would be a mere dot on the screen, and all blue ties look alike at that magnification, so it wasn't *that* hard), a more fundamental problem than paperwork and neckwear gnawed at me: we lacked an actual trial strategy. I knew we should talk to you, the American people, to convince you of the president's guilt by making clear the evidence and how damning it was.

I wanted to win in the court of public opinion—but I also wanted to win in the trial court! In the Senate, sixty-seven votes were constitutionally required to convict. There were just forty-seven members of the Democratic caucus. Three were from red states and could not be taken for granted: Doug Jones of Alabama, Kyrsten Sinema of Arizona, and Joe Manchin of West Virginia. How were we going to hang on to them *and* convince another twenty Republicans? To make matters worse, we faced an implacable foe. Not the president, but his leading senatorial enabler, Majority Leader Mitch McConnell, who had declared that he was "taking [his] cues" from the White House. I knew success was unlikely, but I still wanted to try.

Barry and I had embarked upon this journey under the belief that the Mueller Report would help Republicans see that supporting a criminal president endangered our democracy. When that failed, and the president committed the same kind of abuse and obstruction again in the Ukraine scandal, we had hoped it would break through the partisan divide. We had been told that a dozen Republican members were huddled in a corner during the October 31 House floor vote on impeachment procedures, discussing the decision they faced. But so far the only House conservative to call for impeachment remained Michigan's Justin Amash, who had first spoken out against the president's conduct in May, reacting to Mueller as we once hoped many Republicans would. Instead of bringing members along with him, he ended up choosing to leave the party, now identifying as an independent. That symbolized the challenge we faced in getting GOP votes.

I called Barry from the car on the way into work to tell him our lack of a plan for getting to sixty-seven votes in the Senate was *his* fault. As his laughter crackled out of the speaker, he reminded me that we had not exactly been lazing around. Immediately after finishing the committee vote, the full Judiciary Committee impeachment staff had rushed to finish our 298-page impeachment report, literally sprinting through the tunnels below Congress to deliver it at 11:59 on Sunday night to the House tally clerk, making our deadline with one minute to spare. (The younger staff were impressed that I kept pace with them during that mad midnight dash; I assured them it was due to the terror of blowing the deadline, not athleticism.) Monday had been spent preparing for Tuesday's daylong hearing in the Rules Committee to adopt the rule that would govern today's proceedings. The team had worked until well after midnight on Tuesday night, readying a fifty-four-tab briefing book of counterpunches Jerry wanted to land in response to the GOP arguments expected during today's floor argument.

We hadn't had the luxury of time to feel anxious about what came next. When we rendezvoused in our office, I continued to press until Barry finally had enough: "Would you stop!" He was right. We had come here to hold Trump accountable and were about to attend a House vote on impeachment. There'd be time enough tomorrow—or tonight over a bourbon—to worry about the Senate. "Can you take just one day—just one—to appreciate the moment?" he said.

He had a point. Trump was certainly treating today as a meaningful one. Last night he had sent Pelosi a deranged six-page screed. In it, the president claimed he had done nothing wrong and was the victim of an illegal "attempted coup," and he regurgitated grudges against the Speaker, Schiff, Nadler, Mueller, and many others. He went back more than three years to the FBI's purported "use of spies against my campaign"—a claim that had been expressly rebutted by the DOJ inspector general. Trump recognized the momentous nature of impeachment: he was being taken irrevocably to task for the pattern of his misconduct. At least for today, shouldn't I recognize the same?

By 11:20 A.M., when Barry and I headed over to the floor to meet Jerry, my normal optimism revved back up again. That extended to my hope for some bipartisanship. We couldn't be certain what every Republican would do in the Senate, or for that matter in the House. Some might surprise us, starting right now.

WE PRESENTED OUR "SPECIAL LEADERSHIP Access" passes, white letters on a bright red background, and passed through ornate double doors to the floor of the House. The current of history filled the enormous room, circulating among the nearly 450 seats on the floor, pulsing through the crowded galleries that ringed all four walls, and rising to the grid of brilliant lights on the high ceiling.

At the front of the room, presiding in the Speaker's chair at the top of the rostrum, an American flag draped on the marble wall behind her, was Representative Diana DeGette. She was the Speaker pro tempore, "for the time being," when the actual Speaker has a different role in the chamber. (Today Pelosi would be working the room until the final vote.) DeGette was framed on either side by the symbols of republics dating back to ancient Rome: a bundle of fasces entwined with laurel, the images rendered in bronze and set into the white stone. Farther down the walls, a full-length painting of General Washington was on one side and of General Lafayette on the other, reminders that American freedom could never be taken for granted. It had to be fought for in every generation.

Barry and I made our way down the sloping aisle on the left, Democratic side of the room in the direction of the rostrum. Just behind the front row of seats were two tables with lecterns, one on either side of the aisle. Jerry was already in place at the one on the right. Barry and I took the seats right behind him, where we could lean in and advise him or our colleagues. Arya joined us in our row, her arms wrapped around the rebuttal binder. Aaron and Amy were beside Jerry. Members of the Judiciary staff who had worked so hard on the articles and building our case for impeachment—including Joshua, Sarah, Maggie, and Kerry—occasionally joined us on the House floor throughout the day. Barry and I sat shoulder to shoulder, as we had all year—from the first coffee of the day at our parallel desks to the pizza we split for every lunch to our nightly walk home across the darkened campus.

The buzzing chamber fell silent as DeGette called out, "The Clerk will report the resolution." We listened as the words we had pushed forward with every ounce of our being were sounded out on the floor at last: "Resolved, that Donald John Trump, President of the United States, is impeached for high crimes and misdemeanors." The clerk read out the articles of impeachment, word by contested word. "Article I: Abuse of Power . . . Article II: Obstruction of Congress." We came to Congress to fight Trump's pattern of abuse, corruption, and obstruction, and he would soon be marked for two out of the three. I had scrutinized each sentence of these articles, as a jeweler examines a sachet of diamonds poured out on black baize. Ever in sync, Barry gave me a sharp nudge with his elbow whenever the clerk came to a particulary good passage, whispering, "We wrote that."

After the reading of the articles, Chairman Nadler rose and introduced the woman who had enabled us to be here: "I now yield one minute to the distinguished Speaker of the House." This was Pelosi's "magic minute" (as the Speaker, she could talk for as long as she wished; it would count for only one minute of our carefully husbanded time).

Pelosi strode down the aisle in a somber black lapel-less suit adorned with a gold brooch: the Mace of the Republic. The brooch—an eagle with outstretched wings, balanced atop a globe, perched upon a fasces like the mace on the rostrum—symbolized our American system. She referenced its meaning in her remarks: "For centuries, Americans have fought—and died—to defend democracy for the people. But, very sadly now, our founders' vision of a republic is under threat from actions from the White House." She explained that if we simply allowed the president to engage in the pattern of abuse and obstruction of the past three years—repeatedly encouraging foreign electoral interference and then covering it up—we would be complicit in the threat to our system. "He gave us no choice," she explained.

She was just back, she continued, from the seventy-fifth anniversary of the Battle of the Bulge. The aged veterans she met described how the Europeans had questioned them: "Why did you risk—you don't know us—and give your lives to save us? We are not Americans." Their response: "We came here to fight for you not because *you* are Americans but because *we* are Americans." Now it was my turn to nudge Barry. If not exactly a strategy for the Senate, it was at least an answer to why we were pushing articles toward that body despite the near certainty of defeat.

With that, the debate was launched. Starting with the Republicans' first speaker, Doug Collins, the GOP laid out its case. There were some new arguments, or at least emphases, in the defense of the president. Collins claimed a revelation had hit him the night before. It was not Trump who was subverting American democracy, he argued, it was the Democrats. By Collins's account, we believed "it would be dangerous to leave it to voters to determine whether President Trump stays in office . . . I will tell you right now, Madam Speaker, we on the Republican side have no problem taking our case to the majority and to the people of this country because they elected Donald Trump, and it is a matter for the voters, not this House."

The flaw in this argument was that impeachment is no less a part of our Constitution and our republican form of government than voting. When a president is manifestly unfit and, indeed, threatens a fair vote by inviting—nay, pressuring—foreign attacks on our elections, should we wait for him to do it again as an at-risk election approaches? As Jerry later reminded the chamber, "Impeachment was put into the Constitution as a defense of the Republic in between elections."

Of course, we also heard that the House had denied Trump due process (despite Jerry's open invitation to him, which Trump had slapped aside). As for the substance of the impeachment case, the

GOP defense of Trump centered on "four facts that will never change." Collins, Jim Jordan, and others laid them out over and over again. **1. No quid pro quo:** "We have the call transcript, no quid pro quo"; **2. No pressure:** "We have the two guys on the call who have repeatedly said there was no pressure and there was no pushing"; **3. Ukraine didn't know:** "We have the fact Ukraine didn't know aid was held up at the time of the phone call"; and **4. The aid was released:** "Most importantly, Ukraine took no action and no announcement of investigation to get the aid released."

Jerry, presiding over the first half of the debate, demolished these "facts" one by one. When the GOP said no quid pro quo, he pointed to the president's own officials who disagreed, including the White House chief of staff, Mick Mulvaney. Jerry quoted Mulvaney's October press conference admission that there had been a quid pro quo and that "we do that all the time . . . get over it"—a gift that kept on giving. That evidence also falsified the second purported fact, that there was no pressure. How can there not be when the most powerful man in the world seeks something from a needy ally? As for Ukraine not knowing about the hold, Jerry shot back that within hours of the July 25 call State Department emails revealed that the Ukrainians were asking, "Where is the aid?" Finally, the chairman was at his fiercest on the fact that the aid was released: "This House launched its investigation on September 9. The hold on the aid was lifted on September 11. This is not evidence of innocence. It is evidence of *culpability*."

Jerry's performance was all the more remarkable because his wife of forty-three years, Joyce, had just been diagnosed with cancer. He had raced home on Tuesday to be with her, then sped back in time to lead the floor argument. He was suffering, but he compartmentalized it, and you would never have guessed it to see him in action.

Jerry was such a hard rhetorical counterpuncher that at one point I feared it would come to actual fisticuffs. Representative Louie Gohmert of Texas—a staunch GOP Trump defender on our committee known for his feisty nature—argued that impeachment had stopped the investigation "into the corruption of Ukraine interference into the U.S. election in 2016." As Fiona Hill had powerfully testified, Russia was pushing the claim of a Ukrainian plot in order to obscure its proven misconduct. When the Texan finished, Nadler responded with one of his counterblows: "Madam Speaker, I am deeply concerned that any Member of the House would spout Russian propaganda on the floor of the House." He then passed the mic to the next speaker. But Gohmert was a hot reactor. You could practically see a mushroom cloud form over his head as he leaped up, glowing with rage, and commenced shouting at the chairman, gesticulating with fury and hollering for Nadler to take it back. Nadler simply sat in his seat impassively as DeGette put a considerable amount of elbow grease into gaveling Gohmert into silence. But he wasn't done. Gohmert went steaming up the aisle from his spot and crossed the back of the chamber from the Republican to the Democratic side. "Uh-oh, here comes Gohmert," I heard someone say as he stomped down our aisle to continue his rant, ending up inches away from Jerry. "You called me a Russian agent!" he shouted. "You called me a Russian stooge! You take that back!"

As with Collins, I had always gotten along with Gohmert; we had once mused on the excessive power the legislature had ceded to the presidency over the decades and whether the majority and minority could work together on legislation to take it back. But now it seemed as if he could get violent with the chairman. For a moment I feared a modern-day version of the Brooks-Sumner affair, a pre–Civil War assault by a southern congressman on a northern senator on the premises of the Capitol. I was ready to leap out of my seat to restrain the angry Texan. But Jerry remained perfectly calm. Looking straight ahead, he replied, "I simply said that I wouldn't want *any* member of this body to spout propaganda." Gohmert, still sputtering, turned on his heel and stormed away as we all exhaled.

My hopes of a bipartisan breakthrough had been dwindling throughout the day as I witnessed some of the more violent embroidery of the Republicans' basic points (election theft, due process denial, and those four "facts"). Barry Loudermilk had thundered, "When Jesus was falsely accused of treason, Pontius Pilate gave Jesus the opportunity to face His accusers. During that sham trial, Pontius Pilate afforded more rights to Jesus than the Democrats have afforded this president in this process." Clay Higgins declaimed, "I have descended into the belly of the beast. I have witnessed the terror within, and I rise committed to oppose the insidious forces which threaten our Republic. America is being severely injured by this betrayal, by this unjust and weaponized impeachment brought upon us by the same Socialists who threaten unborn life in the womb . . . who threaten Second Amendment protections of every American patriot, and who have long ago determined that they would organize and conspire to overthrow President Trump." The inflamed tone for these remarks and too many others like them had been set, I felt, by the president's bizarre and ugly letter of the night before.

During one of the more heated moments a bit later, Barry leaned in and whispered to me, "Do they actually believe this shit?" I wasn't sure how to answer. As a former diplomat, I had learned how to appreciate multiple sides of an argument. But I could not fathom what I was hearing from the other side of the aisle. Sure, some were opportunists or charlatans. But many of the speakers seemed to be genuinely committed to what they were saying, and that was far more frightening. The gap between Democrats and Republicans was vast. How could a nation so divided find its way forward?

Hakeem Jeffries had the same concerns on his mind. He was one of our most riveting orators, rising to important occasions in cadences that echoed the long history of the civil rights movement. He did so now: "There are some who cynically argue that the impeachment of this president will further divide an already fractured Union, but there is a difference between division and clarification. Slavery once divided the nation, but emancipators rose up to clarify that all men are created equally. Suffrage once divided the nation, but women rose up to clarify that all voices must be heard in our democracy. Jim Crow once divided the nation, but civil rights champions rose up to clarify that all are entitled to equal protection under the law. There is a difference between division and clarification."

On her own campaign for clarification, the Speaker was everywhere on the floor—engaging with colleagues, coming over to consult with Nadler, praising his work, thanking me and Barry, then moving on to the next huddle. We were in a war of words, and she was our general, roaming the battlefield.

Around 3:35 P.M., Schiff entered with Dan, Maher, and the rest of their small army and occupied the table across the aisle. Adam delivered the case for presidential accountability with his standard elegance. He spoke about the wrenching experience of impeachment, underscoring that it would be taken only in the gravest of circumstances. He referenced Professor Gerhardt's statement that "if what we're talking about is not impeachable, then nothing is impeachable," and locked eyes with me just at that moment, earning me another elbow from Barry.

Other speakers who followed Schiff were prophetic about the consequences of Trump's behavior. My friend Tom Malinowski, now a representative from New Jersey, emphasized the president's insatiable propensity for quid pro quos that had gotten him in trouble in the Ukraine case. "In America, when we call the fire department or enroll our children in school, we do not expect a government official to say to us: 'I need you to do us a favor, though.'" Unfortunately, we now know that Malinowski could have added "or when we call the federal government for help with a pandemic."

Near the end of the debate, the Democrats got an extra surge of energy from Steny Hoyer, a tall, silver-haired representative who has been in Congress for thirty-eight years. Hoyer was from the moderate wing of the Democratic Party and worked as well as anyone in our caucus across the aisle. As the majority leader, he too had a magic minute. He used it to appeal to the Republican sense of reason and duty, asking the entire body to look into their souls and vote their conscience, emphasizing John Locke's adage that "wherever law ends, tyranny begins." He praised Justin Amash for his courage, suggesting that Republicans should take note that the one person in the room who no longer belonged to either party was supporting impeachment, not because of partisan allegiance, but because it was their responsibility to hold a lawbreaker accountable, even when that lawbreaker was their president.

Then Schiff concluded, his remarks harking back to his conversation in the SCIF with me and Barry about the theory of the case:

> What is at risk here is the very idea of America. That idea holds that we are a nation of laws, not of men. We are a nation that believes in the rule of law. When we say we uphold the Constitution, we are not talking about a piece of parchment; we are talking about a beautiful architecture in which . . . no branch of government can dominate another. That is what it means to uphold the Constitution. If you ignore it, if you say the president may refuse to comply, may refuse lawful process, may coerce an ally, may cheat in an election because he is the president of our party, you do not uphold our Constitution. You do not uphold your oath of office. Well, I will tell you this: I will uphold mine. I will vote to impeach Donald Trump.

Eight hours after we began, at 8:08 P.M., Speaker pro tempore DeGette declared that it was time for the vote. She called the question on Article I, first the ayes thundering throughout the room, then the nays. Jerry, as the sponsor of the articles, called for a recorded vote. With that, Pelosi finally ascended to the rostrum as members milled about the floor, inserting their voting cards in card readers affixed to the backs of benches around the chamber. There would be a period of roughly twenty minutes for the votes to be recorded.

Voting intervals are periods of frenetic socializing among the more gregarious members of Congress (which was basically all of them). Barry and I were in the center of the storm, standing in the aisle between Nadler and Schiff as their Democratic colleagues streamed over to thank them and all of us for the hard work that day and all year. Many had heard about Jerry's wife and took an extra moment to lean in and express their sympathies. Doug Collins made his way over to ask Jerry how Joyce was feeling and to say he and his wife were praying for her. He was a pastor and he genuinely meant it. I could not help liking him, and he had some kind words for me as well.

I complimented Schiff on his Churchillian words—just a few feet from where Sir Winston had once spoken—and told him I had been reading the great orator's history of World War II as my inspiration for our battle. Neither of us was naive about the consequences of the sort of disturbing partisanship on display that day. I admitted to Schiff that I feared for our country. He nodded, wearing an expression of thoughtfulness I would come to know well. "It is a dark time," he said, "but we are doing what we can."

Pelosi announced the vote on Article I, 230 to 197. Three or four people began to applaud, either from the floor or from the gallery, but Pelosi snuffed it out with a swift "stop" gesture, pursing her lips and swiping her hand from right to left. She could have silenced the crowd just from the expression in her eyes. She then called for the vote on Article II, which ultimately passed 229 to 198.

Although we had not picked up a single Republican vote (and had lost two Democrats on the first vote and one more on the second), our achievement struck me with the force of a gale. As more well-wishers crowded in on Nadler and Schiff, I turned to Barry. "Brother, we just helped impeach the president."

He shook his head, smiling grimly, and said, "Do you know how many times I thought I had made a terrible mistake in coming here?"

"Yeah," I replied, "but guess what? You didn't."

As we exited along with a tide of departing members to watch the post-vote press conference, I had for the moment forgotten all about the problem of the Senate. But the Speaker hadn't.

• • •

WE WALKED ACROSS THE CORRIDOR and into the Rayburn Reception Room. It was jam-packed with reporters and photographers filling every one of the two dozen available seats and ringing the rest of the room. Opposite them, Pelosi and the six committee chairs were filing in and finding their places below a portrait of George Washington. He gestured in their direction with an open hand, as if he had followed us from his station on the House floor to say, "They did it." Barry, Arya, Aaron, and I worked our way to the front and stood along the right side of the room as Speaker Pelosi stepped to the microphone to the flashes and *clickety clack* of dozens of cameras all working at once.

After brief opening remarks, Pelosi was asked right off the bat if "there are steps you might take to try and ensure . . . a more fair trial in the Senate." She replied, "We cannot name managers until we see what the process is on the Senate side, and I would hope that will be soon." A murmur went through the room as the reporters digested the statement. Standing at the side, I could see them pause, think, then snap to attention as they realized what she had just said. No managers meant the articles would not be transmitted either. The two were part of the same final legislative "sidecar" resolution that everyone had assumed would start moving immediately (and that Jerry was responsible for overseeing).

The idea of delaying the transmission of articles had been rattling around for days. John Dean, who had testified to Judiciary at our first hearing post–Mueller Report, floated it on CNN on December 5, saying, "I think Nancy Pelosi has some real leverage in this. She doesn't have to send articles of impeachment to the Senate . . . [S]he could say, listen, let's just hold these articles here until the Senate gets its act together." (The Speaker happened to be at CNN that night for an appearance and saw Dean on the TV in the greenroom.) Dean had messaged me to press for a delay that night, December 8, and did so again on December 13, saying, "Why not proceed by not proceeding? Make the impeachment a win and not a steppingstone for Trump." The idea had picked up steam in recent days.

Larry Tribe had come around to it too, lobbying me and others, including the Speaker, and penning an op-ed urging that the Speaker hold on transmitting the articles to the Senate. The *Washington Post* columnist Jen Rubin, one of the smartest commentators out there, was also pushing it. I had had an email exchange on the topic with her and Tribe, but I had yet to take a position.

Earlier on impeachment day, Representative Earl Blumenauer had floated the potential strategy on the floor, but there was little indication that it was about to become our official policy. Quite to the contrary, it appeared that when Team Pelosi got a whiff of what he was going to say, he had been held back from speaking for a time while his remarks were vetted to avoid confusion on this very point. One moment he was supposed to speak, and the next minute someone came over and told our colleague, Moh Sharma, who was keeping the list of speakers, that he was on hold. He had finally been allowed to go ahead as the last speaker during our block of time, and had made a very quick pitch to hold the articles, but it had barely registered. Now Barry looked at me as if to say, "Did you know about this?" I shook my head no.

It would turn out to be one of the most brilliant moves the Speaker made all year long, but at the time it surprised everyone. Pelosi's staff and the Speaker herself seemed taken aback by the stream of questions that followed from the press. "Could you wait to send the articles until you understand what the Senate's going to do?" "Could you withhold the articles for weeks until you get what you consider a fair trial?" "Can you guarantee that the impeachment articles will be, at some point, sent to the Senate?" "Is it possible you would *never* send the articles?"

Pelosi attempted to wrench the conversation back to our historic milestone that day, but that was already old news. The vote had been predicted, leaving little journalistic sizzle in that. Here was the same hunger for something new that had given Barr his opening to spin the Mueller Report (and, to be fair, the same appetite that we had been feeding all year long, beginning with the eighty-one letters).

The questions were on one topic and one alone: the revelation that Pelosi was not sending the names of managers or the articles to the Senate.

At last the press conference broke up, and reporters raced back to their cameras to broadcast the Speaker's surprise announcement. Pelosi corralled Jerry and the rest of the chairs for an impromptu meeting back in her office to think through what had just happened. Barry and I headed back to Judiciary, where our colleagues were waiting. When we got back to the office, the staff—who had been watching on TV—was as surprised as the journalists, having assumed that the articles would be transmitted immediately.

I asked them whether they had a better strategy for dealing with the Senate. I certainly didn't, and, I said, at a minimum it would buy us some time to get our act together. But we have no leverage, they noted. Suppose McConnell says, "Fine, keep the articles." And was it even constitutional to hold them?

Before I could reply, Jerry showed up and invited us all to gather. We followed him down to the members' conference room, where take-out Chinese and a bottle of the ever-present Widow Jane, as well as tequila, wine, and soft drinks, awaited. He was bemused about the Speaker's surprise move and relaxed about the outcome, whatever it might be. There had been no consensus among the six chairs on how to proceed, so the Speaker decided to consult with the Senate minority leader, Charles Schumer, and get back to them. In the meantime, all had agreed to focus their comments to the press on what they had done that day, and that's just what Jerry did, saying, "We defended the Constitution and we defended our democracy. Right now, that's the story."

Those sentiments were not just for public consumption. He meant it, and he told us we had all built the infrastructure. "You helped make history," he said. He added that he had two models for how he felt. One was familiar: the Watergate-era Judiciary chairman, Peter Rodino, who, after the committee had passed articles of impeachment, went into his office and cried. His other model surprised me: General Winfield Scott as depicted in the 1941 movie *They Died with Their Boots On*. Nadler now quoted his line at the Battle of Gettysburg from the film: "The Union will be safe."

We all talked about what a rite of passage the year had been, starting with the first meeting we had had with the team in that very conference room. Jerry's long-serving aide John Doty reminded us that there had been several times as many secretaries for the Watergate hearings as we had staff members for this impeachment. Amy chimed in that this would be one night when none of us would be staying late. She forbade us to work after dinner. With that, we dissolved into convivial conversation.

Later, as the gathering broke up, I walked Jerry back to his office. "Norm," he said, "we couldn't have done it without you."

"Well, that's kind of you to say, Jerry."

"It's not kind; it's factual," he replied. I thanked him, said good night, and went to find Barry for our stroll home.

IN THE DAYS THAT FOLLOWED, Pelosi's statement went from trial balloon to jet fighter. She declared the next day, "When we see what they [Senate Republicans] have, we'll know who and how many we'll send over." She wanted to make sure the trial was fair given McConnell's open favoritism to the president. It was controversial, to say the least. Commentators criticized her, including our witness Noah Feldman, who claimed it was unconstitutional. Tribe and others sprang to her defense. McConnell, as our team had feared, signaled indifference, saying, "I admit, I am not sure what leverage there is in refraining from sending us something we do not want. But alas, if they can figure that out, they can explain it. Meanwhile, other House Democrats say they would prefer never to transmit the articles. Fine with me!"

Team Trump was not so nonchalant. First Trump's enablers and then the man himself became enraged. Lindsey Graham said that it was "an incredibly dumb and dangerous idea," and Trump said, "Pelosi feels her phony impeachment HOAX is so pathetic she is afraid to present it to the Senate, which can set a date and put this whole SCAM into default if they refuse to show up! The Do Nothings are so bad for our Country!" He was acutely aware that impeachment represented a blot on the presidential escutcheon for all time, and he was furiously and futilely attempting to rub it away. Trump's violent reaction was a sign that Pelosi was onto something.

Whatever the merits of the delay, it also solved a personal problem for me and Barry: we desperately needed time to prepare for the trial. Jerry would be a manager, and Barry and I would go with him as his trial counsel, together with Aaron and Arya. The rest of the Judiciary crew would pitch in as well. Among other immediate challenges, Judiciary would bear responsibility for the official record. Arya and I began thinking that through the next morning. It was daunting to attempt to predict every shred of evidence that we and the other committees had relied on, and would need at trial, particularly because we had pleaded Trump's pattern of abuse and obstruction sprawling over the past three years. We estimated we would need to collect over twenty-five thousand pages of material, and just sketching the categories out consumed the two of us through Christmas Day.

It was understood by all that Schiff would serve as lead manager, and Dan and Maher were hard at work on Senate trial prep. By agreement of the Speaker and Jerry, Barry and I were designated to work with Dan and Maher to pitch in on everything: motions, briefs, arguments, possibly witnesses. They welcomed us as equal partners, and the four of us began meeting regularly with four representatives of the Speaker: her chief of staff, Terri McCullough; her national security adviser, Wyndee Parker; Dick Meltzer (he of the "Magic Meltzer" line); and Doug Letter, the House counsel. At this stage, the committees and staffs had acclimated to working seamlessly. We had done our work to support Schiff, and vice versa, so now there was a real sense of unity. The small crew proved perfectly leakproof, with nary a peep of our discussions (or even our existence as a group) surfacing. That remained so as our circle gradually widened to include others from our offices and Oversight.

Nadler told us to make the Senate trial just like our Judiciary hearings—tell the story, keep it simple. That had been his mantra all year long. Our members and staff had responded by preparing scripts supported by rich audiovisual materials, breaking new ground in congressional hearings. "Trial magic," as Barry liked to call it, and Nadler, like an old-time movie mogul, wanted more of it in the Senate. When we talked to Schiff, he agreed. Make it like an HBO miniseries, he said. Like Ken Burns (and, he added with a twinkle, not like Mr. Burns, the old codger from *The Simpsons*). To execute that vision into a single integrated whole, our small, leak-free, inter-committee team began working overtime immediately after Christmas.

The Pelosi Pause allowed the organic emergence of the one thing we needed even more than time: a strategy for getting Republican votes in the Senate. We would put on a case so compelling that it would force GOP senators to take a fresh look at the case and to concede, at the very least, that the call was not "perfect." We would focus the debate on making the trial a trial: on getting the Senate to subpoena witnesses and documents that had so far been withheld. Maybe those witnesses and documents, combined with our powerful presentation, might actually blow the case open. Think of it as a virtuous cycle: prove the case to drive the vote on new evidence, then use that new evidence to secure the votes we needed. Getting one or more subpoenas approved required only fifty-one votes. We would target the four GOP senators most likely to swing votes our way: Mitt Romney, Lisa Murkowski, Susan Collins, and Lamar Alexander. Recognizing that that kind of a breakthrough was unlikely, we would measure success by securing the support of the forty-seven in the Democratic caucus (including the two independents who vote with them), and ideally garnering at least *some* Republican votes. Never in history had a senator crossed the aisle to vote to convict a president of his or her own party on impeachment. We aimed to change that.

Finally, we would never forget that we were not just talking to the Senate. This was above all our chance to make the case directly to you, the American people. If we persuaded you, we would succeed—no matter how the Senate voted.

Pelosi's decision to hold the articles had yet another unexpected benefit. While we were preparing, at first a trickle, then a gusher of new evidence began pouring into the space she had created with the delay. It started in late December, when new emails were uncovered revealing that a top presidential official formally held up military aid to Ukraine just ninety-one minutes after the Trump-Zelensky call ended. Then, on December 29, more emails surfaced showing how involved Mick Mulvaney was in delaying aid, how White House lawyers worked to rationalize it, and how much alarm there was within the administration over the decision. On January 2, still more evidence came out, this time of warnings from the Pentagon that the hold on the aid was not legal. On January 3, a judge authorized one of Giuliani's associates, Lev Parnas, to hand over a slew of material shedding even more light on their efforts to smear Ambassador Yovanovitch and to pressure Zelensky to investigate Biden.

It was an evidentiary bonanza that reinforced our account of what had happened in Ukraine and—together with the ongoing Pelosi-McConnell dispute—drove incessant coverage of the looming impeachment trial. And that was all before the biggest revelation yet. On January 6, Trump's former national security adviser John Bolton posted a statement on his website that generated global headlines. He had previously resisted testifying in the House. Now, he declared, he would appear if the Senate subpoenaed him. Bolton was the holy grail: he met directly with the president during the relevant period and was known to be harshly critical of the Ukraine scheme, disparaging it as a "drug deal." His lawyers declared Bolton had information that was both new and relevant.

With the Bolton revelation, it felt like Pelosi would soon press Play. When we met with Nadler and then Schiff that day to discuss what to do about Bolton, no one (the chairmen included) knew exactly when we would send over the articles, but we all sensed things were about to start moving. On Thursday, the ninth, Pelosi called Jerry and told him he should be ready to carry the resolution on the floor of the House the following week. On Friday she made it official in a letter to all her colleagues: "I have asked Judiciary Committee Chairman Jerry Nadler to be prepared to bring to the Floor next week a resolution to appoint managers and transmit articles of impeachment to the Senate."

Jerry told us that Wednesday, the fifteenth, would be the big day. As it approached, we developed a pretty good idea who the other managers would be. We expected a smaller number than Clinton's unwieldy thirteen—likely seven. It was set that Schiff and Nadler would be managers. Zoe Lofgren was almost as certain. She was a close Pelosi ally with the deepest impeachment expertise. Val Demings had excelled, as a member of both committees, so the smart money was on her too. Hakeem Jeffries, with his eloquence and his role as the head of the caucus, was also favored. The sixth name was more of a rumor, but one that came from several sources: Jason Crow, a freshman and a military man from Colorado, a purple state. He had been a relatively early impeachment adopter and a signatory of that all-important *Post* op-ed. The only mystery was the seventh member of the team.

That was solved for us on the fifteenth as Barry and I watched Speaker Pelosi's 10:00 A.M. press conference naming the impeachment managers. Having correctly divined six out of the seven, we found the last came as a delightful surprise: Sylvia Garcia, one of the *tres comadres* from the Judiciary Committee, a former judge and a veteran of many of our script brainstorming and moot court sessions. There was no harder worker in Congress. It was a dazzling group, and one that looked like America. The Speaker used the opportunity to celebrate the delay strategy during the press conference, saying, "Time has revealed many things since then. Time has been our friend in all of this because it has yielded incriminating evidence, more truth into the public domain." I certainly agreed about time's friendship. Like Pelosi's magic minute on the floor of the House, her shrewd delay had given us a magic month.

Now that Pelosi had let the dogs of war off the leash, things started to move quickly. By 1:35 P.M. that same day, Nadler had shepherded the resolution appointing the managers through the floor, and we were having our first official prep session in the Intel SCIF: a lunchtime meeting with no lunch. It was Schiff's home court and he chaired the meeting, sitting at the center of the witness table where I had played Taylor. He and the staff were briefing the managers when Pelosi sailed into the room. "I thought there would be food!" she exclaimed, laughing. After quickly thanking everyone, she sped away.

Schiff sketched out the basic structure of what lay ahead, and gave the managers a stack of materials to read. Then we all returned to the Rayburn Reception Room, where we had last been together for the fateful post-impeachment press conference. This time the managers and the six committee chairs appeared with Pelosi for the engrossment of the articles. As is traditional, Pelosi signed them pen by pen, giving one to each manager as a historical artifact. Just after 5:30 P.M., pens in pocket, Schiff and Nadler led their colleagues across the Capitol to the Senate, where they delivered the articles of impeachment to a largely empty chamber (though McConnell was present to receive them) and withdrew.

At noon the next day, the Senate trial began with the ceremonial reading of the articles of impeachment. The managers once more processed across the Rotunda. Behind them, Barry and I joined Maher and Dan and other counsel and staff for the trial in marching over two by two. We ascended to the gallery to watch Schiff read the articles on the Senate floor. As he stood at the lectern, the other six managers lined up to his right, virtually all one hundred desks were occupied—many of them by friends from my years in Washington. That was true on both sides of the aisle; a majority of the Republicans had voted for me as ambassador, and many had visited or supported me afterward. As we waited for Schiff to begin, I was reminded of how much smaller the Senate was than the House; there was barely room for the two counsel tables, one for the managers and the other for the president's team, between the front rows of desks and the dais.

It was also far quieter. There was none of the murmur that always hummed throughout the House, only a somber silence, punctuated by Schiff's opening remarks. At stake was one of the most momentous decisions any Senate could make. As Schiff read words that I had helped draft, I looked down at the empty House managers' table and spotted the place where I'd be sitting across from Nadler. I thought of the distance I had traveled: from watching Watergate on our little portable black-and-white television in the hamburger stand as a kid; to sitting in my Judiciary office in front of the three stacks of articles from prior impeachments, unsure of where to begin; to where I was now, surveying the floor of the Senate.

As Schiff finished reading the articles, it seemed to me that the silence in the room had intensified, the onus of history settling upon all of us. Some of the last of his words rang in the air. Knowing all that has happened since the impeachment, they reverberate still: "President Trump has demonstrated that he will remain a threat to the Constitution if he remains in office."

I would be responsible for helping the managers convince the hundred members of the court sitting below me, on both sides of the aisle, of that proposition. More important, it would be my job to help convince the ultimate court, you, the American people, of its truth.

CHAPTER TEN

Bolton's Bombshell

THE LIE RANG OUT ACROSS THE FLOOR OF THE SENATE: "IN the Judiciary Committee . . . there were no rights for the President."

My head shot up from my note-taking. It was just past 10:00 P.M. on Tuesday, January 21, 2020. We were nearly ten hours into the first day of President Trump's impeachment trial. I was sitting near the head of the narrow, curved House managers table across from Nadler and Schiff. Along with the other managers and counsel, we were wedged between the first row of Democratic senatorial desks and the black marble dais where Chief Justice John Roberts was presiding.

The deputy White House counsel, Pat Philbin, had just outright lied about our committee's work. Worse yet, he had proclaimed that falsehood to all one hundred U.S. senators while standing a mere ten feet from me, orating in a slightly nasal drawl I knew well. We had spent the better part of the past year negotiating subpoenas and litigation issues with Philbin, an erudite former Bush administration official. I had been on a call on December 5 when we reaffirmed all of Trump's rights, the same ones he was now claiming we had withheld from the president.

Barry and I had been aggressive all year long—and expected similarly forceful tactics from the president's lawyers. What I had *not* expected was for them to appear in front of the chief justice and the full Senate and mirror the president's habit of delivering bald-faced lies. Especially not Philbin, a man recognized for his integrity: he had famously rushed (as had Jim Comey and Bob Mueller) to the bedside of then attorney general John Ashcroft to block the Bush White House from taking advantage of the ailing AG to extend a domestic surveillance program. His insistence on principle had cost him a promotion.

Yet, with cool indifference to his reputation and the truth, Pat advanced one falsehood after another: "The President had no opportunity to present his defense, no opportunity to present witnesses, no opportunity to be represented by counsel, and no opportunity to present evidence whatsoever in three rounds of hearings." That certainly was not true of our committee, and as Pat spoke, Nadler was growing increasingly irate. The chairman's default mode is scholarly bemusement. But he is brutally honest, and when others are not, he flares into ferocity. All day long, the president's lawyers had been pushing the outer boundaries of veracity. Now Jerry was fuming as the bespectacled Philbin recited lie after lie (echoing similar misrepresentations made earlier by another one of the president's lawyers, Jay Sekulow).

I leaned across the table and told Jerry what I thought might have driven Pat and the others over the edge. The White House apparently had not anticipated that the managers would recount the story of Trump's career of abuse and obstruction by using a full array of video clips, graphics, and slides, hammering the need for the missing evidence at every point and from every angle. Four large-screen TVs were set up around the room to show the video and other demonstrative evidence—the first time since the Clinton trial that any video had been played on the floor. In response, the president's team seemed to be winging it. They had evidently expected a dry procedural skirmish, whereas we had come ready to make our case to the Senate and the American people. As one commentator tweeted, "It's like the New York Yankees versus the Bad News Bears."

Nadler looked at me as if to say, "Is that supposed to make me feel better?" He had fought within his own caucus to extend to Trump the very protections Philbin was now claiming we had denied him. I had seen Jerry press a skeptical Schiff to treat Trump far better than the president was treating Congress. "The Constitution demands it," he had told me. Jerry had won the day, and following his meticulous instructions, we had inserted Trump's full privileges into the October legislation approving the impeachment. He got the same basic guarantees that Nixon or Clinton had enjoyed, though Trump had cooperated far less than either of them. In fact, Trump had not cooperated at all.

The managers arrayed down the curve of the table to Jerry's right knew how hard the chairman had fought for these rights. Zoe Lofgren shook her head in disbelief, her blond curls swaying. Demings and Garcia both glared, knowing that Philbin was spouting deceit. Hakeem Jeffries smiled sarcastically. The most junior manager, Jason Crow, a decorated veteran, was slack-jawed. To Jerry's left, Adam Schiff sat erect, jotting notes. The lead manager had been the primary target of outrageous GOP falsehoods for months, and he had grown used to them, learning to maintain a neutral expression. He was one of the great orators in the history of Congress when moved to speak, but his resting mode was stillness—a rhetorical predator ready to fly from his perch and strike in cold blood, whereas Jerry did so in the heat of the moment.

Jerry leaned over to Schiff. Schiff inclined his head slightly as Nadler whispered heatedly into his ear. "Adam, we have to do something. We can't let them get away with this. These are blatant lies about my committee." Schiff pursed his lips and considered—as calm in that moment as Jerry was pugnacious. I could see why Pelosi called Schiff "the General" in private. Both men were brilliant, but their styles were very different.

Barry and I joined in the whispered deliberation of how to respond. Schiff urged us not to stray too far from the plan for the first day of the trial, methodically marching through the witnesses and the documents, demanding subpoenas for each, all supported by our elaborate multimedia presentation. Jerry's turn was coming up, and he had the most important subpoena of all: for John Bolton. The former national security adviser had at last proclaimed his readiness to appear if only the Senate asked. Although the initial votes on witnesses and documents had so far all failed along party lines, today was only the preliminary round. We would get another bite at the apple in a few days, and our four key GOP senators had left open the possibility they might cross party lines then—at least to hear witnesses.

Ultimately, Jerry determined to keep his remarks on Bolton intact, but to preface them with some of the extemporaneous counterpunching he'd displayed on the House floor. I asked him what he was going to say and he replied, "The truth." When it was his time to speak, Jerry made his way to the lectern, covering the distance in short, quick strides. He began with Philbin's statements and the rest of the falsehoods that had accumulated over the course of the day. "They lie, and lie, and lie, and lie," he said. Trump's minions squirmed and glared as Jerry homed in on the charge that we had not afforded due process, and delivered some real-time fact-checking. He noted that he had with him the explicit letter from November 26 in which he, as Judiciary chairman, had written to the president, offering witnesses, cross-examinations, and the opportunity to be present. He followed to devastating effect by pointing out the letter rejecting our offers, from December 1—signed by none other than White House counsel Pat Cipollone, sitting just a few feet away at the defense table.

Turning to the task at hand, Jerry explained why the president and his enablers were afraid to hear from Ambassador Bolton: "Because they know he knows too much." Bolton had been present in the White House from the launch of the Ukraine scheme all the way through his September 10 resignation. What's more, he had made his outrage clear at what he called the Ukraine "drug deal," signifying its illegality. Every day, seemingly, new revelations were emerging about his involvement. Jerry lacerated the president for refusing to make Bolton available, then turned to the Senate. With the bluntness of an Old Testament prophet, he told them, "The question is whether the Senate will be complicit in the President's crimes by covering them up. Any senator who votes against Ambassador Bolton's testimony or *any* relevant testimony shows that he or she wants to be part of the cover-up. What other possible reason is there to prohibit a relevant witness from testifying here?" He emphasized that the failure to bring in witnesses and documents was equivalent to betraying their pledges to be impartial jurors: "I see a lot of senators voting for a cover-up, voting to deny witnesses—an absolutely indefensible vote, obviously a treacherous vote, a vote against an honest consideration of the evidence against the president, a vote against an honest trial, a vote against the United States."

Pat Cipollone stood to respond, white with rage. Pat was a protégé and partner of one of the D.C. trial lawyers I admired most, Jake Stein. Stein's adage was never to lie in court; once you lose your reputation, you can never get it back. Pat's irate counterattack flew in the face of that lesson. He doubled down on the prior misrepresentations, claiming that it was *Nadler* who had been making false allegations. Perhaps playing to his presidential audience of one or simply emulating the Trumpian style of escalation, Pat furiously demanded that Jerry apologize to the president, the Senate, and the American people.

First Philbin and now Cipollone had gone full Trump, and as Jerry had noted, many of the GOP senators in the room were likely to do the same. I flashed back to the floor of the House, where member after member had fallen into the black hole of the president's influence. What had caused them to lose their moral moorings? It was one of the signal features of the Reign of Donald: he sucked all those around him down to his level, and distinguished counsel were no exception (as Barr and Rosenstein had shown). It made the heroism of the Ukraine whistleblower and my State Department and other colleagues who had come forward in the House all the more remarkable.

There had been much speculation surrounding when Chief Justice Roberts would first open his mouth to engage or intervene, and he chose this moment to do so. If his judicial career had not quite lived up to his famous declaration before the Senate during his confirmation—that it was his job to "call balls and strikes"—neither had he been a complete disappointment, issuing Solomonic rulings like joining with the liberals to uphold Obamacare. Having known him for years (he too had been a houseguest of mine in Prague), I was gambling we would not hear from him that first day. I lost, as he issued a warning to both sides: "I think it is appropriate at this point for me to admonish both the House managers and the president's counsel in equal terms to remember they are addressing the world's greatest deliberative body." It would later emerge that Susan Collins had sent him a note requesting he get the parties to turn the temperature down. She evidently had not relished Jerry's candor (or Pat's rejoinder, for that matter).

I looked across at Jerry. His face was studiously neutral, but in his eye was a glint of steel. He leaned across the table and told me and Barry in a low voice, keeping his expression very still, "It *is* treacherous and they *are* lying." He was not one to tolerate dishonor or dishonesty. Still, that was the last of the fireworks—for the moment.

WE LOST ON ALL OUR amendments that night, but as we took our places at the trial table the next day, Wednesday, January 22, the managers and the counsel were in good spirits. We had used the arguments to present the prior witness highlights by video, bringing them into the room. That and the other demonstratives had set up our case beautifully. "Trial magic," Barry pronounced. We knew we would have another crack at arguing subpoenas toward the end of the second week of the trial. We had made a good down payment on our virtuous cycle strategy of proving up the case to drive the vote on new evidence.

As we waited for the chief justice to take the chair, I wondered whether there might be some hangover among the senators from Jerry's brutal honesty the night before. But when Jerry returned to the floor for his remarks that day, he handled the spat deftly: "Before I begin, I would like to thank the chief justice and the senators for your temperate listening and your patience last night as we went into the long hours. Truly, thank you." I was watching Collins and Murkowski, who seemed to approve. Sometimes it is better to ask forgiveness than permission, and he struck just the right tone. Schiff eloquently expressed similar sentiments both during his opening remarks and to the press, deflecting questions by explaining that it had been a long day and that emotions often grew strong after many hours in the courtroom.

That Wednesday was the most challenging day for our strategy, the day for straight factual recital. Thursday would be devoted to arguing why those facts constituted abuse of power, and Friday to why they proved obstruction of justice. They would have analysis and argument, which livened things up. But today served as a chronological march through the details of what had happened, extending over eight long hours (nine, including breaks)—after keeping everyone there until almost 2:00 A.M. the night before.

But something surprising happened as the House members meticulously laid out what the president had done: the senators for the most part listened attentively. The managers made heavy use of video to bring the witnesses into the courtroom: Sondland's and Taylor's testimony about the existence of the quid pro quo; Mulvaney's shocking admission that there *had* been one and that we should "get over it"; Fiona Hill's riveting and implicit warning that Trump was doing Putin's bidding; and Trump's public doubling down on his private demand after he was caught—"Well, I would think that if [Ukraine] were honest about it, they would start a major investigation into the Bidens." On the first break, we learned from the senators that many of them had not had adequate time to keep up with the facts that had become so familiar to us. It was not just our friends on the Democratic side of the aisle who said so. The courtly Louisiana GOP senator John Kennedy welcomed me to the floor and noted that he and many of his colleagues were seeing some of this evidence for the first time.

By the second break, senators started asking to have all the slides printed out and brought to each of their desks. We agreed that going forward we would do that, and we were before long producing a hundred thick packets of slides every ninety minutes or so. (I asked for them to be given to the defense as well, earning me some chaffing from my colleagues who reminded me that the White House hadn't given us a damn thing except for grief.) Fresh sets were distributed after every break by the congressional pages: high school students who were stationed all around the chamber for tasks just like this.

To be sure, the attention of some on the GOP side wandered, particularly after the dinner break, but quite a few remained intently focused. That included all four of our top GOP targets. Murkowski and Collins stayed in their seats and took copious notes. Romney usually did the same, though he alternated between sitting and standing. Alexander sometimes roamed the chamber but appeared to be listening closely from all points. Eight hours after we began, virtually all of the senators were back in their chairs for Schiff's conclusion when he acknowledged that he was asking a lot of senators from states Trump won, then pointed out that the Ukraine witnesses in the House had "risked everything . . . but if they can show the courage, so can we."

Immediately afterward, McConnell noted that today was the last day for the current crop of pages, and the senators stood and applauded them. I leaned over the table and whispered to Schiff, "Let history record that shortly after you finished speaking, the entire

Senate rose in a standing ovation." We concluded at 9:42 P.M., not early, but much better than the night before. As I read the room, the audience had remained engaged, with our two best days yet to come.

AS OF THURSDAY, THE MANAGERS and the trial team had settled into a daily schedule that we would follow for the remainder of the trial. When you're working around the clock with that kind of stress, you need your routines. Mine was liberally laced with caffeine. My touch point in the morning was to stop at my neighborhood 7-Eleven for an extra-large latte from the robot barista. The Ethiopian cabdrivers—from one of the world's great coffee-growing regions—who queued up with me also swore by it. The nose wrinkles I got from more elite coffee drinkers I passed on my way to the Hill only added to the pleasure.

I entered the Capitol using the same south entrance every day (superstition reigns among trial lawyers), speed walking up the ramp, rolling through security, passing from the bright daylight to the hushed, dim halls of Congress, and sliding into the last seat at the table in the Speaker's number two conference room (the second-fanciest one—HC-219, large, but with no windows, no bald eagle, and no Lincoln portrait) for our morning meeting with the managers, generally around 10:00. The day always began with Schiff setting the stage, and as I took my place that morning, he said, "You may not believe me, but I will begin the trial today with a very brief introduction."

"We believe you," Demings replied, "we just don't know how you define very brief." Laughing, Garcia added that there was a Schiff magic minute, just like Pelosi's. But it was good leadership. Now that we were settling in, the lead manager was making an effort to distribute the work evenly.

There would be plenty to go around that Thursday. It would feature the core of the case: arguing Article I, abuse of power. Jerry would kick things off with an hour-long overview of why Trump had committed an impeachable abuse of power—perhaps our most important legal argument of the entire trial. It was one Jerry and I had been collaborating on since just after Christmas when we first discussed what he wanted to say, then started sketching it out on paper, joined by Joshua (whose recent impeachment book was an indispensable resource). Jerry's script—and everyone else's—had been constantly revised ever since. We had been working on them late into the night before to take account of the new evidence that was still coming in, to push the audiovisuals to be as dynamic as possible, and to account for senatorial reactions so far.

I wish every voter in America could have seen what happened next, because it speaks volumes about the work ethic of the managers. After they received updated drafts of their words, these high-powered legislators put their phones to the side, ceased conversation, and launched into an intensive review of the material. Sitting in the room together, they worked silently—sometimes for hours at a stretch. They turned the pages, mouthed the lines, and made tick marks or notes in the margins, occasionally whispering a question, comment, or edit to one of the staff. The halls of Congress had become the study hall of Congress.

Following script review, the full trial team made the formal procession from the House to the Senate for the 1:00 P.M. start, always with enormous press attention. We traversed the Capitol, making the trip from the House side to the Senate through the Rotunda, passing beneath its rounded dome, with murals high above depicting other, slightly more notable journeys in American history, starting with the embarkation of the Pilgrims. Capitol Police and velvet ropes blocked off a path for the managers as we counsel and the other staff trailed immediately behind. Crowds of tourists gawked at the procession passing by. At the end of the trip loomed a holding pen of dozens of TV camera operators and still photographers, bright lights glaring, flashes popping, and shutters clicking. Just beyond them was the main entrance to the Senate floor.

Instead of going straight into the chamber through the double doors, our parade passed the gauntlet of journalists, then veered sharply left and headed to our own holding pen: room S-219. Just off the Senate floor, it was a large and elegant room, with a marble fireplace, a huge gilded mirror, chandeliers, antique tiled floors, and windows overlooking the National Mall. Staff made last-minute edits or worked ahead on the next day's scripts at two rectangular tables with a total of eighteen computer workstations. There were four large-screen TVs (tuned to CNN, MSNBC, Fox News, and whatever fourth channel was of interest that day) and industrial-sized printers and copiers in constant whirring use. The room was as hectic as the study hall had been quiet; Schumer's staff referred to it as Santa's Workshop. Managers did last-minute prep at a seating area of couches and armchairs, eating a quick lunch that was waiting for them. That day I hovered over Jerry as we put final touches on his remarks.

At about ten minutes to one, I tucked my trial papers under my arm and slipped out to the Senate chamber. I liked to survey the room, making sure everything was in order (we would occasionally be missing notepads for the table or be short a chair), before setting down my massive four-inch-thick trial binder at my place. It was bulging with everything that might be—and often was—needed if ever a manager would want to see some piece of evidence to retool his or her remarks or respond to an unexpected point with accuracy. Then it was back to S-219, to wait for the announcement: "It's time, everyone." We would repeat the impeachment parade, first the managers and then the counsel proceeding through the back lobby, entering just to the right of the dais, where our counsel table was located.

Everyone's locations at the trial table had more or less jelled by this point, and we went right to our usual places. In the very first seat was Nick Mitchell, a young former federal prosecutor who operated the trial magic on a laptop; we joked that his index finger should be donated to the Smithsonian since it drove our entire case. Schiff, as lead manager, sat immediately to his left. Across from Schiff and Mitchell at all times were one or more of Dan, Maher, and Rheanne

Wirkkala, a brilliant policy analyst and top Schiff aide who knew the case cold. She also helped manage the trial logistics, keeping all the trains running on time and all the passengers (both the House managers and the staff from so many different offices) happy.

Next to Schiff was Nadler, with me and Barry generally across from him. Going down the table to Nadler's left were the rest of the managers in order of seniority, starting with Lofgren. Across from them, the remaining counsel seats were usually occupied by Susanne Grooms and Krista Boyd from COR, who were our resident experts on the facts of the case and who, with their committee colleagues, shouldered an enormous proportion of the behind-the-scenes work. They also pitched in heavily on the trial logistics. The last counsel seat was usually occupied by Doug Letter, representing the Speaker and weighing in on legal questions, but sometimes another colleague would sit there, depending upon the issues that were cued up at any given time.

Everyone stood as the chief justice entered and ascended the dais. We remained standing for the official commencement of the day: the invocation by the dapper Senate chaplain, Dr. Barry Black. Bowing his head, with a deep baritone voice ringing out above his bow tie, he would offer a prayer that could lend a surprisingly sharp running commentary on the mood of the chamber. That Thursday, he urged the senators to strive for "an empathetic attentiveness that builds bridges and unites" and at every decision point in the trial to "ask which choice will bring God the greater glory." That was followed by the Pledge of Allegiance. I hoped that both the chaplain's words and those of the pledge meant the same thing to the Republican senators (particularly to our Big Four) as they did to all of us sitting at the House table.

WHAT FOLLOWED THAT DAY WAS vintage Jerry. He took the lectern for an hour-long comprehensive overview on what abuse of power encompassed and why it was the most fundamental of the high crimes and misdemeanors that the framers established as a basis for impeachment. Because the Senate had not yet allowed us to have witnesses, Jerry adeptly welcomed our experts from the December 4 hearing into the room by playing video clips from each of them.

Even more powerfully, Nadler used the GOP's own allies against them on a key point of the Trump defense: that we supposedly had to prove a *statutory* crime to establish a constitutional high crime. He started by harking back to my December exchange with the GOP's impeachment expert, Jonathan Turley, and his position that "there is much that is worthy of investigation in the Ukraine scandal, and it is true that impeachment doesn't require a crime." Jerry noted, "Professor Turley is hardly the only legal expert to take that view. Another who comes to mind is Professor Alan Dershowitz, at least Alan Dershowitz in 1998." Dershowitz, of course, had been announced as one of President Trump's lawyers, and Jerry flashed to old video of him stating, "So certainly, it doesn't have to be a crime. If you have somebody who completely corrupts the office of president and who abuses trust and who poses great danger to our liberty, you don't need a technical crime."

The GOP senators might not have agreed, but they were paying attention as Jerry continued, saving the best for last: "I might say the same thing of then–House Manager Lindsey Graham, who in President Clinton's trial flatly rejected the notion that impeachable offenses are limited to violations of established law. Here is what he said." Every head in the room turned to the large screens—though that did not include Graham's. Perhaps sensing what was coming from the earlier videos, he had absented himself from the floor. "What's a high crime? . . . Doesn't even have to be a crime. It's just when you start using your office and you're acting in a way that hurts people, you've committed a high crime." The Republican senators didn't bother to hide their smiles as many leaned toward their neighbors and whispered about what they had just seen. We would hear a great deal more about the "no crime" argument from the president's lawyers, but I don't think it held much water after that day.

Jerry's presentation was followed by equally strong showings from the other managers who filled in the framework he had sketched. Over at the president's defense table, the lawyers furiously scribbled notes, trying to keep up. Philbin and Purpura were back after a mysterious absence the day before (a reporter told me the president had been none too pleased with the Tuesday mismatch, and they had been called on the carpet, but in fairness, maybe they were just preparing the defense, which would start Saturday). Cipollone would occasionally look up and flash me a little smile when we drew blood with a particularly effective slide, like one Garcia put up showing the timing of Trump's sudden interest in the Bidens' Ukraine ties. Trump said nothing about it for years—until Biden emerged as his leading opponent in early 2019 polls. I appreciated Pat's gesture. Although I didn't like what he was arguing, I did like him, and we often chatted on breaks.

When we broke for dinner, the managers and the trial team traded notes. My friend Senator Sheldon Whitehouse—himself a formidable trial lawyer and former U.S. Attorney—suggested to me that we had made the case for the crime, but not for removal. The managers had heard the same point from other senators. We needed to go further to explain why President Trump was a "continuing threat," as Jerry had put it. This was the time to get the point across—not just to the four Republican senators who we hoped would unlock witnesses for us, but also to hold our own: Jones, Sinema, and Manchin. If we couldn't get them, it wouldn't matter if we picked up the four GOPers. But beyond them, we knew we were speaking to you, the American people. As we headed back onto the Senate floor, Schiff agreed to retool his closing to hit removal hard.

I sat across from him as he began lining out portions of his existing script and jotting down additional thoughts. He worked intently, occasionally pausing and pursing his lips or tilting his head as he considered a phrase or a line of argument. After about forty-five minutes, he leaned over to me: "Norm, do you have a copy of the call record in your trial notebook?"

"Adam, I have *everything* in my trial notebook," I replied. The four-inch-thick tome that I kept in front of me at all times had become a running joke among the trial team; whatever we needed, I had it. Trump's call record was high on the list. I clicked open the binder, removed the July 25 memorandum of the telephone conversation marked "UNCLASSIFIED" in red, and passed it across the table—my contribution to what would be one of the greatest speeches I have ever heard, and one of the most far-seeing.

When Schiff rose at 10:05 P.M., he began by acknowledging that the senators had been listening with an open mind, as indeed they had. On the abuse of power that we had been arguing all day, he brought their attention back to the July 25 call record. He didn't only quote the famous line—"do us a favor though." Using the call record, he pointed out how the president had set up his demand for the favor, saying, "The United States has been very, very good to Ukraine. I wouldn't say that it's reciprocal necessarily." That line, with its implicit request, is a crucial piece of what makes the whole call so unsavory: of course it implied a quid pro quo.

After Schiff teased out the meaning of the call record and set the context, he posed a series of crucial questions to the senators: "Okay, he is guilty. Does he *really* need to be removed? We have an election coming up; does he really need to be removed?" And then: "How much damage can he really do in the next several months until the election?" Responding to his own question, switching his tone from hypothetical to grave, he said, "A *lot*. A *lot* of damage." I looked around. All the Republican senators—everyone in the room, actually—was listening closely.

Schiff unraveled more of the president's recurring abuse and obstruction, before peering into the future, and into the heart of the crisis that grips our nation today: "Can you have the least bit of confidence that Donald Trump will . . . protect our national interests over his own personal interests? You *know* you can't, which makes him dangerous to this country; you know you can't count on him; none of us can." He continued, with building intensity, "If right doesn't matter, it doesn't matter how good the Constitution is . . . If right doesn't matter, we're lost. If truth doesn't matter, we're lost. The framers couldn't protect us from ourselves if right and truth don't matter . . . You know you can't trust this president to do what is right for this country; you can trust he will do what is right for Donald Trump. He will do it now, he's done it before, he will do it for the next several months, he'll do it in the election if he's allowed to. This is why if you find him guilty, you must find that he should be removed. Because right matters . . . And the truth matters. Otherwise, we are lost."

It was a statement as prophetic as it was powerful. Today, who believes Donald Trump acted to protect our national interests over his own selfish, political ones in responding to COVID-19? Who feels he has done what is right for our country during the pandemic and the protests over racism and police brutality—or that he has paid the slightest bit of attention to the truth? In great crises, right and truth are our compass. Without them, we are lost—wandering through one of the most challenging times in our history with no national direction.

Although there would be other truly remarkable moments throughout the trial, there were none that exceeded this one, and it has grown only more important with time.

After the chief justice adjourned, Schiff was swarmed by senatorial well-wishers. Even those not known for being fanboys rushed over to congratulate him, from Minority Leader Chuck Schumer on down. I noted the Republicans eyeing the crowd around Schiff; I was sure some of them too would have liked to have come over and acknowledge his brilliance. Game recognizes game, as Barry had said to me during the Hicks testimony. But party loyalty and fear of Trump (and McConnell) held them back. I broke into the scrum around Schiff to say, "I'm honored to be the fourth to shake your hand." On my way out of the room, Whitehouse caught my eye and gave me a nod: well done.

After every session, we gathered in S-219 for a quick postgame review, before scattering home so we could be up early to do it all over again (in my case, beginning with the 7-Eleven robot barista). Tonight, as we formed into a large circle, Zoe Lofgren said, "Adam, we're going to recognize you the way the farmworkers do it back in my home state of California." She started slow clapping, with everyone gradually joining in and clapping faster and faster until the entire group finally broke into rapid applause. "Yes! That's how it's done!" she said. Val Demings said, with her usual sense of humor: "All you needed to do was drop the mic at the end." Because there was no mic, Jason Crow quipped, "You'd have had to push the podium over." Schiff seemed humbled by the attention and was quick to demur, saying, "Everyone did a brilliant job today." They had indeed, but none more than he.

As magnificent as Thursday was, the high point of the trial might have come on Sunday, January 26, when we were not even in session. On Friday we had closed the case by laying out the obstruction of Congress analysis. Jerry had hit hard, pointing out that if the president could "fight all the subpoenas," as he had proclaimed, he would be a dictator. Schiff did not pull punches either, discussing a published report that GOP senators had been warned, "Vote against the president and your head will be on a pike." There was some publicly calibrated grumbling from GOP senators, but I was glad Schiff had raised it. Indeed, I wondered why Chief Justice Roberts had not brought it up first; in a normal court, a news report of threats against judges, even quoting an unnamed source, would garner a vigorous reply.

On Saturday, the twenty-fifth, the president's team opened their three-day defense, using just two of their eight hours and forfeiting the rest. The "four facts that will never change" showed up again in Mike Purpura's presentation, but were subdivided and had become six. (I guess they did change, after all.) On the process side, we were informed by Philbin that Trump had—surprise!—been denied his rights by House Judiciary. Schiff, Nadler, and the other managers held a long press conference afterward decimating the now-familiar arguments, one by one.

But the highlight of the day for me was the delivery and filing of the massive impeachment trial record—all 28,000 pages of it. Working under Arya's supervision, Judiciary's clerks had labored night and day, giving up their December holidays and countless hours of sleep to compile every scrap of evidence supporting our case. As we prepared for the trial, Madeline Strasser, Will Emmons, Priyanka Mara, and their colleagues were commonly still there when I staggered out at 2:00 A.M. to grab a couple hours of rest, and often still at their desks when I came barreling in the next morning. Their iron constitutions were one of the secret weapons of impeachment. Now our junior colleagues were the stars of every cable station, the video playing again and again as they helped wheel a series of carts piled with documents into the Senate, marching side by side with the managers. It was an irresistible visual, intended to make a point about the overwhelming proof of Trump's wrongdoing—and I was glad to see those who had worked so hard get some very public credit as a result.

Because we were in trial six days a week, Sunday was the one day when the full trial team could get an extra hour of sleep, then meet at 11:00 A.M. or so and plan the week ahead in relative leisure. We spent the day back in the Speaker's conference room (the one sans windows; instead, photographs of the Speaker performing her duties adorned the walls). By mid-afternoon, we were deep into preparation for our next speaking role in the trial: two full days of senatorial Q&A later in the week, after the White House finished its defense.

By about 6:00 P.M., the bagels were long gone, we were down to the last bottle of now room-temperature orange juice, and we were discussing how to deal with Trump's "I know you are but what am I" style. Just then, multiple cellphones seemed to light up, buzz, or chime at once. More or less simultaneously, we saw breaking news from *The New York Times,* with the headline "Trump Tied Ukraine Aid to Inquiries He Sought, Bolton Book Says." I almost choked on my juice as I read the subheading: "Drafts of the book outline the potential testimony of the former national security adviser if he were called as a witness in the president's impeachment trial."

The room fell into silence, punctuated by the occasional murmur of excitement, as everyone devoured the article. According to the *Times,* Bolton's book tore a hole in the center of Trump's defense. "President Trump told his national security adviser in August that he wanted to continue freezing $391 million in security assistance to Ukraine until officials there helped with investigations into Democrats including the Bidens," it read. Apparently, Bolton hit more than just Trump. He also implicated Secretary of State Mike Pompeo and Attorney General Bill Barr, as well as further digging the grave of Acting Chief of Staff Mulvaney. "Oh my God," Schiff finally said, "he's throwing *everybody* under the bus."

This could not have been timed worse for Trump's lawyers, who had a plan laid out, scripts written, and slides built around the idea that Trump was innocent. Indeed, Purpura had emphasized just the day before that supposedly "not a single witness testified that the president *himself* said that there was any connection between any investigations and security assistance, a presidential meeting, or anything else." It was the centerpiece of his defense! We had explained at length why that was not true, but if any senators thought that there were no such witnesses, here was their chance to hear from one.

It was a dramatic breakthrough for our strategy of getting witnesses, which had already highlighted Bolton above all. Barry put it simply: "game changer." The group instantly swiveled to what we should do and how to respond. There was discussion of issuing a statement (someone suggested the first word should be "yikes!"), about whether to issue a subpoena in the House (ultimately discarded as too late), and questions about getting our hands on a copy of the book (I asked my publishing sources, who just laughed). No matter: after two more days of the defense case and two of Q&A, we'd have the Senate vote on whether to bring in Bolton as a witness. All of the previous presidential and other impeachment trials in

American history had had new witnesses in the Senate: fifteen out of fifteen. We had just gotten the most powerful boost imaginable for our effort to do the same—the ultimate vindication of the Pelosi Pause.

The Speaker, back from leading a congressional delegation abroad, visited with the trial team the next morning. She praised our effort and was modest about her own. But if not for her deep intuition, the trial might have been over by then, and we would have been too late to benefit from the Bolton bombshell. We discussed how Bolton struck right at the heart of the need to present evidence. How could the Senate not call him? And if they did, would that break the dam? On average, there had been thirty-three witnesses in each of the prior impeachment trials.

I wondered how the defense was going to deal with the Bolton development, particularly because two old and unlikely friends of mine were the guest stars that Monday: Judge Ken Starr, the Clinton independent counsel, and Professor Alan Dershowitz. I had worked for Dersh in law school—my first legal job. Starr had also been kind to me when I was a young lawyer and gofer on the Clinton impeachment. Both had visited me in Prague; by coincidence, Dersh had stayed with us at the same time as Barry, who also had him as a professor. The world of criminal defense lawyers is a small one.

That Monday, Starr had the most successful approach to the Bolton story: he avoided it entirely. In a tone that blended bemusement with professorial detachment, he lamented the partisan nature of our proceeding. He gave a heartfelt peroration about the perils of living in "the age of impeachment." I smiled to myself, considering how his role in the Clinton case had helped construct the age of impeachment. I gave him credit for chutzpah (though it was really the specialty of his co-counsel, Dershowitz; in fact I had been Alan's research assistant on a book with that title). Starr also argued that you *did* have to have a crime to impeach a president, while credibly conceding there was authority both ways. Overall, he focused on law and history and stayed somewhat above the fray.

Dershowitz's approach was the opposite of the high-toned, genial Starr. Rather than sidestepping Bolton, he attempted to pummel his evidence into oblivion. Even if the Bolton story were true, according to Alan, you had to have a statutory crime as a limiting principle for the high crime of abuse of power; otherwise, anything the House didn't like could be portrayed as an abuse. He admitted that modern authorities—including himself in the 1998 video Jerry had played—disagreed with him. He said he had studied the issue more since then, confessed he had been wrong, and claimed everyone else was, too. (Barry rolled his eyes up so far into his head that I thought I might never see his pupils again.)

The Republican senators flinched, squirmed, and looked away every time Dersh mentioned Bolton. The problem was, the White House hadn't told the GOP senators this was coming, and they were visibly irritated. Bolton was a widely respected archconservative who many of them knew and trusted; it was not so easy to dismiss him as a liar. Plus, they didn't know what the next Bolton revelation would be (other stories had emerged revealing Bolton's concerns about Trump's financial ties to dictators he coddled—the good old emoluments clause surfacing again). With the vote on subpoenas for him and others looming at the end of the week, the discomfort was palpable.

I could see the cracks emerging in my conversations with GOP senators. The most fascinating one came when I was chatting with Starr and Mitt Romney on a break. Romney told Starr how much he appreciated his presentation, but proceeded to ask him a series of penetrating questions that spoke to a mind that had not been made up. He focused on Starr's disparaging of this impeachment as a partisan one. "Judge," Romney said, "haven't things changed so much that a bipartisan impeachment might no longer be possible? And isn't it our job as senators—whatever others may have decided—to search our individual consciences and ascertain if it's an impeachable offense or not?"

Romney was grappling with the problem that had gradually emerged for me over the course of the year, coming to the fore during the House floor debate. How do we function as a country in the face of the partisan divide that had opened between us? I believed that Trump had widened that gap into a chasm, attacking truth, evidence, logic, values, and the other foundations of human discourse. Without those commonalities, I was not sure how we could even talk to each other as a nation, much less find a way forward. Romney was offering an answer, one equally applicable to senators and each of us: when you don't know what to do, do the right thing.

Starr reformulated his earlier points in response to Romney's question, urging that we all take a step back from that brink, starting with rejecting the impeachment. But Romney—listening very politely—did not seem to be buying it. I wondered what *his* path forward would be. He finished by complimenting the judge for acknowledging that prior authorities went both ways on the need for a crime—some supported Starr's view and some opposed it. Romney suggested that, based on his study of the precedents, he doubted a statutory offense was necessary for a high crime where there was a profound abuse of power.

Romney was not only a businessman; he too was a graduate of Harvard Law School and his analysis showed it. In fact, he was another former Dersh student, one of many involved in the trial. After Alan's remarks, Romney joined a cluster of us saying hello to our old professor, including Senators Mark Warner and Ted Cruz. Romney proudly proclaimed, "Professor, you gave me an A." Nevertheless, Romney tended to disparage his own legal ability, at another point telling me and a group of the other counsel, "You guys do great with all that litigation stuff; I'm not good at it, which is why I became a business guy." But the exchange I had witnessed with Starr showed that he had a nimble legal mind and a moral conscience to go with it.

• • •

WHEN WE RECONVENED THE NEXT morning, the Bolton issue was still crackling. Our goal was to get witnesses, and there seemed to be fissures on the other side that might enable us to do just that. The Republican senators Lindsey Graham and James Lankford were floating a proposal to take Bolton's testimony, but to do it in a SCIF, like the one where Schiff and the Intel team worked. Even opening the possibility in this way was a major concession. As the defense wrapped its case that day, GOP senators continued to look down and away every time Bolton's name came up.

After the president's legal team completed its impeachment defense, they and key Republicans huddled to discuss whether to call new witnesses. With the GOP caucus still reeling from the Bolton revelations, we were cautiously optimistic. "How can you have a trial without witnesses?" Senator Tim Kaine asked me on the floor, genuinely befuddled. We hoped that we might actually get enough votes to hear Bolton, and perhaps others, in the Senate. And maybe, just maybe, those witnesses would swing votes our way on conviction.

Shortly after 8:00 that evening, *The Washington Post* broke an article with yet another headline that lifted all our spirits: "McConnell Tells Senators He Doesn't Yet Have Votes to Block Witnesses in Trump Impeachment Trial." Apparently, McConnell had informed colleagues in a closed-door meeting that the commitments from his caucus fell short of what he would need to bar subpoenas. In other words, four or more Republicans were still leaving the door open to witnesses.

We knew that it would be very tough to get the votes to convict the president. That would be true no matter how powerful a case we made; no matter how many Republican senators publicly or privately approached us to offer praise; no matter if Bolton testified that the president had confessed to murder on Fifth Avenue. But both Barry and I had seen impossible cases won when a surprise witness stepped forward. And, however farfetched a Senate conviction may have been, if we could get Bolton, we would at least stay alive to fight another day. Potentially many days, if Bolton opened the door to other witnesses as well. And that meant more days of talking to you, the American people, about the essence of President Trump.

If McConnell, as ferocious a caucus wrangler as ever operated in the Senate, did not have the votes, then we were doing our job. As Barry and I headed home, even though it was a cold January night, it appeared that spring was in the air. It was certainly in our steps. The *Post* story seemed too good to be true. I had to pinch myself.

Reality was about to pinch me back.

CHAPTER ELEVEN

Trial Magic

When I woke up the next morning, my first thought was that it had been a dream. But no, as I opened my door to pick up the Wednesday, January 29, *Washington Post,* there it was above the fold, in black and white: "McConnell Says He Lacks Votes to Bar Trial Witnesses." I was still smiling as I ducked into the 7-Eleven. On my way to the coffee machine, I flipped through the pile of newspapers in the rack by the door. There was that beautiful headline, again and again.

With Pelosi back in town for the second week of the trial, we had relocated our morning prep meetings from her suite down one floor to H-142. It was a lovely, light-filled, first-floor corner meeting room that had previously belonged to the Appropriations Committee. (The appropriators control the money, so they get all the good stuff.) More important, it was right near my lucky southern entrance to the Capitol, enabling me to shave thirty seconds off my just-in-time arrival for our meeting. The managers were in a good mood as I slid into my seat and we began preparations for the first day of questioning. They had delivered the case brilliantly to the Senate and the American people. Now we were driving ahead on getting the documents and witnesses, with the latest Bolton revelations unexpectedly powering us forward. Still, almost everyone was more cautious about their enthusiasm than I. True, McConnell not having what he wanted was not the same as us having what we needed. We didn't have fifty-one votes for witnesses in hand. I suppose my desperate optimism was coloring my view of the situation. Even more than caffeine, that attitude had propelled me here every morning and had kept me going over the course of this entire year, through all its ups and downs.

Jerry was back with us after having missed Monday to be with his wife, Joyce, and to deal with some challenging decisions regarding her cancer. Characteristically, though he had had a tough few days at home, he had remembered his colleagues and had brought back a large bag of Zabar's babkas—heavy bricks of Jewish coffee cake that are a specialty of New York delis. A single slice is enough to a knock you out as surely as an Ambien, and he had brought an entire babka per manager. They were spread out on the table as everybody got to work.

As we talked through that day's Q&A session, the focus remained on the Bolton revelations. His disclosures had put Trump and his lawyers in a terrible position. With the threat of Bolton hanging over them, they would have to fall back on the Dershowitz position—that abuse of power without a crime is not impeachable. That was not legally tenable, as Romney had noted in our conversation with Starr.

The final Q&A script was handed out to each of the managers. When our team had been set up in December, Judiciary had taken the first crack at these, sketching out a list a couple of pages long. It had since grown into a 348-page tome of questions and answers, complete with fifty-four slides, exhibits, videos, and graphics. (Like our list of eighty-one letters back in the day, the document had taken on a life of its own.) The topics were loosely divided up among the managers based on expertise. Jerry, as a constitutional expert, would handle questions dealing with legal issues relating to abuse, obstruction, and impeachment power. Garcia would take burden of proof, hearsay, and due process questions; all were within her bailiwick as a former judge. And so on, with each manager taking a selection of the anticipated queries, and all of us working off a cheat sheet indicating these topics. Once we got to the trial, staff at the table would figure who answered what, in consultation with Schiff. We had little idea what the Republicans, or the Democrats for that matter, were going to throw at us. The Senate Democrats had not offered the questions in advance, and we accepted that. They took their oath of impartiality seriously, even if McConnell did not.

After the managers received their binders, they fell into their usual quiet study—on this occasion fueled by the mountain of rapidly dwindling babkas of every flavor. Barry and I chatted in a corner. Exactly twelve months prior, we had been negotiating our employment contracts; now we were in the middle of an impeachment trial and on the brink of getting one of the president's former closest advisers to incriminate him.

Barry whispered, "Norm, did I ever tell you about the 'look-good loser'?"

"No."

"Some trial lawyers go to court, and they don't really believe they are going to win, but they just want to look good while they lose. I don't want to be that guy. I want us to take Bolton's deposition and I want to persuade these senators!" Then he asked, "You know what I like?"

That question was a Barryism. He constantly posed it. The first time he had done so, at a Judiciary staff meeting, we had all fallen for it, replying, "What do you like?"

"Winning!" he said. He made that his mantra, so whenever we were in a tight spot in a meeting, he'd pipe up, "You know what I like?" and everyone would answer, with a groan.

This time, I replied, "Yes, I know what you like." And, I thought, we might just get it.

THE CHALLENGES TO MY OPTIMISM started coming as soon as I made the long noontime walk from the House to the Senate. I ran into one of the most senior members of the Senate Democratic leadership staff on my way into the chamber and stopped to chat with him about the state of play.

"Norm," he told me bluntly, "you can't count on Alexander." He proceeded to unsettle me with a litany of disappointing moments when Alexander had let down Democrats, going as far back as George W. Bush. "He's best friends with McConnell! If it comes down to him, we're screwed." Who was I to argue with an expert? But I did. I pointed out that Alexander had confronted McConnell, working with the other three GOP potentials to ensure there would be an eventual vote on getting witnesses. Why would he bother doing that if he wasn't open to actually hearing from some? And what about the *Post* article? My friend smiled and said, "McConnell likely leaked that himself, as a way of reminding his caucus to wake up and smell the coffee."

I knew he was capable of such a move. I had seen the power of McConnell up close at my own nomination as U.S. ambassador to the Czech Republic. At one point during the vote, he stood in front of the dais and appeared to personally manage the voting to ensure that I had enough support to get through, but evidently not so much that my Republican Senate opponents would be embarrassed. As some of his caucus approached, he had indicated to them how they could vote with a thumbs-up or a thumbs-down. From everything I had seen, he still had that power.

I hoped my friend was wrong, but nonetheless entered the Senate chamber with Alexander on my mind. We had a fallback plan. Even if we lost him, a 50–50 vote would, according to the rules and to historical precedent, allow us to argue that the chief justice should break the tie. Chief Justice Salmon P. Chase had done so in the Andrew Johnson impeachment. But that was in 1868, and we did not know how Roberts would rule. It would be much better to just secure 51 votes.

The next warning sign came with the first question of the day. The Q&A process was ritualistic: one of the senators would rise to announce he or she had a question, either alone or on behalf of a group of colleagues. There were uniform four-by-six-inch question cards, and the senator would then pass the card to a page. The page would shuttle it to the dais and hand it to the parliamentarian, who in turn would hand it up to the chief justice, who would proceed to read the question, indicating which side was requested to answer. McConnell and Schumer took turns choosing who on their respective sides would ask questions.

McConnell doled out the opening query, which was posed by Susan Collins to the White House lawyers on behalf of herself, Romney, and Murkowski. It was an important one: how the Senate should proceed if the president had "more than one motive," that is, if the president had asked Ukraine to attack the Bidens *both* for selfish, corrupt reasons and because of legitimate concern about corruption. It was a good sign for us that those three senators were at least considering the possibility that the call was less than perfect. The only thing that gave me pause was that just three of our four targets had asked it. "You can't count on Alexander" echoed in my mind as Philbin answered the question, attempting to deny the general legal rule that even partial bad motive established corrupt intent. Perhaps, I thought, Alexander was saving up his chit for a question of his own.

Evidently, I was not the only one trying to decipher the tea leaves. On the break, I started hearing from multiple reporters, all of whom echoed the refrain that we did not have fifty-one votes for Bolton or any other witness. The Republicans had been putting out the word since earlier in the day. McConnell was apparently feeling more confident, and the rumor was that he had gotten further GOP assurance. I didn't think that could have come from Romney. Perhaps Collins or Murkowski had tipped her hand, but it certainly didn't look like it as they sat beside each other, listening attentively and scribbling notes. Murkowski had had a private meeting with McConnell earlier that morning, but she said she had not made up her mind and, by all appearances, she meant it.

That left Alexander, who was seated in the first GOP row across from me. Tall, balding, mild-mannered, and slightly stooped, given to wearing sweaters under his jacket, Alexander harked back to another era and he looked it. He had been the protégé of Senator Howard Baker (who famously asked, "What did the president know, and when did he know it?" during Watergate), a university president, and education secretary for George H. W. Bush. Alexander had a reputation for bipartisanship, had publicly admitted Trump was not his first choice, and had (selectively) critiqued his policies. He would not have to face Trump voters, because he was soon retiring. Now he listened with an air of pensive senatorial integrity. Surely, anybody concerned with upholding his oath to do impartial justice would at least allow us to examine a witness as important as Bolton.

But, just as I could feel the positive charge that had electrified the Hill on important days all that year, now I could sense a kind of invisible negative current circulating in the Capitol. Somehow, all at once, everyone knew the votes we needed to get witnesses had slipped away. I felt it most palpably when I stepped away from the trial table and went back to our normally bustling Santa's Workshop to retrieve a document we needed. It was as if Christmas had been canceled. The room was completely deflated. I didn't think it was going badly with the questions at all—on the contrary. Everything in the Senate chamber was going fine, but our team had picked up on the vibe too. As I went from person to person, trying to buck them up, there seemed to be a consensus that Alexander, and maybe others, had turned. I asked the Speaker's fierce communications director, Ashley Etienne, who helped manage our impeachment trial reporter relationships (and much more), where it was coming from. She always had the dirt; talking to her was like getting an exclusive advance edition of Twitter. "Norm," she replied, "it's just in the air."

I took it with a grain of salt. I had lived inside such buzz for the past year. Rumors and gossip can be, by definition, exaggerated, miscalculated, or outright false. As far as I could tell, our four Republicans could still go either way, plus we had a plan to deal with a potential 50–50 vote; I saw no advantage to relinquishing hope.

At 2:11 P.M., we got just the morale boost we needed. Chief

Justice Roberts was handed a question addressed to the president's counsel: "As a matter of law, does it matter if there was a quid pro quo? Is it true that quid pro quos are often used in foreign policy?" Professor Dershowitz leaped up to respond. He began with a discussion of foreign policy negotiations before stating, "Every public official whom I know believes that his election is in the public interest. Mostly, you are right. Your election is in the public interest. If a President does something which he believes will help him get elected—in the public interest—that cannot be the kind of quid pro quo that results in impeachment."

A low buzz rose all over the room. Had we just heard what I thought we heard? None of us at the trial table, managers or staff, could believe our ears. If a president thinks that his reelection is in the public interest, "that cannot be the kind of quid pro quo that results in impeachment." It was perhaps the single most shocking declaration made over the course of a trial with plenty of them. I was astonished by the categorical nature of that "cannot," of the extreme subjectivity of measuring justice on what a president believed. Alan made no qualifications; there was no "generally" or "usually." Barry leaned over to me and whispered one of his favorite family sayings: "He may be smart, but he sure isn't clever." Alan had gone too far.

An immediate Democratic question was sent up to the chief justice, asking us to respond. Schiff was at the lectern practically before Roberts finished his question. "I would be delighted," he said with a smile. Schiff pounced on the argument, as he would continue to do for the following days, whenever this newly minted Dersh Doctrine came up (and when it didn't, raising it himself). Using a hypothetical scenario in which Barack Obama had demanded a quid pro quo from the then president of Russia, Schiff asked, "Are we really ready to say that would be okay, that Barack Obama asked Medvedev to investigate his opponent and would withhold money from an ally that needed to defend itself to get an investigation of Mitt Romney?" I glanced over at Romney, who looked up from his notes with a good-natured smile. We had to have his vote, and we were not above letting him know it.

The Republicans seemed shocked by Alan's argument too. Even Pat Philbin—who had so mischaracterized our due process offers to Trump—later seemed to distance the White House from Dershowitz's view, referring to the "more radical portion of his explanation of his theory." The response from the media and experts was ruthless and immediate. A Watergate prosecutor said the statement was "the most ridiculous thing I've ever heard," and many others piled on. Schumer later held a press conference, warning that "the Dershowitz argument frankly would unleash a monster; more aptly, it would unleash a monarch." We would not see Dershowitz the next day; he was not at the counsel table, blaming a prior commitment in Miami and difficulties in rebooking his plane ticket owing to the Super Bowl. Indeed, Wednesday was the last we would see of him in the Senate for the remainder of the trial.

I was also encouraged that day by witnessing three out of four of our potential GOP allies experiencing our ongoing challenge: trying to squeeze actual information out of the White House. At 8:53 P.M., Romney asked, "On what specific date did President Trump first order the hold on security assistance to Ukraine, and did he explain the reason at that time?" It was a penetrating question, and earlier Collins and Murkowski had attacked the same salient, questioning whether Trump had ever mentioned Joe or Hunter Biden in connection with Ukrainian corruption before Vice President Biden entered the presidential race. Philbin dodged the questions, including by saying he was limited to the record. As Schiff was quick to point out, that was not true. Purpura had made that clear earlier when he cited a brand-new *Daily Beast* story. I thought we had gained some ground. But where was that first question from Lamar Alexander?

THAT EVENING, I SPOTTED REPRESENTATIVES Pramila Jayapal and Mary Gay Scanlon from Judiciary. I slipped away from our table to go sit with them at the back of the room, where there is always a row of red-cushioned seats reserved for members of the House who drop in. We got to discussing the Dershowitz Doctrine, and I told them about my history with him. They were surprised to hear that I had been trained by and owed a lot to the man who was making these arguments.

From our vantage point in the back of the room we noted how smoothly the question process operated on the Democratic side. (We couldn't see how the GOP was running things from that spot.) The staff members maintained a list of who had spoken and who wanted to. As senators proposed or deliberated possible questions, they huddled with the staff to avoid repetition and achieve sufficient coverage of important topics. When a question was agreed upon, it was walked across the hall to the minority leader's office, typed up, and printed out in fourteen-point type for ease of reading by the chief justice. Then it was affixed to the question card and returned to the senator in time for him or her to send the question to the desk.

The three of us kept chatting as the battle for Bolton raged. The White House had finally come up with a defense to calling Bolton, but it was one that left Jayapal and Scanlon shaking their heads. If the Senate subpoenaed Bolton, Trump would sue to fight it on privilege grounds and call witnesses of his own, dragging out the trial and grinding the Senate to a halt. That argument suffered from several flaws, one being the fact that the litigation might well have been thrown out. But we had a strategy up our sleeve for that possibility: set aside a week for depositions and let the chief justice decide right then and there which witnesses requested by the parties were material. "We have a perfectly good chief justice," Schiff argued, "we are willing to do that." The other side, he pointed out, was not—because they didn't want the information to see the light of day. We needed all the help we could get with those four Republican votes; perhaps they would perceive ceding authority to Roberts, a GOP icon, as a token of our good faith.

Still hopeful we would get witnesses, Barry was hard at work back in S-219 on an outline of the possible examination of Bolton. He was teaming on the project with Sarah Istel (the cheerful young litigator we had poached from Paul, Weiss earlier in the year) and Dan Noble of Intel (a sandy-haired former federal prosecutor known for his bulging biceps and big brain). We were anticipating a Friday vote on subpoenas—meaning the Bolton deposition could be as soon as the weekend.

I had kept close watch on Alexander throughout the day. He continued to make eye contact with the House team. A trial lawyer knows that when your jurors start evading your eyes, you've lost them. But I was troubled when the end of the day came, and he still had not spoken. A weary Schiff, in shorter than usual remarks back in the war room, praised the managers' arguments, said we had finished strong, and should all get some rest. He needed it most of all; you never would have known it from seeing him in action, but he had a terrible toothache, had been pounding Advil all day long, and needed a root canal as soon as we could manage a day off.

THE NEXT MORNING, THURSDAY, AS we gathered back in H-142, we were treated to live TV images of Trump's former co-conspirator Lev Parnas wandering the Capitol. He had continued to provide important documents to us; he wanted to see for himself what we were doing with them. (Because he wore an ankle bracelet, he was not able to gain access to the Senate galleries to watch the trial.) As we settled in and the managers dug through their bags to pull out their Q&A notebooks and highlighters, we discussed polling data that boosted all our spirits. You, the American people—by overwhelming numbers ranging as high as 75 percent—wanted a fair trial, meaning witnesses. Even many Republicans and Trump supporters felt that way. In our era of polarization, that unity was welcome. It also meant that there would be a price to pay for refusing to subpoena Bolton.

The day got off to an exciting start when Senator Rand Paul sent up a question evidently identifying the whistleblower. The chief justice refused to read it; it was the only question that was rejected out of hand. His decision was confirmation of his common sense, which we might have to rely on very shortly if he was called upon to break a 50–50 tie on witnesses. True to form, Paul immediately marched outside like an insolent teenager, read the question aloud to the press, then tweeted it. Of all one hundred senators, he was the only one who tried a stunt like that.

Finally, at 6:19 P.M. came the moment I had been waiting for: Alexander rose from his seat to pose his first question. For the first time in the trial, we heard the mellifluous voice with its Tennessee intonation. He thanked the chief justice for recognizing him, then said, "I send a question to the desk on behalf of myself, Senator Daines, and Senator Cruz." Uh-oh. That was not a good sign. Steve Daines and Ted Cruz were *never* going to support impeachment. I waited anxiously as the senator handed his card to a page, who then walked it to the dais. Here it came: "The question is . . . for the House managers." So far, so good. "Compare the bipartisanship in the Nixon, Clinton, and Trump impeachment proceedings. Specifically, how bipartisan was the vote in the House of Representatives to authorize and direct the House committees to begin formal impeachment inquiries for each of the three Presidents?"

Damn. My heart fell, although I maintained a poker face. I could see my colleagues attempting the same. The question certainly suggested we would be looking to the chief as the tiebreaker. Zoe Lofgren was the perfect manager to handle our response, having worked on all three impeachments. She did so adeptly, by pointing out that historically, while senators initially dug in on their respective sides, there had been a coming together once evidence was released, the kind of coming together she believed could be achieved if the senators would just agree to hear from Bolton. I continued watching Alexander and saw his eyes shift away from Lofgren and all of us—a telltale sign that you have lost a juror.

Back in our war room for the dinner break, we huddled with the managers. Schiff joked, "When this is over, who's up for a root canal?" Though his tooth was still bothering him, apparently adrenaline was the best medicine. After the break, he went right back at the White

House and the senators on the witnesses, energetically returning to our offer: let the chief justice decide who is material, take a week for depositions, and see where we are.

We thought this plan was eminently reasonable, but the signal we got back from our GOP hopefuls was ominous as Alexander pulled Murkowski into his orbit. Her first question after the break delighted us: "Why should this body *not* call Ambassador Bolton?" That was a query that contained its own answer, and one sharply in our favor. But a little later she pivoted, joining with Alexander and a group of others, including Graham (one of the president's most ardent champions), in rephrasing the question. It was still leading, but now in the exact opposite direction: even if Bolton testified, she asked, "Isn't it true that the allegations still would not rise to the level of an impeachable offense and that, therefore, for this and other reasons, his testimony would add nothing to this case?"

It wasn't conclusive of course. Maybe this was simply Murkowski tagging along to get the other side of the answer, I told myself. Still, it didn't send a message of hope. If we lost both her and Alexander, there would be no 50–50 tie for us to ask the chief to break.

I told Barry and Jerry that I was going to go to the back of the room to take the temperature of the senators while they remained at the trial table with the others. The message I got was not good. Senator Chris Coons told me, "You guys have done great, but the room has shifted." He attributed it to McConnell's cracking down, as well as the exhaustion of the long trial days. Even Romney, perennially cheerful, was frustrated. He felt he could not get answers to his questions from the White House team and that now he could not even get the chance to pose them. "As you may see," he said to me, "I'm not getting called on a lot." Senator Michael Bennet, whom I had known since we both started out as young lawyers in D.C. nearly three decades ago, lamented the loss of GOP moderates who he felt would of course have voted for witnesses in days gone by. My friend Sherrod Brown put it more bluntly: the Republican senators were scared. I guess Schiff's "head on a pike" comment had been on the mark.

As I was talking with the senators at the rear of the chamber, a swell of confusion washed across the floor. There seemed to be a misunderstanding involving Amy Klobuchar and the question shuttling process that had been working so flawlessly for the past two days. Something was amiss with the card she had sent. The chief justice was trading different cards with the clerk, trying to find the correct one. People were laughing or muttering. Then Klobuchar—clad all in red, tired at the end of a long day, eager to get back on the campaign trail—put her midwestern can-do attitude on full display. She simply grabbed a pen, wrote her question out, never mind the whole page system, marched it right down the aisle, elbows pumping, and delivered it to the dais herself.

It was a benign, open-ended question directed at the House managers, but everybody had been thrown off and distracted by the commotion. The next thing I knew, there was some kind of a hubbub at our trial table and Nadler was marching to the lectern with as much gusto as Klobuchar had exhibited on her descent down the aisle. Once there, he called out the president's counsel for their "usual nonsense," his voice filled with passion and purpose. As I had been trying to get clues to where we stood with our four Republicans, Jerry had already sensed we were not going to get the votes that we needed. The "usual nonsense" had worked. We'd been hearing the same lies about due process, about four facts that would never change (until they became six), about executive privilege and immunity; the president's counsel had been using slants on these weak arguments to justify their client's conduct all year.

Jerry pointed out that we were on the verge of having a trial with no witnesses, which was absurd, as "any ten-year-old knows." Then he cut to the heart of the matter, stating the central question before us: "Did the President abuse his power by violating the law to withhold military aid from a foreign country and extort that country into helping him—into helping his reelection campaign—by slandering his opponent?" Yes, he did. Jerry listed the irrelevant distractions presented by the defense and dismissed them, literally with the wave of his hand. And with that, the time expired and the chief gaveled the day to a close. It was another strong blast of truth from the chairman.

As I mingled with the senators in the back of the room, the consensus seemed to be that Senator Collins would vote for Bolton and perhaps other witnesses. We were confident of Romney, so that meant forty-nine if we held our own caucus. It was so close. Then the blow fell: Senator Debbie Stabenow whispered to me that Alexander would be a no, making fifty-one votes impossible. It didn't come as a shock but was profoundly disappointing nonetheless. (Although if I had to hear it from anyone, I was glad it was Stabenow, a grandmother of five who had a comforting manner—as if she were taking me aside to tell me my parents were getting divorced.) And indeed, a little after 11:00 P.M., Alexander released a public statement: "The Constitution does not give the Senate the power to remove the president from office and ban him from this year's ballot simply for actions that are inappropriate."

I huddled with Barry, who snorted. "Inappropriate? Inappropriate is when you belch at a dinner party; not when you extort a foreign leader to attack our elections!" Alexander had conceded that we had established the quid pro quo that we had so worried about proving back in September: "There is no need for more evidence to conclude that the president withheld United States aid, at least in part, to pressure Ukraine to investigate the Bidens; the House managers have proved this with what they call a 'mountain of overwhelming evidence.'" No matter: without Alexander we would not be getting 51 votes for witnesses. Now it was all down to Murkowski and the chief justice. We were still hoping for a 50–50 tie that Roberts would break. On her way out of the Senate that night, Murkowski told the press she was deliberating, brandished her two big trial notebooks, and promised she was going to go back to her office and study them.

I asked Barry what the confusion had been at our table before Nadler's remarks. Apparently, it had not been his turn to speak. As he headed to the lectern, Schiff had called out repeatedly to try to signal him, but a focused Nadler had blown right past him. Jerry was thinking about the question and his powerful, passionate response; he hadn't realized it was the last slot of the day and had been assigned elsewhere.

"Dude," I asked Barry, "how did you let that happen?" Counsel was supposed to be directing traffic.

"Fuck you," he shot back, "you couldn't have stopped him either. He moved like a gazelle!" As we were squabbling, Aaron (the father of two young and boisterous boys) approached us. "Am I going to have to separate the two of you?" he said, smiling. Growing serious, he lowered his voice. He said that Jerry had been preoccupied with difficult news from home that day. Joyce's health had taken a downturn, and Jerry was going to head back to New York a day early. That made sense to us. It was a miracle that Nadler had performed as well as he had these past months, considering the strain he had been under, from every front.

Trump, of course, attempted to make hay of the late-night crossed wires. He claimed on Friday morning, in true playground-instigator form, that Schiff and Nadler were fighting. In fact, when Schiff saw me at our morning meeting, the first thing he asked was how Joyce was doing. He was understanding and gracious, telling me to send his warmest wishes to her and Jerry.

FRIDAY WAS RESERVED FOR FINAL arguments on witnesses and documents, followed by the vote on those issues. Right before we entered the chamber, we learned through the grapevine that we had lost Murkowski (she made it official shortly thereafter). So we knew from the moment we started the trial on Friday that we would not have even fifty total votes.

We were strangely cheerful nonetheless. As we settled into our seats, I took stock of where we were on our trial strategy. We had powerfully told the story as planned, convincing many of the senators that Trump had done what we said. Alexander had admitted the quid pro quo, and Senator Ben Sasse had said that "Lamar speaks for lots and lots of us." If that meant even half of the GOP caucus, then about seventy senators accepted the core factual proposition we had worked so hard to prove. That was a blow to the White House defense that the call was perfect and the president had done nothing wrong. Senator Marco Rubio even went so far as to admit the president's actions "meet a standard of impeachment" (though he hastened to add that not everything that met that standard merited a vote to convict). So far, none of the Democrats had come out against us on the ultimate conviction vote, and we were hearing that we would hold all three of our red-state Ds on the subpoena votes that day, in addition to picking up Romney and Collins on at least some of them.

We had come oh so close to getting Bolton and perhaps other witnesses, and possibly breaking things open. It was not meant to be, but we had helped convince about 75 percent of Americans that it was wrong for the Senate not to hear from those witnesses, according to poll after poll. Whatever the Senate did, the country was listening, and that mattered. Schiff had articulated it well the night before, prior to sending everyone home to get some rest: "Now we're going to make our argument straight to the American people." Indeed, Friday was the day when we truly began our primary appeal to you.

We had some help. A bit past noon, *The New York Times* broke its latest story on Bolton: his book said Trump had advanced his pressure campaign against Ukraine during an Oval Office conversation in early May. The president had told Bolton to call Zelensky to ensure a meeting with Giuliani to discuss the investigations of the former vice president. The participants at the meeting included Mulvaney, Giuliani, and none other than my friend Pat Cipollone, who would soon be seated just a few feet away from us.

Shortly after 1:02 P.M., when we were already seated at the trial table, a page rushed in and handed me an updated version of the *Times* article: Trump was now denying the conversation had happened. That put the factual dispute front and center just in time for our argument about the Bolton subpoena. I leaned over to Goldman and whispered,

"There is a God." Manager after manager hammered away at the sheer absurdity of the Republicans' position, and of the fact that they would not hear a single witness when there had been a previous average of thirty-three witnesses at Senate impeachment trials. It was like *Darkness at Noon,* the 1940 novel of Stalinist justice. Or maybe Kafka was the better comparison. It was just *so* ludicrous you had to laugh. The combination of seeing the absurdity of it all and knowing we had held on to all of our Democrats buoyed our morale.

My spirits were also lifted by a whispered conversation I had with Schiff during the presentations. He had an antique Waltham pocket watch that he would leave out on the table with a white face and a many-faceted edge. I pointed to it and asked what the story was. "It was my grandfather's," he explained. I was wearing my dad's wristwatch, and he gestured to it and said, "That's a beautiful one too." I explained to him that it was also a family heirloom—a rectangular gold Bulova, purchased after my dad got out of the army in World War II. I told Schiff my dad must have known that someday his son would be an ambassador, because the model is called Excellency. He laughed, then commented on how amazing it was that they used these watches all those years ago and now we do; it's a deep connection with the past.

I flashed back to watching the Watergate hearings with my father in the hamburger stand, how he admired that fight for American values. I told Schiff how proud my dad would have been of our effort, win or lose. I felt that pride too, and a sense of coming full circle, irrespective of how the Senate voted.

The atmosphere in our war room had also recovered. I took the pulse of its regulars, including Ashley Etienne, the Speaker's sharp comms aide; her equivalent on Schiff's staff, the thoughtful Patrick Boland (projecting calm no matter the crisis); and our big Judiciary contingent, including Sarah, Kerry, Maggie, Sophie, and Joshua. Everyone seemed sanguine.

Our feelings were captured by Senator Elizabeth Warren, who came in on a break to speak with us. "You got up to defend what is decent and right," she said, making eye contact with each of us. "You made us all proud in the Democratic caucus: proud to be Democrats, proud to be in Congress, and proud to be Americans." Though she was clearly a woman on the campaign trail, I knew she meant every word. "So I just wanted to say thank you for all you've done."

She told us we had been especially effective that day by playing back opposing counsel's own words, revealing their contradictions. In particular, we had used the clip of Mike Purpura saying there was not a single witness, even as we were calling for Bolton to appear. She praised the team effort and the amazing staff work. Schiff told her that the staff had moved into this room and hadn't left for two weeks. "Well, that explains why it smells in here!" she said, making us all laugh.

Her tone turned more serious as she shook her head, speaking freely: "It's incredible that we can't find *four* Republicans—we don't need the entire Republican Party! Just four. That was not a proud moment for our country . . . but things will get better." Warren spoke to the issue of the collapse of bipartisanship. "Sadly," she continued, "the lesson is, if you can get the party behind you, you can do whatever you like. If they would only hang together, the fever would break—but they're getting what they wanted: tax breaks; freedom for polluters; right-wing judges . . ." Despite this grim diagnosis, it was clear that she believed that eventually the country would move past this divide.

After we returned from the break, Schiff concluded our daylong argument. Harnessing all his Churchillian eloquence, he urged a packed, rapt room to consider that "the importance of a fair trial here is not less than in every courtroom in America; it is *greater* than in any courtroom in America, because we set the example for America."

Before the vote on Bolton and the other witnesses, there was a long quorum call—a procedural device that allowed McConnell to take an indefinite time-out and hold everyone on or near the floor. He needed to do this because his caucus could not agree on how to proceed. A third of the GOP wanted to go directly to a vote on the articles and end that day. They wanted it to be over as soon as possible. A third wanted to vote on Monday to avoid the appearance of rushing justice, and a third wanted to vote on Wednesday, to look even more reasonable. Under Senate rules, McConnell also had to have the Democrats on board, and we were holding out for Wednesday to use our bully pulpit to continue making the case to the American people. (It would also mean Trump would have to deliver the State of the Union on Tuesday night, while his impeachment trial was still going on.)

The extended break gave people who had been in this room together for trial days of up to fourteen hours a chance to relax and talk informally. For me, it was an opportunity to stroll around the chamber and visit with those on both sides of the aisle. Ted Cruz—a man who didn't agree with us on virtually anything—said to several of us, "I've tried a lot of cases, and you did a great job. You did not persuade me, but I admire your skills." He was not alone. I spoke with other friends on the Republican side like Jim Inhofe, an arch-conservative who had been one of the champions of my ambassadorial nomination after we hit it off on my courtesy call. He had some kind words for our effort but added that he was ready for it to be over ("beyond ready," he added, with a piercing Oklahoma stare). I knew him and many of his colleagues to be people of principle, though I wondered how many of them would have rushed to convict a Democratic president of the same conduct.

The long hiatus also gave me the opportunity to probe a new idea for getting the Senate to hold Trump accountable. I had talked on and off throughout the trial with Senator Joe Manchin. He was the longest serving of the three Democrats we were worried about. We were relieved to have held on to all three on the coming witness vote and hoped to do the same on conviction. He told me he still hadn't made up his mind on the ultimate question, but that he had another idea. What about a censure resolution—that is, a statement by the Senate condemning Trump? Because it was clear we were not going to have the votes for witnesses or a conviction, why not do censure instead? "It's better than nothing," he told me. Manchin showed me two censure resolutions that he had already prepared: one that was more politic and one that was very tough—or, as Manchin put it, "an ass-kissing and an ass-kicking" version. I would have been fine with either, but I told him I doubted it would work unless he got a Republican co-sponsor. Unfortunately, he could not find a single GOP adherent for the concept of censuring the president—even those like Alexander who believed the conduct was "inappropriate." When Sasse had said, "Lamar speaks for lots and lots of us," that also—evidently—referred to an aversion to taking any action.

At 5:35 P.M. the quorum call ended, and it was time for the votes on new evidence. First the Senate would be polled on the general question of whether consideration of *any* witness or document subpoena was in order. It failed as expected, 51–49. Before voting on the specific subpoenas for Bolton and the others, we learned even if we had held on to Murkowski, it wouldn't have mattered. In response to a parliamentary inquiry from Schumer, Chief Justice Roberts stated that he would not have broken a tie, rejecting the precedent set by Chief Justice Chase in 1868. Roberts felt it would be antidemocratic for him to intervene if the Senate itself couldn't decide. I suppose that was some backhanded consolation for the fact that we lost the vote on Bolton by that same 51–49 margin.

We did get our way in terms of the timing of the final vote on the articles of impeachment; that would be postponed until Wednesday, February 5. Every additional day allowed us to talk to the country at large and keep people focused on the magnitude of Trump's abuse and obstruction. If we could not persuade all the senators, we would use the remaining days of the trial to persuade their bosses: you, the American people.

We were about to get some help in that effort.

CHAPTER TWELVE

"An Inescapable Conviction"

THE TRIAL DAY HAD LASTED INTO SHABBAT, SO I WOULD BE walking home through the darkened D.C. streets. As Barry raced to grab a train to New York, I began the nearly hour-long journey through blocks of empty office towers alternating with bustling sidewalks crowded by Friday night restaurant goers and bar hoppers. As I strolled, I reflected on all that had come to pass. My optimism had suffered some blows over the prior three years, but it had been repeatedly resuscitated by Americans in and outside government; by colleagues in the legal Resistance who were and are still fighting Trump indefatigably; by the press who (with occasional stumbles) have vigorously exposed the president's wrongdoing; by those in Trump's own executive branch who defied his misconduct, including Mueller and his team, for all their failure to go the distance; by the voters who had given the House the power of accountability in 2018; by the work of my House colleagues to expose Trump's two-step of abuse and obstruction; and now by an overwhelming 75 percent majority of the American people supporting a fair Senate trial with witnesses.

History hung in the balance as we made the pivot that Schiff had urged: arguing directly to you, the American people. With Alexander and Murkowski and virtually all their caucus unwilling to stop the serial abuse, a heavy responsibility would fall on Americans to determine which direction the country would travel. We would all be tested. Trump had called Ukraine the very day after the Mueller hearing, and our hearings were just about to end. History suggested that Trump's next batch of sins were nearing. I wondered if they had commenced already as I headed north, passing under streetlamps and shadows along the nighttime boulevards of downtown Washington.

Well, nobody—least of all those fifty-one senators who had voted against all witnesses—would be able to say they did not know what was coming. They had heard about it from everybody on our side, from Schiff to Nadler to Professor Karlan. As Barry had argued to the Judiciary Committee, "Our imagination is the only limit to what President Trump may do next." All had expressly warned, on repeat, that the president would keep up the abuse of power and obstruction, if he was given the opportunity. My Judiciary colleagues and I had written the pattern into the articles in black and white and included the "continuing threat" for all posterity. The American people would know whom to hold accountable when the next crisis hit. Walking amid crowded groups, then through deserted stretches, I wondered what horror might be slouching toward me, and toward all of us.

We reconvened at 11:05 a.m. on Monday, February 3, for the closing to the Senate. The weekend had been a relatively quiet one. Schiff had gotten his root canal on Saturday and was feeling much better. We had taken one last run that weekend at getting Bolton's testimony in the Senate by inviting him to submit an affidavit. A flat refusal was the reply from his lawyer; he would appear only under Senate subpoena. Bolton seemed to be playing a game: he evidently wanted to be seen as offering to tell his story so he would not be criticized later, but not to be viewed as cooperating with the Democrats. Who knew if he really wanted to talk at all (he certainly had passed up enough opportunities), or if he just wanted to have a rebuttal point when interviewers hit him after the book came out.

The managers planned to split our two hours, using the first for a traditional closing, with Crow, Demings, and Jeffries summarizing our case. After the defense wrapped, the managers would utilize the last hour to speak from their hearts about what they'd seen, taking one last and more personal run at the Senate. Although we would not convict, there was plenty to do in that chamber. We would be addressing the three Democrats we needed to hold, as well as the two Republicans who were still up for grabs, Romney and Collins. The final appeal would be intensely human and individual. Instead of crowding into our stuffy room that weekend, staff had worked from our respective offices and homes on the slides and helped to structure the arguments into a logical sequence. Jerry, as ever, continued to push us, even from Joyce's bedside. Just tell the story, he advised. Keep it simple, and make it compelling.

Crow was the first to walk from the managers' table to the lectern, anchoring our endeavor in the full span of American history. He began by quoting extensively from Daniel Webster's famous Seventh of March speech, emphasizing the role of the Senate: "a body to which the country looks with confidence, for wise, moderate, patriotic, and healing counsels." He also invoked the words of Alexander Hamilton about the Senate's "independent" role in impeachment, urging the legislators to set partisanship aside and hold the president accountable for his abuse and obstruction. Paraphrasing Barry Goldwater during Watergate, Crow ended with his own fiery question: "How many falsehoods can we take? When will it be one too many?"

Demings then brought the senators to the present day, outlining one last time the vast evidence the Republicans had refused to acknowledge. "President Trump abused the extraordinary powers he alone holds . . . He then used those unique powers to wage an unprecedented campaign to obstruct Congress and cover up his wrongdoing." With her characteristic intensity—that of a former law enforcement officer confronting a lawbreaker—she used the five chapters Judiciary had set out to organize the vast detail.

With the past and present covered, Jeffries took the lectern and pivoted to the future: "Once we strip the president's obstruction of this legal window-dressing, the consequences are as clear as they are dire for our democracy." He warned that a president who is not held to account is "more likely to engage in corruption, with impunity. This will become the new normal, with this president and for future generations." How can we be assured, he asked, that this president will not do wrong again? Tragically, that question has since been answered, at the cost of tens of thousands of American lives.

When we returned from lunch, the defense took over. I liked many of them personally, but they were firmly in the thrall of Trump, clear victims of his corrupting influence. I eyed them with both respect and sadness. After very brief words from Cipollone on the theme of "leave it to the voters," Starr kicked things off—perhaps a recognition that he had been their most effective advocate. Like Crow, his references ranged across our history, from Lincoln to RFK to Martin Luther King. He argued that we had not done enough to prove our case under American standards of "freedom and justice" and that our evidence did not rise to the "level of a high crime or misdemeanor." He received an attentive reaction, although I was sure that privately a majority of the chamber concurred with Rubio: an impeachable abuse of power had been established. Unfortunately, that did not mean they intended to act on it.

Purpura was up next, reverting to the six facts that would never change, but he had already lost the battle to prove the perfection of the president's call. That included a waning of interest among the GOP senators, judging from their wandering gazes and shifting posture while Mike spoke. Sasse had admitted that many of them agreed with Alexander, not the White House. Philbin took up the other half of the core defense case, addressing the unfairness of the process—repeating one last time the misrepresentations about how the House had behaved. Sekulow made the brazen suggestion that Trump was in fact extremely bipartisan, and went as far as showing dated footage of bills he had passed—on everything from fentanyl to farm bills—as proof. He too was addressing the question that so concerned me of our nation's terrible divide, if only to say it's not the president's fault. But surely even the president's most ardent defenders did not believe that Trump modeled cross-party relations. Cipollone closed by picking up on one of Starr's themes, urging that the members vote against conviction to "end the era of impeachment, once and for all."

The final hour in the arguments was ours, a time for the managers to speak freely to the senators and to the American people about judging Trump. Each offered a different compass to guide the way and, I thought, to navigate our nation through the partisan straits we faced. Lofgren's words reflected her faith in the Constitution, going back to the founders and their writing of that document after they had fought another abusive ruler. She spoke of the acts of Republican courage in defense of that document that she had witnessed while working on Watergate early in her career. Garcia cited scripture and said that it was our responsibility to look out for the vulnerable. "Sometimes fighting for the most vulnerable means holding the most powerful accountable." As a Catholic, she emphasized how important forgiveness was to her and how willing she had been to give Trump the benefit of the doubt. But there was no further doubt: "We all know that he will do it again."

Crow returned to the lectern to discuss his touchstone: his fellow veterans and what they had given for this country. He explained the meaning of the oath they had sworn, and Trump had betrayed, urging accountability for that betrayal. Demings recalled that her North Star as a chief of police was "always [being] concerned about the message we were sending." What message were we sending to the nation, she asked, were we to let Trump get away with what he had done? Jeffries followed, delivering his most majestic speech yet: "If the Senate chooses to normalize lawlessness . . . then America is in the wilderness." He finished by also quoting scripture, urging the senators and all of us to "walk by faith"—whatever that faith might be. Each of the managers had a different take on what guided them, and I thought back to McBath's prayer and Raskin's coda the morning before Judiciary voted back in December. For the final messages to the Senate, the managers had offered articles of faith to accompany the articles of impeachment. So many different guides, from the Constitution to scripture to our oaths, all pointing in the same direction. That gave me hope.

And then it was time for one last set of remarks from Schiff. We were on the edge of our seats, as were the Republicans. Even they recognized they were witnessing one of the greatest orators ever to speak in this chamber. Schiff's mind too was on our partisan polarization—the same issue we had discussed on the floor of the House the night impeachment was voted out. He began by quoting Lincoln, telling the senators, "'We are not enemies, but friends. We must not be enemies.' If Lincoln could speak these words during the Civil War, surely we can live them now and overcome our divisions and our animosities." He summarized our case and responded to the defense: "If abuse of power is not impeachable—even though it is clear the founders considered it the highest of all high crimes and misdemeanors—but if it were not impeachable, then a whole range of utterly unacceptable conduct in a president would now be beyond reach. Trump could offer Alaska to the Russians in exchange for support in the next election or decide to move to Mar-a-Lago permanently and let Jared Kushner run the country . . . Because those things are not necessarily criminal, this argument would allow that he could not be impeached for such abuses of power." He described the pattern that had brought us to this moment: "Can we be confident that Americans and not foreign powers will get to decide, and that the president will shun any further foreign interference in our democratic affairs? The short, plain, sad, incontestable answer is, no, you can't." And he sounded the theme that had brought me and Barry to work in the House almost exactly one year before, one that had resonated all year long, one that would echo loudly in the months ahead and still does today:

> You can't trust this president to do the right thing, not for one minute, not for one election, not for the sake of our country.

> You just can't. He will not change, and you know it . . . He has made that clear himself without self-awareness or hesitation. A man without character or ethical compass will never find his way . . . You will not change him. You cannot constrain him. He is who he is. Truth matters little to him. What's right matters even less. And decency matters not at all.

He also focused the full force of his rhetoric away from Trump's conduct and directly onto that of the senators. "Every single vote—even a single vote, by a single member—can change the course of history. It is said that a single man or woman of courage makes a majority. Is there one among you who will say, 'enough'?" He was addressing the senators, but he was also speaking to the members of the American nation—to each one of us, and the momentous choice we will face come November 2020.

Afterward, a line of senators swarmed our table. Schumer pounded Schiff on the back so vigorously I was afraid he would knock him over. Others took a lighter tone, with Mark Warner telling Schiff, "You did great, even though you had Norm Eisen as one of your lawyers." We had resolved not to let down our own side as the Clinton managers had done theirs, and we had succeeded in that. But had we hung on to our three Democrats, and would we get any Republican votes? Now we and the president's trial team would leave the chamber, and the senators would proceed to three days of stating their views. One by one they would cycle through the chamber to give ten minutes of remarks on what *they* thought and how they would vote. On my way out I asked Manchin, as good a proxy as any, for his reaction. Schiff's was a hard-hitting speech, he readily acknowledged, but his mind was not made up. He needed to digest everything and wanted to see whether the president would express any remorse at the State of the Union address on Tuesday, the following night.

• • •

There was no sign of contrition whatsoever in the State of the Union address. Trump was belligerent and defiant, beginning the evening by refusing to shake Speaker Pelosi's extended hand. Although impeachment was not expressly mentioned, Trump decorated one of his most ardent anti-impeachment attack dogs in the middle of his speech. The first lady pinned a medal on Rush Limbaugh as Trump saluted him in his remarks, which added more falsehoods to a rapidly growing pile of them. Jerry was back from New York, where Joyce was doing better, thankfully. He very visibly read his pocket Constitution while awaiting Trump's stream of falsehoods (the final tally was more than thirty, according to fact-checkers). After listening to his screed, Pelosi spontaneously tore up her copy of the presidential address. I was only sorry that there was no room on the rostrum for an industrial shredder through which she could feed his sheaf of self-congratulatory fabrications. Not that I expected a redemptive performance. After all, within twenty-four hours the Senate would be voting on whether to remove him from office, and historically speaking, the man is not at his best when he feels cornered.

Wednesday, February 5, was the final day of the trial. The senators would make the last of their individual remarks and then come together again for their final judgment. Before the 4:00 P.M. vote, Barry was taking Sarah Istel and Joshua Matz out for lunch. It would be a luxury to join them, but I decided not to go. Instead, I made the long walk from our office in Rayburn down through the tunnels and over to the Senate floor to hear Mitt Romney deliver his ten-minute speech explaining which way he would be voting. For good luck, I went along the path that took me by the bust of Winston Churchill in the small House Rotunda on the first floor of the Capitol. His writings had been my guide to the past three years and had helped bring me to this moment. The sculpture was a massive bronze rendering of Sir Winston's head that captured his bulldog tenacity, his brow furrowed above a steely gaze and pursed lips. I said a silent prayer that Romney would show the kind of courage radiating from the bust. There had been no Republican senator with whom I had spent more time talking over the course of the trial, and I was grateful that he had been so willing to vote for witnesses—defying party to do so.

Based on his sincere inquisitiveness during our interactions, I also had reason to hope that, were there to be that one member among the Republican Party who would be willing to say "enough!" to Donald Trump, it would be Mitt Romney. When I got to the floor of the Senate, I was practically alone in the room. I was surprised that my expectations for Romney's remarks were not shared. But I was glad to have the time to just sit and listen in relative isolation, after a year of relentless frenzy and expectation.

I arrived shortly before 2:00 P.M. and took a seat at the back of the room just as Chris Murphy was delivering his justification for his vote to remove the president. Murphy—a Democrat from Connecticut whom I had known since my ambassadorship—was explaining that his parents had been Republicans; his mom was still a Republican. They voted for members of both parties, and believed that "what mattered in politics wasn't really someone's party. It was whether you were honest and decent." He spoke about the fragility of democracy and picked up on Jerry's theme of treachery and betrayal by the Senate, saying, "What happened here over the last two weeks is as much a corruption as Trump's scheme was. This trial was simply an extension of Trump's crimes. No documents, no witnesses; the first ever impeachment trial in the Senate without either. John Bolton practically *begging* to come here and tell his first-hand account of the president's corruption? Denied . . . This was a show trial: a gift-wrapped present for a grateful party leader. We became complicit in the very attacks on democracy that this body is supposed to guard against."

Murphy identified this moment as exceptional because Republicans had put party before decency. He hoped that if a Democratic president had done this, we would have the "courage to stand up to our base." With characteristic thoughtfulness, he recognized that it would not be easy. He had thought about it and struggled with it, but ultimately believed that he would hold the Democrats to this same standard and vote to remove. We need that spirit if our country is to survive, if our democracy is to survive, and if *we* are to survive.

Although it was surely a coincidence, there could not have been a better introduction for Romney. He entered as Murphy was discussing the challenge of voting against your own party. I watched him, with his handsome face and graying hair, listening thoughtfully to the end of Murphy's remarks. Murphy finished his speech by mentioning the cult of Trump's presidency and how it required a recalibration of our entire system.

As Romney rose at his desk, the floor remained largely vacant. Murphy stayed and Brian Schatz showed up, as did Pat Leahy. Those three made up the Democratic senatorial contingent. The only Republican members I saw were Senator Roger Wicker and Senator David Perdue, who was presiding. A handful of Senate staff and I were the only other people on the floor as Romney readied his remarks on his lectern. The press gallery was relatively empty as well, with just over a dozen of the seats occupied.

Then Romney began: "The allegations made in the articles of impeachment are very serious. As a Senator-juror, I swore an oath, before God, to exercise 'impartial justice.' I am profoundly religious. My faith is at the heart of who I am. I take an oath before God as enormously consequential," he said, getting choked up. He paused to get ahold of himself. From my vantage point across the floor, he seemed to be fighting back tears.

He recovered and proceeded to dissect the case, but not before acknowledging that judging the president and leader of his own party would be the most difficult decision he had ever faced in his long and consequential life. He boiled down the president's case: that there could be no impeachment without a statutory crime, that the Bidens' conduct justified the president's actions, and that we should let the voters decide. Harking back to his and my conversation with Starr, he systematically refuted each. He explained that his reading of the law put the lie to "no crime, no impeachment." As for the facts, it was hard to explain the president's motives as being anything other than personal. "There is no question in my mind that were their names not Biden, the President would never have done what he did." He then addressed the keystone of the president's case, the democracy defense, explaining that it got the law backward: "The verdict is ours to render under our Constitution."

By this stage, the media had realized that something was going on; the press gallery now had more than thirty reporters, with more streaming in by the moment. They furiously scribbled down what came next, the core of Romney's presentation:

> The grave question the Constitution tasks senators to answer is whether the president committed an act so extreme and egregious that it rises to the level of a "high crime and misdemeanor."
>
> Yes, he did.
>
> The president asked a foreign government to investigate his political rival.
>
> The president withheld vital military funds from that government to press it to do so.
>
> The president delayed funds for an American ally at war with Russian invaders.
>
> The president's purpose was personal and political.
>
> Accordingly, the president is guilty of an appalling abuse of the public trust.

Romney proceeded to indicate that he had supported "a great deal of what the president has done." But, he said, "were I to ignore the evidence that has been presented, and disregard what I believe my oath and the Constitution demands of me for the sake of a partisan end, it would, I fear, expose my character to history's rebuke and the censure of my own conscience." He acknowledged that the president and his supporters would attack him for his comments and his forthcoming vote. But he asked, "Does anyone seriously believe that I would consent to these consequences other than from an inescapable conviction that my oath before God demanded it of me?" He knew that it would not be enough to remove the president from office. But "with my vote, I will tell my children and their children that I did my duty to the best of my ability, believing that my country expected it of me. I will only be one name among many, no more no less, to future generations of Americans who look at the record of this trial. They will note merely that I was among the senators who determined that what the President did was wrong, grievously wrong."

He ended on a poignant note—one that spoke to all Americans who would soon decide on the fate of the president at the ballot box: "We're all footnotes at best in the annals of history. But in the most powerful nation on earth, the nation conceived in liberty and justice, that distinction is enough for any citizen."

Schiff's call for just one senator to demonstrate such courage had been answered. So had the defense's point that no Republican supported impeachment. It was no footnote, it was an exclamation point, written in bold red ink. Romney had just become the first American in the 231-year history of our constitutional republic who would vote to convict a president of his own party in a Senate trial. I sat, astounded by what I had just witnessed and heard. The full Senate vote would acquit a high criminal and enable him to continue his abusive career. But to suggest that he would be doing so unchecked no longer seemed accurate. A member of his own party had just checked him and set an example for all Americans come November. I felt lucky, and moved, to have been among the few to have seen it.

As I walked down the hall afterward, I encountered Senator Schatz, who was visibly crying. Romney's speech, he said, had restored his badly shaken faith in human nature. He later explained his tears to a reporter: "Because we all need to believe that this place can work, and this place can only work if people occasionally put country over party." He was talking about the Senate, but he might as well have been talking about the entire idea of America.

Infused with inspiration, I went into Schumer's office and talked with my friends there who had been running the mechanics behind the scenes. I joked that Romney's words were an antidote to their usual cynicism; they were some of the most brutal realists I'd encountered in Washington. But they objected to my characterization: "We are institutionalists, Norm. We believe in the Senate; that makes us optimists." I was delighted to have the company, and we discussed how impeachment was only the penultimate safeguard in the Constitution; the will of the American people was the ultimate protection.

THE SENATE AND STAFF ALL gathered together in the chamber at 4:04 P.M. for the final vote on the articles of impeachment. Jerry took his usual seat, and Barry and I took ours, directly across from him. The clerk read the articles from poster-sized cards—another tradition of the Senate, and one that made for error-free scansion from large type. It was an ephemeral moment that I took a pause to cherish. I had helped assemble these words over many months, read the earlier iterations to myself again and again sitting at my desk, and heard the final version read at critical junctures in the Judiciary Committee, the House, and the Senate. Now the articles were being proclaimed for the last time. I hung on to every word.

Chairman Nadler listened contemplatively, running his finger along the ornamental nails decorating his chair as the articles were read. He had labored so hard to bring this day about. We would not be here if not for his leadership over the past year. A slight, sardonic smile flickered when the clerk came to the sentence about Trump's pattern of conduct. Jerry had been fighting that pattern longer than any of us.

Then the senators cast their votes in alphabetical order. We began with Article I: Abuse of Power. The first of our once-hoped-for

GOP swing votes to state his verdict was Lamar Alexander. He pronounced his "Not guilty" in a halfhearted fashion, far from the thunderous tenor that some of his colleagues would employ. We hear what we want to hear, but I thought I could detect in his tone that he knew he was not doing the right thing by choosing party and policy over principle. Collins was the next to bow to her president and party, stating "Not guilty" in the tone of one who was proving a point. I repressed a jolt of nausea, the disappointment punching me in the gut, though I should have known better. Murkowski, on the other hand, had an expression and cadence of regret as she uttered her vote. In her comments she had hardly been triumphal: she focused on the failures of the institution as a whole. I knew she had wrestled with her decision, and I found it difficult to feel much opprobrium toward her.

Any queasiness I had felt from hearing Collins's acquittal was settled with each one of the "guilty" votes that the Democrats cast—first Jones, then Manchin and Sinema. I admired Jones, whose vote perhaps was even more personally and politically difficult than Romney's. Jones was coming up for reelection in the heart of Trump country, Alabama. Mitt's next cycle (if he even ran) was years away, and his state of Utah contained many who were ambivalent about Trump even if they ultimately voted for him. Manchin's vote was up in the air until the very last second. He had brought two speeches with him, one to acquit and one to convict. He made up his mind only shortly before he spoke. I wondered what the likes of Rubio and Cruz must be thinking, as senators who had actively opposed Trump, even warning their fellow Republicans and the country of his unfitness, yet who were now passing up the opportunity to do something about it. The final vote was 52–48.

The second article failed along party lines, 53–47. Even Romney fell for the White House position that we had been too hasty in not litigating. It was a Catch-22: Trump argued in the McGahn and grand jury cases that we had no right to court relief, and in impeachment that we had to go to court. We did hold on to all three of our swing Democrats on the obstruction count, after fearing that one or more might split the baby.

Within fifteen minutes, we were done. Barry and I were lifelong defense lawyers, and as the verdict came in, Barry whispered to me that he had never been so sorry to hear the words "not guilty." Afterward, more senators came to the table to thank the managers and us, but the mood was naturally more muted. We said goodbye to senators Jack Reed, Bob Menendez, and Debbie Stabenow, who sat directly behind us, the edges of their desks just inches away from our chairs in the close quarters of the Senate floor. They had been an unceasing source of encouragement and advice, and I told them how much we appreciated that. Stabenow gestured to our table and said, "I will never look at that space the same way again." Perhaps that was just her kind way of saying she would be glad to have a little breathing room once more, but I think she was complimenting us as well.

For the last time, we walked down the hall to the war room, where the clerks were already taking things apart. Schiff reminded us of how easy it would have been to lose Democrats, and how amazing it was that we had kept the caucus intact and even secured one Republican. Schiff described it as a phenomenal result, one we could all be proud of. He thought Romney's vote was one of the greatest acts of political courage in the last century. He said that it was an honor and a privilege to work with everyone, and after other managers spoke, the whole trial team posed for a picture—all seven managers plus thirty-one counsel and staff, who had helped make history.

When we walked back to the House with Jerry, he said our efforts to pick up Republican votes had reminded him of Abraham's negotiation with God to spare Sodom from destruction. Abraham starts by asking if the Lord will spare the city if fifty righteous people can be found, and works his way down from there. Every time God agrees, Abraham bids him down further. I rattled off one of the verses, Genesis 18:32: "And Abraham said to the Lord, 'Possibly ten shall be found there, and he said I will not destroy it for ten's sake.'" Without missing a beat, Jerry responded, "We only found one Republican here, but it might have been enough to save us all from destruction."

At the end of the day, Nadler gathered our Judiciary team together back in the members' conference room for one last meeting. "Some of you have been here from the beginning of this effort; some came along later; some of you will now scatter," he started. "We knew the House leadership would come along eventually, and they did. We also knew that the GOP was not going to convict, no matter what. Do not be disappointed in the outcome; we knew it was foreordained. But it had to be done anyhow, to lay down the markers and to prevent Trump from being able to get away with the pattern. We exposed the pattern, and in so doing you helped save the country. You did a great service—you should remember that; we will remember that."

Returning to my office, I sat down and looked for Barry, who had been right behind me. A few minutes later he walked back down the hallway.

"Where were you?" I asked.

"I just handed in my resignation. We did what we came here to do. I'm going to throw my things in a bag and get the train home to my family as soon as I can."

We took out the Widow Jane and our bags of Trader Joe's rice crackers and raw almonds for the last time. We toasted each other and the long year we'd shared. "Crazy that it's over," I said.

"Over? You think it's over? Buddy, it's not over," he said with a sideways grin. "Fasten your seat belt for tomorrow." We knew Trump's instincts as well as anybody. We knew, as we sat there, that the pattern would continue. All we could hope was that the next time Trump betrayed his oath, it would be easier for the American people to connect the dots because of the work we had done. Barry laughed, lifted his plastic cup, and said sardonically, "Whatever's coming next, Trump's probably already deep into it, right now!"

And he was.

Closing Argument

The tests are all perfect, like the . . . [Ukraine] transcription was perfect, right? This was not as perfect as that, but pretty good.

—Donald J. Trump, March 6, 2020,
Centers for Disease Control, Atlanta

Shortly before Mitt Romney gave his historic February 5 speech, and just hours before the final impeachment votes were cast in the Senate, a group of senators from both parties gathered with senior members of the administration in a Capitol Hill briefing room. The secretary of health and human services, Alex Azar, filled them in on a new, deadly disease that had spread from Wuhan, China. A few hours later, one of the senators who had attended the briefing, Connecticut's Chris Murphy, headed to the floor to explain why he was voting to convict the president of impeachment. It was the moving speech that I was lucky enough to catch, sitting among scattered press and a handful of others in the near-empty chamber. Murphy was already anticipating the next Trump disaster. He had laid it out earlier that day on Twitter right after leaving the briefing, stating, "Bottom line: they aren't taking this seriously enough. Notably, no request for ANY emergency funding, which is a big mistake. Local health systems need supplies, training, screening staff etc. And they need it now."

Senator Brian Schatz—among the few Democratic senators in our tiny floor audience, who soon after told me Romney had restored his faith—had also been at the Azar meeting. He told the press he was equally disturbed by the administration's lack of preparation or concern. He had challenged the secretary on the dearth of requisite materials that would allow his state of Hawaii to complete its own testing kits. He offered to personally carry a test kit home with him, but Azar refused.

Murphy and Schatz were not the only two expressing concern that the White House was underplaying what could become an unprecedented crisis for our lifetimes. The Republican senator Tom Cotton was one of the most implacable opponents of impeachment. But he was so disturbed by the news coming out of China that he endeavored to personally call everyone he could in the administration, from Jared Kushner to the president himself.

Trump's response unfolded in the days that followed the impeachment vote: "Looks like by April, you know, in theory, when it gets a little warmer, it miraculously goes away. I hope that's true. But we're doing great in our country. China, I spoke with President Xi, and they're working very, very hard. And I think it's going to all work out fine" (February 10). "The Coronavirus is very much under control in the USA. We are in contact with everyone and all relevant countries. CDC & World Health have been working hard and very smart. Stock Market starting to look very good to me!" (February 24). "Now the Democrats are politicizing the coronavirus . . . One of my people came up to me and said, 'Mr. President, they tried to beat you on Russia, Russia, Russia.' That didn't work out too well. They couldn't do it. They tried the impeachment hoax. That was on a perfect conversation. They tried anything, they tried it over and over . . . And this is their new hoax" (February 28).

Adam Schiff had warned the Senate, "He will not change, and you know it." Members of the jury, President Trump's response to COVID-19 follows the same pattern as the one exposed in his impeachment and trial: putting his personal and political well-being first—not American interests and certainly not American lives. "This conduct is not America first, it is Donald Trump first," as Chairman Nadler said, and that is what happened with the pandemic. By the time Trump was claiming "this is their new hoax," he had been informed repeatedly by Azar; starting at the beginning of January, his classified daily briefings warned him of the threat of a coming pandemic more than a dozen times, with the urgency reiterated face-to-face by the end of the month; and his top trade adviser had written a memo suggesting that the virus could devastate the economy and take as many as 500,000 lives. Trump was informed through every channel possible: in person, by phone, in daily briefings, by watching the news, or on the odd chance that he might have glanced at a newspaper. He knew a pandemic was coming. He knew, and yet he falsely termed concern about the pandemic a hoax—*himself* categorizing it with the same term he used for the Russia investigation and the Ukraine scandal.

In the face of this evidence, and of the pattern we have set forth going back to the beginning of Trump's career, can anyone doubt what drove Trump's initial lies about COVID-19? They were colored by the same pathologically selfish motivations that drove him to invite Russia to hack Clinton's email, or to ask Ukraine to investigate Biden. Only this time it was not the lives of Ukrainian soldiers on the front lines with Russia that were at stake. It was American lives.

Trump and those around him viewed the booming economy as central to his reelection, and so they feared the effects of speaking and acting forcefully about coronavirus. According to press reports, Trump made that explicit calculation on the advice of his son-in-law, Jared Kushner; more tests and more ventilators would only spook the stock market, which would in turn hurt his campaign. In early March, while a cruise ship full of sick travelers floated off the West Coast, Trump's first thought was not for their safety. It was for his image, his reputation. He stated he'd rather the ship not be allowed to dock, asserting zero empathy for the ill, highly contagious passengers in need of medical assistance. "I like the numbers being where they are—I don't need to have the numbers [of coronavirus cases] to double because of one ship." The examples are legion: Trump did what he thought was right for *him,* not for the nation. Indeed, he acted at the expense of the nation.

The similarities to Trump's prior misconduct run through every aspect of his response to the pandemic. As soon as he was forced to acknowledge COVID-19, he demonstrated his propensity for quid pro quos that led to his 2016 statement "Russia, if you're listening . . ." or his 2019 one to Ukraine to "do us a favor though." As I have listened to Trump these past months, I have thought often of Professor Karlan's hypothetical question about how we'd react if Trump made demands on governors during a disaster. That came to mind on March 27, when the president, asked about refusing to speak to the governors of two American states during a global pandemic, declared: "All I want them [governors] to do, very simple, I want them to be appreciative . . . If they don't treat you right, I don't call." He was unabashedly building on an earlier statement that, "You know, it's a two-way street. They have to treat us well also."

The president's demands for fealty and flattery have been coupled with barely veiled threats. "Tell the Democrat Governors that *Mutiny on the Bounty* was one of my all-time favorite movies," he wrote. "A good old-fashioned mutiny every now and then is an exciting and invigorating thing to watch, especially when the mutineers need so much from the Captain. Too easy!" We all know the ultimate punishment the captain could mete out for mutineers.

As the crisis has worn on, the president has become even more blunt about his partisanship. The president has said, "So what's happening is the Democrats have come to us, and they'd like to do a phase four" of funding. "They want to help the states, they want to help bailouts, and bailouts are very tough. And they happen to be Democratic states. It's California, New York, Illinois, you start with those three . . ."

"Maybe the Democrats should have brought this up earlier when we wanted certain things," Trump carried on, deepening the partisan chasm with every word. "I think we want to take a little bit of a pause" on the relief packages, Trump said, "but if we do that, we will have to get something for it. Okay?"

No, members of the jury. Not okay. Trump demanded quid pro quos with our own country's governors in a time of disaster, unapologetically telling the nation that what they get depends on what they give him. But this time, he was not dangling desperately needed taxpayer-funded aid to a foreign ally. His bargaining chip was help for you. For Americans. For those he is meant above all to be serving and protecting.

All of that constitutes an abuse of power, and Trump's abuses of power are always followed close behind with obstruction. "This president sees no limits on his power or on his ability to use his public office for a private gain. And of course, the president also believes that he can use his power to cover up his crimes," Nadler recognized. COVID-19 is no exception. On the contrary, Trump's response to it bears all the features of his prior cover-ups that Barry and I and all our colleagues battled over the course of our impeachment year.

There is the nonstop flow of lies. His most persistent falsehood was that anyone who wants a test can get one, an outright fabrication he began peddling in early March at the CDC: "Anybody that wants a test can get a test. That's what the bottom line is." He said it again in mid-May: "If somebody wants to be tested right now. They'll be able to be tested." Of course it was not true, and has had profound consequences. As we've seen in countries that have handled the virus properly, rapid, pervasive testing is key to safely ending stay-at-home orders. Of course, the falsehoods are ongoing: Trump claims that the United States has tested more than the rest of the world combined, when in fact the rest of the world, even excluding China, has performed three times as many tests. He's gone as far as claiming that the reason the testing system has been inadequate is President Obama's fault. "We started off with bad, broken tests, and obsolete tests," he told a reporter in April. Needless to say, the virus is new, so there were no tests with which to start off. It was *his* responsibility to oversee a new testing system.

The cover-up doesn't stop there. Trump has refused to cooperate with congressional oversight, just as he did on Russia and on Ukraine. In March, while Congress was drafting legislation creating trillions of dollars in new coronavirus relief programs, Trump rejected any inquiries into how he would use the money. "I'll be the oversight," he asserted. When the legislation ultimately passed, it was coupled with reporting and oversight requirements, but Trump still rejected the legislature's role wholesale. In a signing statement he asserted that "a requirement to consult with the Congress regarding executive decision-making . . . intrud[es] upon the President's power and duty." In breathtakingly sweeping language, Trump gave Congress the back of the hand. He followed it up by asserting without any basis in law or fact that he could adjourn Congress because it was obstructing him! "They've been warned," he threatened. His actions extended beyond statements: Trump barred Dr. Anthony Fauci, the director of the National Institute of Allergy and Infectious Diseases, from testifying before the House of Representatives, saying that it was full of "Trump haters." In May, the White House barred all members of its coronavirus task force from testifying before Congress unless Chief of Staff Mark Meadows personally okayed it.

Trump's obstruction has featured another old favorite: attacks on inspectors general. Over the course of two months, Trump ousted a spate of them—the very people charged with investigating and exposing corruption and waste in the government. Among them were the inspector general of the Department of Health and Human Services (who revealed that many hospitals faced equipment shortages) and the inspector general who was set to oversee coronavirus relief. And of course, no Trump crisis would be complete without assailing whistleblowers. The most prominent (though not the only) one in the COVID-19 crisis was the man in charge of the government agency overseeing the development of a coronavirus vaccine. After he repeatedly pushed back on Trump's promotion of dubious cures, warned about equipment shortages, and fought cronyism in contract awards, Dr. Rick Bright was removed from his position and placed in a less prominent job. He filed his whistleblower complaint in May.

Lest there be any doubt about what Trump is up to, these attacks on COVID-19 oversight have been commingled with post-impeachment retribution against the inspector general and witnesses in the Ukraine case. In a wave of retaliation after the impeachment trial, Trump fired the IG who handled the Ukraine whistleblower's complaint, and Lieutenant Colonel Alexander Vindman was also fired from his job at the White House. Trump's rage extended to Vindman's twin brother, who was also removed from a job he had held for two decades. Then the EU ambassador, Gordon Sondland, was fired. John Rood, a Defense Department official who had taken a position viewed as contrary to the president's on Ukraine, was forced out of his job. Another Pentagon official, Elaine McCusker, who had questioned the military aid freeze, had her nomination to be Pentagon comptroller withdrawn.

All of this—the abuse and the cover-up alike—has unfolded in Trump's five stages of grievance that kill the truth, which we have seen him employ with each major crisis. February's **blanket denials** proceeded to Trump's **attacking and accusing others** in the form of his relentless blame of mayors, governors, the Chinese, the WHO—anyone but himself. Then he **slowly admitted what happened** by calling for social distancing and revising national death totals, all the while **testing rationalizations** ("I'm a cheerleader for the country," or "I've felt it was a pandemic long before it was called a pandemic"), then finally **embracing the wrongdoing and claiming perfection:** as he did on May 11, when he announced, "We have met the moment, and we have prevailed!" (Meanwhile, infection rates were on the rise, and a memo was sent out the same day instructing White House staffers to wear masks.)

Members of the jury, you have come to know Trump's serial misconduct. It is what I came to the Judiciary Committee to expose and to fight. It is why Barry left his family and his law practice and moved to D.C. to join me in the battle, and why Arya considered leaving the office at 2:00 A.M. an early night. You have witnessed the results of the Russia investigation and the Ukraine one, culminating in members of the House warning repeatedly that the president would continue to do wrong. "He has shown neither remorse nor acknowledgment of wrongdoing . . . Do you think if we do nothing, it's going to stop now?"

It hasn't. And the terrifying reality, members of the jury, is that this will keep going unless you stop it. The ongoing COVID-19 tragedy is not the end, although it is certainly bad enough. As of this writing, U.S. deaths have gone beyond 100,000, millions more Americans are ill, and tens of millions have been thrown out of work, on a scale that has brought comparisons to the Great Depression.

What new bottom will we hit after this? Trump has gone from encouraging a Russian attack on our democracy, to extorting a Ukrainian one, to recklessly enabling a pandemic. What is next? Will he intentionally provoke or bumble into an armed conflict with one of our dangerous adversaries around the globe—or perhaps with one of our allies? Will he be guilty of further economic miscalculations, when our prosperity has already been rocked to an extent rarely seen? If reelected, will he do as other leaders of his illiberal ilk have done all over the world, from Hungary to Turkey to Russia, and treat his return to office as an invitation to systematically dismantle the elements of our democracy and our freedom?

No one knows how low Trump is capable of sinking over eight years. Toward the end of April, a band of armed men and women descended on the Michigan state capitol demanding an end to shelter in place orders. Several hundred—some carrying assault weapons, others carrying Confederate flags or signs with swastikas—rallied. Many forced their way into the building, leading to a tense confrontation with state law enforcement. Trump's reaction was to encourage them, in language reminiscent of his declaration that "there are good people on both sides" after neo-Nazis marched in Charlottesville.

"The Governor of Michigan should give a little, and put out the fire," Trump tweeted. "These are very good people, but they are angry . . . See them, talk to them, make a deal."

He was not so solicitous in June 2020 to peaceful demonstrators against racism and police brutality in the park outside the White House. They were teargassed and shot with rubber bullets followed by the president having a photo op of walking through the park and posing in front of a nearby church. That day, and since, I have thought often of Nadler's warning to the Senate that Trump "wants to be all powerful . . . only his will goes. He is a dictator." Instead of healing, Trump offers hate to his followers. Where will such a man lead them, if we let him?

"Our imagination is the only limit to what President Trump may do next," we warned during impeachment. With Trump, the next outrage always lies around the corner. There is always that tenth article we worried about when we were drafting—the coming wrongdoing. And it is always one step worse. The only solution is for the American people to convict and remove him at the ballot box.

That brings us to you, ladies and gentlemen of the jury. After all the judgments of the past three years plus, your turn awaits, come November. Some say that we have to turn to you as a last gasp because the system has failed. That prosecutors, the courts, Congress, the press, and all the safeguards of our democracy have proven powerless to address his behavior. That the impeachment trial was a failure—because Trump was not convicted and removed.

I don't see it that way. It was never going to be easy to remove a democratically elected president of the United States, and it never should be. But valiant efforts have been made. They form a foundation for ultimate justice. The final verdict is now yours to deliver. It would not be fair to ask you to do everything in your power unless we had done everything in ours. In our democracy, you represent the ultimate safeguard.

Now you have the evidence of the president's entanglements with Russia. You also know about his actions to obstruct Mueller's investigation: ten incidents of obstruction of justice, five of which were so egregious that they would have led to the prosecution of anybody else in America. You have the details of Trump's shakedown of Ukraine as well, and know that Trump demanded the president of Ukraine investigate his political opponents in the coming election. You know he tried to cover it up, ultimately refusing to produce a single page of documents in response to congressional subpoenas and withholding critical witnesses from congressional examination.

The House indelibly marked Trump with the stain of impeachment. The Senate fell short of conviction. But come November you can follow the courageous examples on both sides of the aisle, the Mitt Romneys and the Doug Joneses, and vote to remove the president.

If Trump had been removed on February 5, his denial and deflection, his refusal to deal with the virus, could have been avoided. Tens of thousands of American lives could have been spared, and millions of American jobs. If any other president were in the White House, surely there would have been an effort to address the discrimination and police violence that have led millions of Americans to protest. Instead, Trump inflamed tensions and responded to complaints of excessive force with more of the same, denying it all the while. He went so far as to claim tear gas was not fired on peaceful protesters outside the White House even though the world saw it with their own eyes. In the months since the impeachment trial, we have the latest turns in Trump's endlessly repeating pattern of abuses and obstructions. As a commentator once said, there are not many Trump scandals. There is just one. And it has turned deadly.

You have the power to stop the next scandal, and the one after that too. By voting. By doing so in such large numbers that there can be no challenging the results or our message. By turning out across the country and making your choices known not just at the top but all the way down the ballot. By ousting not just Trump but his enablers in the Senate and the House.

Will that solve all our nation's problems—the underlying ills that gave us Trump? No. But until the uncivil war is over, the peace cannot begin. Judging the president in numbers too large to ignore is our starting point. The electoral judgment must be so vast that even he cannot deny it or attack it. A vote that will be loud and overwhelming is the first step to reclaiming America.

Many people have worked to get you all the evidence you need about the high crimes and misdemeanors of President Trump. I have been proud to be one of them. Now it is up to you.

Justice and the future of our country depend on it.

Acknowledgments

I must begin by thanking Domenica Alioto, my editor at Unfurl Productions. We somehow produced these fourteen chapters in fourteen weeks. I doubt there is another human who could have helped me (or, more like it, made me) hustle to make the case to the American people when it mattered most. Her brilliance has shaped every word of this volume. I also thank her husband, Michael Howard, and their daughter, Mae; anyone who has been involved in producing a fast book knows why.

My co-counsel and friend Barry Berke was side by side with me for the events chronicled herein, and has continued to be a font of advice, wisdom, and recollection. His family endured a lot giving him up to D.C. for a year (and tolerating my incessant phone and Zoom calls since), so I thank Alison, Olivia, Rebecca, Elizabeth, and Benjamin as well.

My deepest gratitude also to my friend Dan Berger. I spoke to him almost every day during my tenure on the Hill, and then during the writing of the book. He provided constant encouragement and insight and otherwise supported the book in every way.

For my extraordinary experience on the Hill, I wish to thank Chairman Jerrold Nadler, all the members of the House Judiciary Committee, and particularly those of the majority. Passionate fighters for the Constitution all, I was fortunate to spend so much time with Representatives Mary Gay Scanlon, Zoe Lofgren, Sheila Jackson Lee, Steve Cohen, Hank Johnson, Ted Deutch, Karen Bass,

Cedric Richmond, Hakeem Jeffries, David Cicilline, Eric Swalwell, Ted Lieu, Jamie Raskin, Pramila Jayapal, Val Demings, Lou Correa, Sylvia Garcia, Joe Neguse, Lucy McBath, Greg Stanton, Madeleine Dean, Debbie Mucarsel-Powell, and Veronica Escobar. (Don't worry, I won't thank all their family members—although I should!)

My deepest appreciation also to Speaker Nancy Pelosi, Chairman Adam Schiff, their wonderful staffs and those of the Committee on Oversight and Reform, the House Foreign Affairs Committee, and the House Rules Committee. For making possible such magnificent staff colleagues, and for all their leadership, I thank the chairs of those committees: the late and much missed Chairman Elijah Cummings, Chairwoman Carolyn Maloney, Chairman Eliot Engel, and Chairman Jim McGovern. Thanks also to Representatives Jason Crow, Jackie Speier, Jan Schakowsky, Gerry Connolly, Jim Himes, and Juan Vargas, and to the many other members of the House majority for their kindnesses.

To my dear House Judiciary majority staff colleagues, thanks from the bottom of my heart for how you welcomed me and fought for our democracy. There is no better way to meet a constitutional crisis than by doing battle side by side with Amy Rutkin, Perry Apelbaum, John Doty, Aaron Hiller, Shadawn Reddick-Smith, Daniel Schwarz, Moh Sharma, David Greengrass, John Williams, Arya Hariharan, Ted Kalo, James Park, Sophia Brill, Charles Gayle, Maggie Goodlander, Sarah Istel, Joshua Matz, Matthew Morgan, Matthew Robinson, Kerry Tirrell, Madeline Strasser, Rachel Calanni, Jordan Dashow, William Emmons, Julian Gerson, Priyanka Mara, Elizabeth McElvein, Jessica Presley, and Kayla Hamedi. I tried to tell good stories about all of you in the book and mostly succeeded until my ruthless editor told me something along the lines of "This is not your high school yearbook." So if I failed, know that I love you none the less.

My other staff colleagues from across the House who were so kind to me and who are unsung heroes of our democracy have my deepest appreciation. They are, in the Speaker's office, Terri

McCullough, Dick Meltzer, Wyndee Parker, Keith Stern, Ashley Etienne, Mike Tecklenburg, Jesse Lee, and Mia Ehrenberg; at the House Permanent Select Committee on Intelligence, Timothy Bergreen, Daniel Goldman, Maher Bitar, Rheanne Wirkkala, Patrick Boland, William Evans, Daniel Noble, Patrick Fallon, Diana Pilipenko, Sean Misko, Ariana Rowberry, Nicolas Mitchell, and Wells Bennett; at the Committee on Oversight and Reform, Dave Rapallo, Susanne Sachsman Grooms, Peter Kenny, Krista A. Boyd, Janet Kim, Russell Anello, Aryele Bradford; at the House Foreign Affairs Committee, Jason Steinbaum, Laura Carey, and Jamie Bair; at the House Rules Committee, Don Sisson, Liz Pardue, Nate Perkins, and Matthew Price; and at the Office of General Counsel, Doug Letter, Todd Tatelman, Megan Barbero, Jodie Morse, Adam Grogg, Will Havemann, and Jonathan Schwartz. Thanks also to outside counsel at the Institute for Constitutional Advocacy and Protection, including Executive Director Josh Geltzer and all his colleagues, and at Debevoise & Plimpton, including Dave O'Neil and all his team.

The United States Senate welcomed us for the impeachment trial, and ninety-nine of the members were gracious even if they did not agree with everything (and in some cases, anything) we said. I thank them and their staffs and the staff of the Senate itself.

The president of Brookings, John Allen, and the head of my program, Darrell West, were great allies, including allowing me to go to work on the Hill first part-time, then to take a leave and go full-time, and then welcoming me back to Brookings and encouraging me to write about my experience.

My publisher and editor at Crown, Gillian Blake, fired me up with enthusiasm for making the case, urged me to address events subsequent to impeachment that were predicted by it, and brilliantly shaped the book in innumerable other ways. David Drake ignited the project, and continued to guide it, with his vision, exuberance, and curiosity. Mark Birkey coordinated the production process on an unconscionable schedule; Julie Cepler was invaluable as ever at finding the audience, and Dyana Messina and her publicity team discerned the ideal channels and outlets to speak to you, the American people. Behind the scenes was the crucial support of Matthew Martin, Annsley Rosner, Sally Franklin, Chris Brand, Susan Turner, and Richard Elman.

My agent, Eric Simonoff of WME, has provided his usual sage counsel every step of the way. Special thanks to his assistant, Jessica Spitz, who not only facilitated various WME matters for me but also volunteered to join our book research team and was a wonderful colleague. Also at WME, thanks to Bradley Singer and Lauren Rogoff.

From the moment I began writing, my research assistants and research interns were stellar in every way. I could not have written this book (especially in fourteen weeks!) without Kelsey Landau, Colby Galliher, Theodore Becker-Jacob, Carolina Hernandez, Angela King, Catherine Conrow, and Lica Porcile. My friend and frequent co-author Victoria Bassetti has also lavished loving care on every page of the volume and in particular on helping me unpack thorny legal and factual questions for readers. Deep appreciation also goes to others in our Brookings family who provided invaluable assistance: Brigitte Brown, Michael Cavadel, Courtney Dunakin, Emily Horne, Sarah Chilton, and Robin Lewis.

Thanks Noah Bookbinder and all your brilliant CREW colleagues for your work to hold government accountable and for making me look good during my two-year return to the organization starting at the end of 2016, and to Richard Painter, Larry Tribe, Fred Wertheimer, Walt Shaub, John Bonifaz, and all the members of what I call in these pages the legal Resistance (though they may not agree with that nomenclature). You have fought for the life of our nation as if your own lives were at stake.

As always, I thank my wife, Lindsay, and my daughter, Tamar, for their love and support during my impeachment year, during the writing of this book, and in every part of my life.

The views expressed in the book, and any errors herein, are, of course, the author's alone.

About the Author

Norman Eisen was special counsel to the House Judiciary Committee from 2019 to 2020, including for the impeachment and trial of President Donald Trump. He previously served as ethics czar for President Barack Obama and then as his ambassador to the Czech Republic. Eisen is a senior fellow in Governance Studies at the Brookings Institution, and his previous books include *The Last Palace* and *Democracy's Defenders*. He lives in Washington, D.C., with his family.

Notes, an index of names, and other additional material can be found on www.normaneisen.com

About the Type

This book was set in Fairfield, the first typeface from the hand of the distinguished American artist and engraver Rudolph Ruzicka (1883–1978). Ruzicka was born in Bohemia (in the present-day Czech Republic) and came to America in 1894. He set up his own shop, devoted to wood engraving and printing, in New York in 1913 after a varied career working as a wood engraver, in photoengraving and banknote printing plants, and as an art director and freelance artist. He designed and illustrated many books, and was the creator of a considerable list of individual prints—wood engravings, line engravings on copper, and aquatints.